Praise for

THE ONLY GAME IN TOWN

"What better moment could there be for a book subtitled *Central Banks, Instability, and Avoiding the Next Collapse*? And who better to write it than Mohamed El-Erian—the man who captured the essence of the present era of low growth, low inflation and low investment returns better than anyone else with his memorable concept of the 'new normal'? . . . It is refreshing to read a policy book with the confidence to say that it is pointless to dispense elevator-pitch solutions to epochal economic challenges."

—*Financial Times*

"El-Erian expertly offers a balanced view, commending the central banks for their necessarily aggressive policy views while noting, for example, the failure of the Fed to recognize the pre-crisis housing bubble. But title aside, this is hardly just a book about central banks. Instead, El-Erian offers a grand tour of the challenges we face, along with ideal solutions and more likely outcomes."

—*The New York Times*

"An indispensable guide to understanding the rapid expansion and current role of central banks in the global economy, as well as the challenges and opportunities that they will confront in responding to future economic shocks."

—James Poterba, professor of economics, MIT, and president and CEO, National Bureau of Economic Research

"*The Only Game in Town* says it is about central banks, but it really is about so much more: everything from the investment strategy needed in today's macroeconomic environment to the hard choices about taxes and public works that our politicians face to the economics underlying the still relevant 'new normal' (which he coined). El-Erian has an incredibly rich worldview, far greater than the sum of his impressive diverse experience, and seeing today's world economy through his eyes offers a real education."

—Dr. Adam S. Posen, president of the Peterson Institute for International Economics

"This book is a must-read for anyone interested in the global economy. A masterful account of how central banks became the only game in town after the global financial crisis but also how other structural and fiscal policies are necessary to resolve key global economic issues. El-Erian is the best thinker on the key global issues of our times."

—Nouriel Roubini, chairman, Roubini Global Economics and professor of economics, Stern School of Business, NYU

"Mohamed El-Erian knows the global economy as an investor, a public servant, and an analyst with a rare ability to grasp its essentials. He has an urgent message to convey here: Central banks cannot [continue to] carry the global economy on their backs for much longer without a high risk of a very bad global outcome. If he's right—as he has often been before—all of us, governments, business, finance, and individuals, need to understand why and how to take evasive action."

—Jessica Mathews, former president
of the Carnegie Endowment for International Peace

"Widely regarded as one of the most astute observers of global economic trends, Mohamed El-Erian is famous for having coined the now-ubiquitous phrase 'the new normal.' Five years ago, he was worried that the global economy might take years to regain its footing. Now El-Erian worries it could fall off a cliff. The good news from this book is that if policymakers get their act together, things could be a lot better. The bad news is that this seasoned and influential veteran isn't at all sure this will happen. *The Only Game in Town* is simply a must-read for anyone trying to understand how the global economy might unfold in the next five years."

—Kenneth Rogoff, Thomas D. Cabot Professor of
Public Policy at Harvard University, and former chief economist
and director of research at the International Monetary Fund

"In his next book, *The Only Game in Town,* Mohamed El-Erian has done several important things superbly. First, he has presented the first really comprehensive assessment of the multiple challenges to sustainable and inclusive growth facing a wide range of countries and the global economy. Second, he does it through the illuminating lens of central banks and monetary policy—with few exceptions, the only game in town. Third, he then deftly and insightfully dissects the limits and risks of this almost ubiquitous one-handed policy response. And fourth, he argues persuasively that this is a journey we cannot continue; that we will break either right to a much superior level and quality of growth, or left to declining performance and rising instability. He then suggests mind-sets that will help everyone—policymakers and the rest of us—navigate this complex and uncharted territory. It is a tour de force."

—Michael Spence, Nobel Laureate and professor of economics, Stern School of Business, NYU

THE ONLY
GAME
IN TOWN

BY MOHAMED A. EL-ERIAN

The Only Game in Town:
Central Banks, Instability,
and Avoiding the Next Collapse

When Markets Collide:
Investment Strategies for the
Age of Global Economic Change

THE ONLY GAME IN TOWN

CENTRAL BANKS, INSTABILITY,
AND AVOIDING THE NEXT COLLAPSE

Mohamed A. El-Erian

RANDOM HOUSE

NEW YORK

2017 Random House Trade Paperback Edition

Published in the United States by Random House, an imprint and division of Penguin Random House LLC, New York.

RANDOM HOUSE and the HOUSE colophon are registered trademarks of Penguin Random House LLC.

Originally published in hardcover and in slightly different form in the United States by Random House, an imprint and division of Penguin Random House LLC, in 2016.

LIBRARY OF CONGRESS CATALOGING-IN-PUBLICATION DATA
Names: El-Erian, Mohamed A., author
Title: The only game in town : central banks, instability, and avoiding the next collapse / Mohamed A. El-Erian.
Description: First Edition. | New York : Random House, 2016. | Includes bibliographical references and index.
Identifiers: LCCN 2015035534 | ISBN 9780812987300 (trade paperback) | ISBN 9780812997637 (ebook)
Subjects: LCSH: Banks and banking, Central. | Monetary policy. | Economic policy. | BISAC: BUSINESS & ECONOMICS / Banks & Banking. | POLITICAL SCIENCE / Public Policy / Economic Policy. | BUSINESS & ECONOMICS / Economics / Macroeconomics.
Classification: LCC HG1811 .E44 2016 | DDC 332.1/1—dc23 LC record available at http://lccn.loc.gov_2015035534

Printed in the United States of America on acid-free paper

randomhousebooks.com

2   4   6   8   9   7   5   3

Book design by Christopher M. Zucker

Dedicated to my daughter, my mother,
and my sister
In memory of my late father

Thank you for your amazing love, your terrific
companionship, your enduring support,
and your awesome inspiration

CONTENTS

PART VI: THE KEYS TO
NAVIGATING A BIMODAL DISTRIBUTION

PART VII: BRINGING IT ALL TOGETHER

INTRODUCTION TO THE PAPERBACK EDITION

Thank you so much for reading the paperback edition of *The Only Game in Town*. Published a year after the original hardcover version, the discussion has been updated to reflect an eventful twelve months—a period characterized by developments that, not so long ago, were deemed improbable if not unthinkable. Rather than constitute "noise," they are all signals; and they speak directly to the book's thesis, analysis, and predictions.

The message of this book remains simple yet both consequential and action-oriented. It postulates an end to the path that the global economy has been on, particularly when it comes to central banks' ability to single-handedly deliver stable low growth and to repress financial volatility. It sets out the policies needed to ensure that what follows is a pivot to higher and more inclusive growth, together with genuine financial stability; and it shows why, in the absence of a determined policy response, low growth could turn into recession, and artificial financial stability could become unsettling financial instability.

This book is not just about consequential destinations that affect the well-being of both current and future generations. It is also about the ongoing transition that is likely to feature even more improbables and unthinkables becoming reality. And since this context of "unusual uncertainty" inevitably challenges sound decision making, the book also discusses what can and should be done to minimize mistakes at the corporate, government, and household levels.

Many developments since the first publication of the book in January 2016 support the book's central thesis—so much so, that a growing number of experts have started to take on board the messages of the book and now caution against policy overreliance on central bankers. Indeed, it is not just external voices that are speaking out. Central bankers themselves have also expressed warnings in the face of mounting evidence of the declining effectiveness of their unconventional policies and their higher risk of collateral damage and unintended consequences—be they economic, financial, institutional, political, or social.

While these views have also been evolving, many in the economic forecasting profession, however, have insufficiently internalized the implications for what lies ahead.

Having initially resisted the concept of the "new normal"—that is, a period of unusually sluggish economic growth during which western economies confront unusual cyclical and structural headwinds— consensus has now adopted it with open arms. With that, and having in the past underestimated its effects, too many in the prediction business are now eagerly extrapolating it forward without comprehensively assessing how it is evolving and, crucially, morphing.

Rebranded by some as "the new mediocre" and by others as "secular stagnation," too many simply forecast that low and stable growth is likely to prevail for the period ahead, along with the continued repression of financial volatility by central banks. However, for those willing to look closely, this consensus view is now being challenged, due to an ever-increasing list of internal tensions and contradictions. These tensions explain the growing list of improbables that, just in the last twelve months, have included:

- The surprise election of Donald Trump as president of the United States;
- The shock decision by British voters to take their country out of the European Union;
- Francois Fillon coming out of nowhere and upsetting both Nicolas Sarkozy and Alain Juppé to win the center-right's primary for the upcoming presidential election;
- Italian Prime Minister Matteo Renzi losing the referendum on constitutional reforms and having to resign;
- Investors having to pay (rather than receive) interest on over 30 percent of global government debt that has been trading at negative yields; and
- The breakdown of long-standing correlations among asset classes and, with that, a rather dismal performance on the part of "smart money" and other active investors, some of which have decided to exit the business.

Along with the already considerable list of improbables cited in the hardcover edition of this book, these newer ones share an important common characteristic: that of being heavily influenced by the direct and indirect damage of a prolonged period of low and noninclusive growth. And, for the following reasons, it's a list that will grow as the current global economic configuration comes to its exhaustion point:

- Years of growth that is too low and insufficiently inclusive are eating away at economic potential, making the underpinnings of the economy more volatile and fueling a warranted backlash against the worsening in the inequality trifecta (income, wealth, and inequality);

- The more this persists, the greater the impact of the "politics of anger." With that, a growing number of antiestablishment movements upend traditional politics on both sides of the Atlantic. Many of them are clear on what they wish to dismantle but have yet to come up with credible alternatives.
- Economic and financial regionalization and globalization go from unquestioned beneficial paradigms to political liabilities. Europe faces mounting challenges to an historical integration project that was once viewed as a given. And the United States threatens to undo free-trade pacts that have served the country well overall.
- Cross-border policy coordination falls to its lowest levels in decades, with the resulting vacuum also encouraging political adventures (including Russia's involvement in Syria and Ukraine).
- Meanwhile, on the financial front, ultra-low and negative interest rates erode the integrity of the financial system. While some have worried about the outlook for banks, my concern is elsewhere. It speaks to the extent to which providers of long-term financial security products to consumers (including life insurance and retirement options) can continue to supply the protection services that are so vital to a sense of durable economic security.
- And the list goes on. . . .

All this pertains to disruptions that are shaking the world from above, and that are compounding those shaking the world from below.

The last twelve months have provided further support to the hypothesis that the combination of artificial intelligence (AI) and big data, along with mobility and fast-moving innovation, is turbocharging technological disruptions that upend a growing number of sectors. This is no longer just about Uber and Airbnb. As Andrew McAfee puts it, we are now in the second half of a chessboard in which already-considerable incremental change is compounding in an accelerating fashion.

This mix of top-down and bottom-up disruptions is accelerating the journey to the global economy's historic inflection point, or what the book calls the "T junction"—one whereby the recent period of low but stable growth and repressed financial volatility gives way to one of two very different outcomes. And, as demonstrated in the book, as yet there is nothing automatic about which will prevail. Nothing is predestined.

Much depends on how politicians respond to the unusual uncertainty they face on multiple fronts, be they economic, financial, institutional, political, or social. In addition to determining the scope for economic well-being at the individual country level, this will influence whether the international economic and financial order fragments or evolves into a more effective mode of globalization—and, for Europe, also regionalization.

What is crucially needed is a durable policy pivot along the lines described in the book. Its engineering is known and, by now, commands considerable support among economists. But it is also a pivot that is unlikely to materialize without a catalyst for traditional political systems that have become too complacent.

The catalyst can come in the form of an endogenous political shock, with the emergence of antiestablishment movements (including Donald Trump's election) raising intriguing questions; or it can come from outside in the form of a new economic and financial crisis, a wake-up call that shocks the political establishment into action.

Much will be determined in the months and years ahead, with consequences not just for this generation but for future ones as well. I hope that this updated book can shed light on what could happen, what should happen, and the steps we can take to turn the desirable into the feasible.

PREAMBLE

"*What is needed is not more finance, but better finance.*"

—MARTIN WOLF

"*The world has largely exhausted the scope for central bank improvisation as a growth strategy.*"

—LARRY SUMMERS

In the last few years, the global economy has evolved in ways once deemed highly unlikely, if not unthinkable. It is a phenomenon that continues today and, as will be made clear in this book, will intensify in the period ahead.

The global financial crisis that shook virtually every country, government, and household in the world in 2008–09 gave way to a frustrating "new normal" of low growth, rising inequality, political dysfunction, and, in some cases, social tensions—all despite massive policy interventions on the part of central banks and transformational technological innovations.

Now this new normal is getting increasingly exhausted. For those caring to look, signs of stress are multiplying—so much so that the path the global economy is on is likely to end soon, and potentially quite suddenly.

As we approach this historic inflection point, unthinkables will become more common and insecurities will rise, especially as it becomes clearer that, rather than transition smoothly and automatically, the current path could give way to one of two very different new roads. The first promises higher inclusive growth and genuine financial stability. But, in stark contrast, the second would see us mired in even lower growth, periodic recessions, and the return of unsettling financial instability.

Fortunately, there is nothing predestined about what will come after the exhaustion of the new normal. The road out of the upcoming "T junction" can still be influenced in a consequential manner by the choices that we make, as households, companies, and governments. But to make better choices, we need to understand the forces at play and their likely evolution. There is no better way of doing so than through an examination of the world's major central banks . . . past, present, and future.

These once-staid, unexciting institutions have emerged as the major and often sole policymakers. Having fallen asleep at the switch while irresponsible financial risk taking went wild, they pivoted to an aggressive intervention mode during the global financial crisis. In doing so, they saved the world from a multi-year depression that would have devastated lives and fueled social unrest.

Sensing that other policymakers were paralyzed by dysfunctional politics, central banks then found experimental ways to keep the global economy on a growth path, albeit a somewhat artificial one, and they did so even though the underlying engines of economic prosperity were yet to be revamped.

Now these monetary institutions are expected to continue producing miracles. But their ability to repeatedly pull new rabbits out of their policy hats has been stretched to an increasingly unsustainable degree. We are nearing the point of ineffectiveness as both willingness and ability wane.

This central casting role is new and unusual for central banks. For decades, they operated away from the spotlights. The majority of those who cared to follow these tradition-prone and proud institutions—and there weren't that many outside the rather small circle of monetary economists and policy wonks—saw them as consisting of highly conventional technocrats who quietly worked behind the scenes using complex technical instruments.

The establishment of the first central bank goes all the way back to Scandinavia in the seventeenth century, a century that also saw the creation in 1694 of the Bank of England, which is widely viewed as the parent of modern central banking. Despite the demise of the British Empire, the "Old Lady of Threadneedle Street," as the bank is fondly referred to—after all, it has influenced the design of most other central banks in the world—is still one of the most influential members of this rather exclusive and enigmatic club.

Yet its power and reach pale in comparison to two other institutions that feature prominently in this book: America's Federal Reserve, the world's most powerful central bank; and the European Central Bank (ECB), the issuer of Europe's common currency (euro), which is currently used by nineteen member countries, and is the most advanced component of the region's historic integration project.

Both of these two institutions are much, much younger than the Bank of England. The Fed was not set up until 1913, in response to financial turmoil. Today, as the central bank of the fifty American states and the territories, and operating under delegated authority from Congress, the Fed has a mission to "provide the nation with a safe, flexible, and stable monetary and financial system."

The ECB became operational in 1999. Working with national central banks that are also part of the Eurosystem, its goal is to maintain price stability, safeguard the common currency, and supervise credit institutions (predominantly banks).

To pursue their objectives, all central banks are empowered to manage the country's currency and money supply with a view to delivering specified macroeconomic objectives—universally, that of low and stable inflation, as well as, in some cases, high employment and economic growth. In more recent years, a growing number of central banks have also been charged with supervising parts of the financial system and ensuring overall financial stability.

At the most basic level of their operations, central banks control the price and amount of money in circulation, whether directly (by altering the interest rates they charge banks and the amount of credit that banks are allowed to create) or indirectly (by influencing the risk appetite of the system and its overall financial conditions). In doing so, they have been granted over time greater operational autonomy from their political bosses.

Acting directly or through a parliamentary process, governments set the macro goals for central banks. Many are then left alone to pursue the objectives using the instruments of their choice. This process has been generally viewed favorably as it insulates central banks from short-term political adventures by governments whose eyes are on their reelection prospects. And the related power and influence of central banks have grown by leaps and bounds.

Take the Fed as an illustration. Like other central banks, it has experienced a dramatic increase in its to-do list, tools, and influences— from something as simple as becoming the sole issuer of the currency to much more complex management and regulation of the banking system. Specifically, and to quote from its mission statement posted on its website (http://www.federalreserve.gov/aboutthefed/mission .htm), the Fed is now responsible for:

- conducting the nation's monetary policy by influencing the monetary and credit conditions in the economy in pursuit of maximum employment, stable prices, and moderate long-term interest rates;
- supervising and regulating banking institutions to ensure the safety and soundness of the nation's banking and financial system and to protect the credit rights of consumers;
- maintaining the stability of the financial system and containing systemic risk that may arise in financial markets; and

- providing financial services to depository institutions, the U.S. government, and foreign official institutions, including playing a major role in operating the nation's payments system.

Despite this notable expansion in responsibility, might, and impact, nothing prepared central banks for the dramatically unprecedented conversion that they have gone through in the last few years—both during the global financial crisis and in its aftermath.

Forced out of their mysterious anonymity and highly technical orientation, central banks have been dramatically thrust into the limelight as they have become single-handedly responsible for the fate of the global economy. Responding to one emergency after the other, they have set aside their conventional approaches and—instead—evolved into serial policy experimenters.

Often, and very counterintuitively for such tradition-obsessed institutions, they have been forced to make things up on the spot. Repeatedly, they have been compelled to resort to untested policy instruments. And, with their expectations for better outcomes often disappointed, many have felt (and still feel) the need to venture ever deeper into unknown and unfamiliar policy terrains and roles.

For those accustomed to the conventional operation of economies and financial systems, all this constitutes nothing less than an unthinkable transfiguration for central banks. Yet the structural breaks have not stopped there.

What central banks have been experiencing is part of a significantly broader change whose effects will be felt by all of us, our children, and, most likely, their children, too. It is a change that speaks to much bigger—and consequential—evolutions in the global economy, in the functioning of markets, and in the financial landscape. And the implications go well beyond economics and finance, extending also to national politics, regional and global negotiations, and geopolitics.

Understanding the unplanned and, for them and many others, uncomfortable conversion of central banks from largely invisible institutions to the only policy game in town, provides us with a unique perspective on the much larger changes impacting our world. It speaks to the how, why, and so what by:

- explaining how the global system has fallen further and further behind in meeting the legitimate aspirations of hundreds of millions of people on multiple continents, including those related to economic betterment, remunerative employment, and financial security;
- detailing why the world is having such difficulties growing, why countries are becoming increasingly unequal, and why so many people live with this recurrent sense of financial instability and even distress;
- shedding light on why so many political systems and regulators struggle mightily just to understand fast-moving realities on the ground and catch up with them, let alone direct them to better destinations; and
- helping to put into context the remarkable growth of anti-establishment political movements, together with the general loss of trust in expert opinion, traditional parties, and established companies.

By living in this world, most of us have already observed either directly or indirectly a set of unusual, if not previously improbable, changes. It is a phenomenon that is being felt at multiple levels. And, so far, all this is just the beginning.

In the years to come, this extremely fluid world we live in is likely to pull us further out of our comfort zones; and it will challenge us to respond accordingly. And we shouldn't just wait for governments to make things better.

Unless we understand the nature of the disruptive forces, including tipping points and T junctions, we will likely fall short in our reaction functions. And the more that happens, the greater the likelihood we could lose control of an orderly economic, financial, and political destiny—both for our generation and for future ones.

Looking at the world through the eyes of central banks, this book aims to increase the probability of your managing much better what lies ahead for the global economy. By analyzing the causes and implications of central banks' historical and unexpected transformation and, importantly, by linking them to much broader societal changes, the book briefly explains how and why we got to this important juncture.

Yet this is not a history book, and it is certainly not just about central banks. Instead, by providing a diagnosis of the world we live in today, it is predominantly about what's ahead for the global economy we all share, and what to do about it—thus specifying what is needed to pull the global system out of its doldrums, how likely this is to occur, and what is likely to happen if it fails.

For all these reasons, and a few more that will be apparent as you read through the book, my hope is that your main takeaways will extend well beyond an understanding of the critical role of central banks, including how intertwined this has become with the fate of the global economy. You will also come away with a few analytical frameworks that are actionable and will help you improve the probabilities of better outcomes.

THE ONLY
GAME
IN TOWN

PART I

THE WHY, HOW, AND WHAT OF THIS BOOK

CHAPTER 1

SETTING THE STAGE

"Like ancient doctors, who tried to explain the causes of diseases while knowing nothing about germs or bacteria, academics sought to describe the functioning of developed economies while ignoring the financial sector and the risks it contained."

—FERDINANDO GIUGLIANO

This is a pivotal moment for the global economy. Our romance with the financial service industry—"finance"—has come crashing down in the midst of loud recriminations. With trust broken and the blame game continuing, it is simply not feasible to restore a close and warm relationship, and any relationship that does survive certainly shouldn't be as intimate and exclusionary as the one that prevailed in the run-up to the 2008 global financial crisis. Yet breaking up is also not an option. The interconnectedness and interdependencies among real economies and the financial system are too deep for them to ever go their own separate ways—and so their interaction is still critical in determining growth, jobs, and financial stability.

Recognizing the importance for both current and future generations of establishing a better working relationship between global economics and global finance, central banks have been working overtime since the global financial crisis to buy time. They have engaged in a series of unprecedented policy initiatives using experimental measures—and taking enormous risks.

The stakes are extremely high and, as yet, no specific outcome is preordained—if only because, acting on their own, central banks cannot deliver the needed good outcome involving that important and quite elusive combination of high and inclusive growth, plentiful well-paying jobs, low and stable inflation, and genuine well-anchored financial stability. Governments and politicians need to be more constructively engaged in the endeavor with central banks, and we, as individuals, through our preparedness and actions, also have a lot to do with what eventually transpires in the collective effort to overcome the damage left by the failed romance.

Parts of the global economy are healing and regaining their composure, led by the United States, which now also faces new political realities. But others, such as countries in Europe and Japan, continue to languish and are still a ways from decisively turning the corner. Still others, such as Greece and Venezuela, face the risk of awful tipping points. Meanwhile, a less than fully rehabilitated financial sector continues to deliver one anomaly after the other. These are not just confined to obscure technical corners. They are visibly relevant for you—whether you are an investor looking for relatively safe returns on your savings, a small company looking for working capital, or a family looking to reclaim your financial destiny and establish a durable sense of long-term stability and security.

There was a time—and it was not so long ago—when governments would pay you interest income in order to convince you to hold the bonds they issued to finance their spending overages. After all, shouldn't you be compensated for assuming risks for your money? Today a sizable amount of government bonds in Europe and Japan is trading at negative nominal yields—that is to say, investors are paying governments for the opportunity to lend them money!

There was a time—and, again, it was not so long ago—that banks would compete for your deposits. From free toasters to cash handouts, they were eager to get their hands on your money. It is no longer the case. A growing number of banks in Europe and, now, in the United States actively pursue approaches to discourage deposits.

There was a time when society trusted the banking system's role in channeling loanable funds to productive uses, and society trusted the regulatory and supervisory skills of governments and central banks. This went out the window when banks' irresponsible risk taking, coupled with lax regulation, took the world economy to the edge of a great depression. It will take a long time to restore the trust. In the meantime, alternative platforms, such as Lending Club and Payoff, are springing up and looking to better connect marginalized borrowers and lenders.

There was a time when financial and economic globalization was seen as a given, as were the integrity and coherence of the European Union. That is no longer the case, as antiestablishment movements on both sides of the Atlantic shake national, regional, and global setups.

And there was a time when the political system celebrated central banks, respecting their technical expertise and trusting them with enormous operational autonomy. This is less so today. Again on both sides of the Atlantic, as well as in Japan, there are recurrent political efforts to subject these influential institutions to greater oversight and auditing.

It is not just noise. It constitutes a signal as all this speaks to a much deeper and more consequential phenomenon. As stable as it may seem on the surface to some, the current configuration of the global economy and the financial system is getting harder to maintain. Below the façade of the unusual calm of the last few years, interrupted by relatively few bouts of instability since 2008–09, tensions are rising and the effectiveness of central banks is coming under stress, so much so as to raise serious questions about the durability of the current path that the global economy is on.

The tremors being felt, and the improbables associated with them, are not just economic and financial. The world is going through unusual political and institutional fluidity. And it seems that nothing can be taken for granted anymore.

In 2016, the United Kingdom shocked much of the world by voting for "Brexit," thereby opting to dismantle long-standing trading and political relationships with the European Union that have served Britain well. The United States experienced one of the most bizarre election seasons ever, with both Democrats and Republicans being unusually influenced by less traditional and hitherto irrelevant factions within their parties. The end result was the surprising election of Donald Trump to the presidency, this on the wave of a significant antiestablishment movement. And several European countries scrambled to confront the realities of angry politics that fuel the emergence of disruptive extreme parties there.

Believe it or not, this is both good and bad news.

It is good news because it can serve as a catalyst for us to exit a frustratingly prolonged phase of economic mediocrity and artificially priced financial markets—one that has been dominated by a global economy that operates well below its potential, thereby holding back job creation, fueling political dysfunction, contributing to geopolitical tensions, and aggravating inequalities.

Already there is unusual consensus among economists on the components of a durable solution. Its impact would be turbocharged by exciting innovations and the engagement of lots of cash that is currently sitting on the sidelines or being used defensively and for financial engineering. All it takes is for our politicians to step up to their national, regional, and global responsibilities—by pursuing more comprehensive national policy agendas, by coordinating better regionally, and by improving global policy cooperation; and for the private sector to respond to a more enabling environment, including deploying more of its accumulated cash into productive activities.

The bad news is that politicians generally don't have a great track record of pursuing comprehensive solutions in recent years, and the more the national agendas struggle, the harder it is to coordinate and cooperate across borders. Meanwhile, acting on its own, the private sector as a whole is unable to deliver the decisive breakthroughs needed for economic liftoffs; the pockets of excellence that are delivering transformation benefits are unlikely to have as much impact as they could and should; and some could even be contaminated by the challenging neighborhood.

If we fail to pivot to better outcomes we risk losing generations of economic growth. In addition to alarmingly high pockets of youth unemployment, financial instability, and a real sense of insecurity for many, this would reduce the potential for future growth. Political polarization, dysfunction, and gridlock would grow, as would geopolitical tensions, inequalities, and alienation, all of which will affect millions of young and old around the world.

The central banking community has worked notably hard trying to tip the balance in favor of the successful outcome. Acting both individually and collaboratively, they have bought time for the private sector to heal and for politicians to get their act together, and this after they acted boldly to help the world avoid what would have been an incredibly damaging multi-year depression.

While we should be thankful and praise central banks for their involvement, we must also recognize that their effectiveness is waning, and not surprisingly so, since they could use only the limited instruments available to them. As such, today's global economy is best viewed as traveling toward what the British call a "T junction." That is to say, the current road we are on, one engineered and maintained by hyperactive central banks, will likely end within the next two to three years, if not earlier, to be replaced by one of two roads that fundamentally contrast in their implications and destinations.

One road out of the T junction ahead involves a restoration of high-inclusive growth that creates jobs, reduces the risk of financial instability, and counters excessive inequality. It is a path that also lowers political tensions, eases governance dysfunction, and holds the hope of defusing some of the world's geopolitical threats.

The other road is the one of even lower growth, persistently high unemployment, and still-worsening inequality. It is a road that involves renewed global financial instability, fuels political extremism, and erodes social cohesion as well as integrity.

At this stage, there is about equal probability of the two very different outcomes, with unusual political fluidity playing an ever-greater role. Both the public and the private sector still have the potential to determine which of these two roads will eventually become our course. And it is only by better understanding this most recent, rather unusual, phase of economic and financial history that we can tip probabilities in favor of the better road out of the T.

We can—and must—do everything possible to steer ourselves onto the better road, thereby unleashing the untapped potential of so many people around the world, and, most important, the under- and unemployed youth. Nothing today is more consequential.

CHAPTER 2

THE ONLY GAME IN TOWN

"Sometimes it is the people who no one imagines anything of who do the things that no one can imagine."

—THE IMAGINATION GAME (FILM)

"In recent years monetary policy has been the rich world's main, and often only, tool to support growth."

—THE ECONOMIST

On a rather pleasant November day in Paris, Christian Noyer, the respected then governor of France's central bank, welcomed participants to the Banque de France's International Symposium "Central Banking: The Way Forward?" A who's who of the central banking world was gathered to hear him and to participate in the 2014 edition of this prestigious symposium held at the Westin hotel, substituting for the more ornate Banque de France room, which was being renovated.

Sitting in a rather intimate setting were many central bank governors from both advanced and developing countries. Janet Yellen, the chair of the U.S. Federal Reserve, was there along with several of the presidents of the regional Feds. Bank of England governor Mark Carney and then Governor Raghuram Rajan of the Indian central bank were also there, as were other governors from Africa, Asia-Pacific, Latin America, and the Middle East.

This impressive gathering of officials was joined by leading academics, thought leaders, and commentators on monetary policy. Private sector participants from major financial firms were also there, as were members of the media (though, due to space constraints, most had been seated in the balconies overlooking the nearly overflowing room).

Presenting his preview of the day's much-anticipated panels, Governor Noyer verbalized up front what many in the room viewed as both the strength and weakness of modern-day central banking. Acknowledging that "central banks have been considered the only game in town," he wondered whether "the very high expectations placed on them [might] backfire in the future."[1]

The participants had no way of knowing that just a few weeks later, the world of central banking would be shaken, and not by the actions of large institutions but rather by the unexpectedly abrupt and surprising behavior of smaller ones whose brands and reputation had been carefully aligned for many years—at least until then—to be synonymous with stability and predictability.

In the span of a few weeks, the Swiss National Bank would suddenly dismantle a key element of its exchange rate system, and do so in what proved to be an incredibly disruptive manner for markets; Singapore would alter its own exchange rate system; and Denmark would declare that it would refrain from issuing any more government bonds.

The next few weeks would also witness a market collapse in government yields, including negative levels all the way out to the nine-year point in the German yield curve and the benchmark ten-year bond there trading at just five basis points (that is, 0.05 percent). They would see investors rush to buy many newly issued bonds directly from some European governments, agreeing to pay (rather than receive) interest income for doing so. And they would witness large banks actively discourage depositors from keeping money with them.

These were just some of the many unthinkables. Switzerland's negative interest rate structure would surpass that of Germany as the central bank there battled hard to weaken the Swiss franc, long seen as an indisputable currency of strength. Even rates on more "risky" European government securities, such as those issued by Italy and Spain, would reach ultralow record levels, while Greece, another "European peripheral," would face the risk of economic implosion and threaten to default on loan payments to the International Monetary Fund, one of the world's very few "preferred creditors." (Greece did eventually default on those payments for a short period.)

Adding to the unthinkables, the Swedish central bank would join Denmark and Switzerland in opting for negative policy interest rates. Commenting on this, one observer noted that there was "no history book to turn to," adding that it was "like learning to drive backwards."[2]

The world of modern central banking and global finance was evolving in previously unthinkable ways. It had now entered a new phase of even more obvious artificiality and distortions. And it was doing so in a manner that both fascinated and deeply troubled me.

Reflecting my economics training and professional experiences in both the private and public sectors, I had grown to greatly admire central banks and cherish the important way they contribute to economic well-being. I had no doubt about their critical importance in any well-functioning ecosystem, and especially in a market-based economy.

Over the years, I had also developed quite a bit of affection for those mysterious and often ill-understood institutions of economic and financial soundness—ones whose skillful management of the price and quantity of money in an economy was key to containing inflation, promoting economic growth, and avoiding financial crises. And I had lots of respect for the very talented technocrats who were devoted to their important jobs there (and often underappreciated for the good they were responsible for).

Because of all this, I had become increasingly anxious about the growing policy burden placed on central banks, including the consequences for their future credibility, impact, and reputation. Their operational prospects were becoming more uncertain by the day. Their continued efforts since the global financial crisis to repress market volatility and promulgate a paradigm of "liquidity-assisted growth"—that is, economic growth derived from financial market booms buoyed by exceptional liquidity infusions (rather than fundamental drivers)—was failing to transition fast enough to "genuine growth" and orderly policy normalization. Meanwhile, a growing number of politicians were taking potshots at central banks while also looking into ways to rein in their operational autonomy—an autonomy essential to their effectiveness.

Ever since the 2008 global financial crisis, central banks had ventured, not by choice but by necessity, ever deeper into the unfamiliar and tricky terrain of "unconventional monetary policies." They floored interest rates, heavily intervened in the functioning of markets, and pursued large-scale programs that outcompeted one another in purchasing securities in the marketplace; to top it all off, they aggressively sought to manipulate investor expectations and portfolio decisions.

Because all this was so far away from the norm, neither central banks nor anyone else, for that matter, had tested playbooks and historical precedents to refer to. It was bold policy experimentation in real time, and for an unusually prolonged period of time.

Given all that, it soon became obvious to me that I was not the only one feeling anxious in the room in Paris. Many of us felt inherently uncomfortable about where central banks had been forced to operate, and many of us wondered about what might lie ahead.

These feelings were also evident in the fact that the organizers of the symposium had placed a question mark at the end of its title that day: "Central Banking: The Way Forward?" The organizers were rightly signaling uncertainties in one of the most important areas for the global economy, markets, and policy management, and many in the room recognized that the implications extended well beyond the economic and financial domain. There were also consequential institutional, political, geopolitical, and social issues in play.

In feeling (as one central banker put it to me) "morally and ethically" compelled to take on more and more responsibilities, central banks were reacting to realities on the ground that few if any of the other policy-making entities seemed able and willing to confront. Yet those others possessed in their policy arsenals tools that were much better suited to address the challenges in hand. Somehow, the world was now depending on the one set of institutions—central banks— with one of the narrowest sets of instruments at their disposal given the tasks at hand.

Repeatedly since the 2007–08 global financial crisis, central banks had found themselves having to do a lot more than they expected, and for much longer than they ever imagined. Their heads were increasingly telling them to stop this experimentation and start "normalizing" policies, but their hearts urged them to do even more, and to look for something new in their bag of tricks. Like a doctor tending to a sick patient, they could not walk away even though they lacked the right medication and even though they worried about the side effects of using the wrong one.

No one that I know of had accurately foreseen the length and depth of this policy dilemma.

From day one in the financial crisis, the hope had been that our courageous and responsive central banks would succeed in handing off the baton to high growth, robust job creation, price stability, and financial system soundness—either directly or, more likely, by buying enough time for the private sector to heal and for politicians to enable other policy-making entities to finally step up to their economic governance responsibilities. And with economic prosperity and jobs returning, the world would be able in the medium term to grow out of its debt problems, avoiding the need for disorderly deleveraging, devastating austerity, debt defaults, etc.

To their credit, central bankers had recognized early on that this course of action was not without risk and uncertainty. In an August 2010 conference at Jackson Hole, Wyoming, a prominent and exclusive annual gathering of central bankers from around the world and their privileged guests, Fed chairman Ben Bernanke had made the point quite explicitly. In a speech that marked the pivot in U.S. monetary policy—from targeting the normalization of financial markets (something that central banks can do well) to taking on the primary and enormous responsibility to deliver high economic growth, jobs, low and stable inflation, and overall financial stability—he observed that the use of unconventional monetary policy entailed not just "benefits" but also "costs and risks."[3] And the longer such policy was in play, the greater the probability that the costs and risks would start outweighing the benefits.

Concerns extended beyond the possibility that unconventional policies would be unsuccessful in delivering the desired policy outcomes, including what was referred to as either the "liftoff" or "escape velocity" for the economy. There were a host of other worries, some valid, others much less so.

Would prolonged central bank experimentation, and the willingness to do even more, act as a negative incentive for politicians and other economic policy-making entities to get their act together? Would the artificial pricing of financial assets, repeatedly boosted by central bank liquidity and a generalized perception that these institutions were markets' BFF (best friends forever), lead to excessive risk taking and larger resource misallocations that would come back to bite growth and stability? Would a big surge in inflation materialize down the road? Would central banks be forced to unload their ballooning balance sheets, destroying value and destabilizing financial markets? Would repressed volatility give way to damaging "volatile volatility"?[4]

These were some of the multiplying questions. At their root was a fundamental issue: To what extent were central banks risking to transition from being a major part of the solution to becoming a significant part of the problem? That is to say, rather than facilitate an orderly gradual deleveraging in the context of a growing global economy, they would end up enabling an additional accumulation of debt and resource misallocations that would leave Western economies mired in an even deeper growth malaise—one coupled with recurrent financial instability that would disrupt the economic well-being of countries in the rest of the world, including well-managed developing economies.

The worries were not limited to economic and financial issues. There were also important political, institutional, and social aspects.

Europeans in the room needed no reminder of how economic malaise was fueling political extremism and the emergence of non-traditional parties, both right and left wing; and they didn't need to hear from the Americans, who had lived through the emergence of the Tea Party a few years earlier and were about to experience unprecedented twists and turns in a presidential election campaign heavily influenced by antiestablishment candidates such as Donald Trump and Bernie Sanders. And, with all that, few in the room realized the extent of growing popular mistrust of institutions and expert opinion.

Those from Africa and the Middle East did not need to be reminded of the disruptive and violent role of nonstate actors—be it in Iraq, Libya, Syria, or Nigeria, just to name a few—and of a West too distracted to inform, influence, and coordinate a proper response, let alone impose more peaceful outcomes. And the historic surge in refugee migration was not that far away.

And no one in the room needed to be reminded of the shocking worsening income inequality within nations—one that was contributing to a gradual hollowing out of the middle class in the context of an ever-growing contrast between spreading poverty and unthinkable wealth.

Those sitting in that Paris room knew very well that there was a lot riding on central banks' crucial, unique, and experimental policymaking role, and not just for the institutions but, more broadly, for both current and future generations. It was without precedent. And it was a situation—a policy bet if you like—that central banks had stumbled into rather than carefully planned.

CHAPTER 3

CENTRAL BANKS' COMMUNICATION CHALLENGE

"The highly abnormal is becoming uncomfortably normal."[1]
—CLAUDIO BORIO, BANK FOR INTERNATIONAL SETTLEMENTS

"Houston in the blind . . ."
—SANDRA BULLOCK IN *GRAVITY*

M ost people spend little if any time thinking about how central banks impact them—not only in their daily lives but also in influencing (and even defining) the opportunities that their kids will have. Indeed, despite the substantial reach of these powerful institutions and the critical role they have played, there is still little societal recognition as to how much citizens have riding on their judgment, wisdom, and success—from protecting and enhancing their financial savings to securing credit and helping to find well-paying jobs.

The gap between awareness and reality is big, really big. It is one that cannot be justified by the irrelevance of the issues at hand (they are very relevant to our individual and collective well-beings) or by the lack of information. (Indeed, I try to highlight this point by heavily favoring in this book references that are easily available to the general public, such as newspaper articles, rather than more obscure and less-accessible academic sources.) Yet it is a gap that is not particularly surprising, because of certain legacies of central banking.

For a very long time, central banks purposely flew well below society's radar screens, opting to operate in obfuscating mystique. Indeed, as a *Financial Times* editorial put it, "Central banks used to hide their deliberations from public view more jealously than the papal conclave."[2]

To be fair, this was partly due to the highly technical nature of most of what they do on a daily basis. But it also reflected an important strategic choice.

Until the latter part of the 2000s, their leadership willingly opted for limited transparency as a means of protecting the institutions from the excessive interference of politicians (which interference many central bankers rightly feared, as it tended to be driven by short-term political objectives rather than longer-term societal ones). For decades, "Fedspeak"—as the peculiar wording of Federal Reserve remarks got to be known—was regarded as a "turgid dialect of English," involving "the use of numerous and complicated words to convey little if any meaning." It was, as Alan Greenspan, the long-serving head of the Federal Reserve (1987–2006), observed, a "language of purposeful obfuscation."[3] And it is one that Fed officials learned to "mumble with great incoherence."[4]

Chairman Greenspan's predecessors had taken a similar approach, and done so in their own particular manner. This was especially the case for Chairman Paul Volcker, whom history books rightly celebrate as being most responsible for overcoming the inflationary curse that had crippled the United States and most of the world in the 1970s. In his case, "constructive ambiguity" was delivered with such authority and assertiveness that few had the courage to question him, and those who did often regretted their decision to do so.

But the world changed in two important ways—one had to do with the analytics of central banking, the other with its practicalities.

In their quest to cement their victory over the scourge of inflation, which had eroded living standards around the world, especially in the 1970s and early 1980s, central banks realized they needed help—a realization that was backed by academic work and drove significant operational and institutional changes around the world, especially in the 1990s.

They needed a more robust degree of operational autonomy from a political system that was prone to opt for pro-inflationary actions as a means of buying short-term political support. They also needed to manage forward-looking inflationary expectations in a way that influenced wage negotiation and thus preempted excessive wage settlements that could fuel future inflation.

This led central banks to seek to influence a broader set of behaviors and expectations than had hitherto been the case, and to do so while enjoying much greater independence from their political bosses. It was no longer only about looking to directly determine the price and quantity of money. Central banks heavily got into the business of influencing expectations and the deployment of other people's money. As noted in the *Financial Times*'s editorial, "Monetary policy steers the economy through its effect on sentiment as much as any financial channel such as interest rates."[5]

Central banks initially opted for public inflation targets. The process started a quarter of a century ago in New Zealand, where, battling persistent high inflation, the central bank adopted a highly publicized inflation target of zero to 2 percent after it was approved by parliament. Looking back on the history of an action that started a worldwide phenomenon, Neil Irwin of *The New York Times* observed that this seemingly little step constituted a huge communication revolution back then: "At the time, the idea of a central bank simply announcing how much inflation it was aiming for was an almost radical idea. After all, central bankers had long considered a certain man-behind-the-curtain mystique as one of their tools of power."[6]

Another factor pushing for greater transparency involved the extent to which central banks were assuming greater power, responsibilities, and prominence—and, with that, the realization that the potential costs and risks of political misunderstanding had grown concurrently. Moreover, the "unrivalled power" displayed by the subsequent move into unconventional policies involving trillion-dollar/euro expansions in balance sheets "requires accountability towards politicians without caving in to their short-term needs."[7]

For these reasons, Chairman Greenspan's two successors at the Fed felt a strong need to evolve this tradition. And the changes proved dramatic.

First, under Chairman Bernanke starting in 2011 and then under Chair Janet Yellen, the Fed began using press conferences to explain its decisions and thinking. It engaged in many more public forums, including having the head of the Fed appear on the CBS News show *60 Minutes* and give an in-depth interview to the popular *New Yorker* magazine.[8]

Second, central banks began spending a lot of time developing their approach to "forward policy guidance"—that is, indicating to markets what the probable course of future monetary policy actions would be. This effort entailed careful wording permutations ("linguistic gymnastics"), including various specification of "thresholds" and policy time periods. They evolved from covering triggering economic developments (such as the 2013 reference to a specific level of unemployment) to calendar guidance (such as the phrase "considerable period of time" to signal a minimum six-month period of unchanged and abnormally low interest rates, and, in early 2015, "patient" to signal an interlude of at least two policy meetings before a change in policy stance).

Finally, the Fed started publishing the "blue dots," that is, the individual forecasts of members of its policy-making Federal Open Market Committee, or FOMC. As such, markets were regularly informed of the evolution of these members' numerical and timing expectations for the evolution of interest rates, including "central tendencies" (though no specific names would be disclosed).

But this increased transparency was certainly not without its critics.

While politicians were keen to push for more and, in some cases, formal auditing of its decisions, some economists felt that the Fed may have already done too much: The more it tells markets about its intentions, the greater investors' appetite to take on more risks, and do so to excessive levels, and the greater the risk of market dislocations when Fed officials would decide to change course, especially if this had to be done in an unanticipated fashion. In the process, greater communication would go from being a boost for policy making to risking Fed policy ineffectiveness.

Some individual U.S. central bankers have been more outspoken in public about the issue of potential ineffectiveness of unconventional monetary policies, and they were involved in the decision-making process, albeit from a "hawkish" perspective. As Charles Plosser noted in early 2015, "The history is that monetary policy is not ultimately a very effective tool at solving real economic structural problems. It can try for a while but the problem then is that it's only temporarily effective."[9]

Yet the most important shortfall has to do with the political system and the general public. Despite all that the Fed and others have done on "transparency" and "communication," there is still quite a bit of confusion out there on the what/how/when/why of modern central banking, and the combination of these four decisive factors— that is to say, what actually comes out of central banks—remains puzzling for many people. The vast majority of the population still does not understand well what central banks do and why; they underestimate the extent to which central banks have been driving economic and financial developments, and, as such, they have only a weak handle on what lies ahead and how they will be personally and collectively affected.

By venturing so deep into the use of experimental measures to stimulate growth and jobs, central banks have opted for some immediate relief against the increasing risk down the road of both financial instability and a meaningful erosion in their credibility and political autonomy. It's a trade-off born of prolonged reliance on "unconventional policies"—and one that already has prevailed for much longer than the central bankers themselves anticipated—results in unprecedented central bank involvement in the functioning of markets, in forcefully repressing volatility, in artificially boosting financial asset prices, in influencing how investors allocate their capital, and in impacting the distribution of income and wealth.

Of all these effects, it is the dominant influence on the pricing of stocks and bonds around the world that has attracted the most attention. In responding to my inquiry back in August 2014 as to how they assess the state of the financial markets, many of the readers of my *Bloomberg View* columns focused on the role of the Fed in pushing asset prices higher, be it directly through its large-scale purchases or indirectly by encouraging investors to take on more portfolio risks. They characterized the Fed as the "800-lb gorilla in the room and it looks like they are not in a hurry to leave." In the process, the central bank is changing the "laws of physics," spinning "straw into gold," and sprinkling "fairy dust"—all of which lulls investors into "a state of complacency" that drives investors "into a manic phase," thus turning "unpredictable" long-established relationships between asset classes.[10]

This is a world that also exposes central banks to the political accusation of being "quasi-fiscal" agencies in that they are seen by some as risking taxpayer money, buying government bonds that finance budget deficits, and deciding who gets taxpayer support, and doing all this without parliamentary approval or under executive order. And it is one of the reasons why some parliamentarians have sought to tighten the rein on central banks.

It hasn't been easy for the central bankers to deal with posturing politicians who often lack a deep enough understanding of economic and monetary policy, let alone the intricate plumbing of national and international monetary systems. And even the most collected and calm central bankers, in this case Mario Draghi, the president of the ECB, have been known to lapse—albeit very infrequently—into a visible state of irritation.

Commenting on the tone that President Draghi used "to upbraid a Spanish member of the European parliament," *New York Times* reporters Jack Ewing and Binyamin Appelbaum reminded us of a very unusual occurrence, not only for the ECB but for the vast majority of central bankers—that of Mario Draghi "raising his voice and sweeping his arm dismissively during an appearance in Parliament," and doing so "with an irritation unusual for an otherwise supremely composed central banker."[11]

The historic bet on central bank policy that Western society collectively has placed these days—and that, by implication, the rest of the world is materially exposed to—will succeed fully only if the trio of the United States, Europe, and Japan are able to emerge decisively from their low-growth malaise, and do so without contributing to excessive inequalities or fueling financial market instability. (Note that, unlike others, I worry less about the threat of inflation down the road, something that will become clearer later in the book; nor do I worry that central banks will feel compelled to unload on markets the trillions of dollars of securities they have purchased. But I do worry, a lot, about future financial instability and what that does to economic and social well-being—agreeing with Fed chair Yellen's remark that "a smoothly operating financial system promotes the efficient allocation of saving and investment, facilitating economic growth and employment."[12])

This is an unprecedented policy configuration, and the outcome so far is mixed.

CHAPTER 4

HOW AND WHY
THIS BOOK IS ORGANIZED

"Today, the growth picture is foggier. We have fear about secular stagnation at the same time as cheer about secular innovation. The technological tailwinds to growth are strong, but so too are the sociological headwinds. Buffeted by these cross-winds, future growth risks becoming suspended between the mundane and the miraculous."[1]

—ANDY HALDANE

"I am describing the outlook that I see as most likely, but based on many years of making economic projections, I can assure you that any specific projection I write down will turn out to be wrong, perhaps markedly so."

—JANET YELLEN

In this book, we will discuss how and why we have gotten to such a key juncture in our economic lives. Indeed, the purpose of the book is to shed light on how far we are from the neck of the "T junction," where we could end up subsequently, and how we can increase the probability of a good turn. To this end, it is organized into four main analytical parts following this introductory discussion.

Part II seeks to provide the historical context, and do so in a concise way that captures the essence of what has already been written (including my own book on the run-up to the 2008 global financial crisis, which set out its evolving causes and potential consequences).[2] To this end, we will travel through the recent past, viewing developments through the prism of what have been wild fluctuations in the reputation of central banks—from the mid-1990s, when they were seen as able to do no wrong (and were celebrated for having ushered in a period of great economic prosperity and financial stability), to finding themselves accused of being naïve enablers of enormous malfeasance by banks and others that brought the world to its economic knees, to rehabilitating themselves as the only effective policy responders, and brave and imaginative ones at that.

Part III takes a central bank perspective to detail the ten main issues facing society today. Having already persisted for too long, these are eating away at economic, financial, institutional, and political stability. They have been amplified, often inadvertently, by the previously unthinkable role of central banks as the "only game in town" when it comes to responsive policy making. In doing so, the discussion highlights the degree to which politicians have delegated (willingly and unwittingly) excessive responsibilities to central banks—a situation similar to highly irresponsible parents leaving their baby at the door of the fire station because they are unwilling or unable to step up to their parenting responsibilities.

Part IV deals with the outlook and what needs to be done to increase the probability and reach of good outcomes.

In explaining what lies ahead and why, my strong preference would have been to do so by asserting a single high-probability baseline. Such an approach provides clarity, assertiveness, and confidence as to outcomes. It avoids the dangers and accusations of appearing wishy-washy and indecisive. And, as a friend joked with me, it is much better to sell books! Yet as attractive as such an approach is, it is simply not a feasible option given present realities. Indeed, it would also be intellectually dishonest and analytically irresponsible to do so in the times in which we live.

There is simply too much fluidity in each of the four major factors that currently impact much of our collective well-being (economic, political/geopolitical, market, and policy issues), and the intersection of the four—which is where the real world operates—is even more fluid. As such, it is important, if not paramount, to think more broadly, including breaking away from the usual confines of well-behaved bell-shaped distributions that have the comforting attributes of very high expected outcomes and thin tails. We need to be able to embrace the increasing possibility of bimodal distribution—that is, probabilistic outcomes in which the previously most common outcome (the so-called belly of the curve) has a lower chance of materializing when compared to more extreme outcomes, both good and bad.

Accordingly, rather than pretend that we can confidently predict a single high-likelihood outcome—and though I really wish we could—this book opts for a scenario analysis that does more than highlight what Chairman Bernanke once referred to as an "unusually uncertain outlook" (that is, not just uncertain but *unusually* uncertain). Using the concept of bimodal distributions and interdisciplinary insights from behavioral science and neuroscience, I explain why the world ahead of us is likely to fundamentally challenge us as decision makers, whether we operate in companies, governments, households, or investment firms.

By taking us out of our comfort zones and keeping us there for a while, this is a world that is liable to lead us to poor decision making and sequential mistakes that can build on themselves rather than self-correct quickly. Yet none of this is predetermined or automatic. We can improve our prospects, and so Part V discusses tools for better navigating this "unusually uncertain outlook."

While government economic measures will be the most critical in determining what road the global economy takes out of the T junction—specifically, whether such measures successfully join central banks in addressing the unusual combination of cyclical, secular, and structural issues, or don't—the rest of us are by no means helpless. There are things that we can and should do to improve the prospects not just for this generation but also for future ones.

It is important to stress that there is nothing preordained at this stage about global economic outcomes. Choices matter more than destiny. And most of the choices we make require open mindsets, cognitive diversity, and the ability to function smoothly outside our traditional operating zones.

None of this is easy. But my sincere wish is that this book will do more than show you how the perspective of central banks—the most powerful, engaged, and yet still-mysterious policy-making entities in the world—provides us with important insights about the past, present, and future of the global economy. I hope that it will also provide you with analytical frameworks that can be usefully applied to other situations you may face, especially tricky ones. I, for one, have found such frameworks particularly useful over the years. I hope they will prove the same for you, too.

PART II

CONTEXT: THE RISE, COLLAPSE, AND RESURRECTION OF CENTRAL BANKING

"Consider the past quarter century: a credit boom in Japan that collapsed after 1990; a credit boom in Asian emerging economies that collapsed in 1997; a credit boom in the North Atlantic economies that collapsed after 2007; and finally in China. Each is greeted as a new era of prosperity, to collapse into crisis and post crisis."

—MARTIN WOLF[1]

THE GOLDEN AGE OF CENTRAL BANKS AND "BUBBLISH FINANCE"

A BRIEF HISTORICAL PERSPECTIVE

"It is true that a train cannot move when the brake is on, but it would be foolish to say that the cause of motion in a train is that the brake is removed."

—JOAN ROBINSON[1]

By the mid-2000s, central banks had acquired power, influence, and a reputation that went well beyond the traditional textbook characterization. Their standing was unmatched. Their actions were greatly admired. And their accomplishments were celebrated.

From seeing them as the deliverers of multi-year prosperity to promoting Chairman Greenspan as the "maestro" who had not only consolidated the Volcker victory over the dreaded enemy of inflation but also overcome the fluctuation of the business cycles, there was little if any questioning of the dominant narrative that advocated the supremacy, effectiveness, and wisdom of central banks. Looking back at this era with the benefit of hindsight, however, one sees it was only a partially warranted golden age.

Part of the golden phenomenon was warranted by the central banks' multi-decade conquering of inflation. But there was another component, a particularly dark one: the extent to which central banks' golden age involved the underregulation and supervision of a banking system that was increasingly pursuing irresponsible risk taking and excessive leverage. But before we go there, let us look at central banks themselves.

The golden age was structurally enabled by central bankers being granted greater operational autonomy by politicians, as well as an unusually favorable operational environment occasioned by an unprecedented set of global secular developments that translated into massive productivity gains and a non-inflationary boost for the world economy (including the rise of China and the integration into the global market economy of parts of central and eastern Europe).

As notable as these factors were—and they were real and consequential—their visibility obfuscated other, less comforting developments. And few took the trouble of looking properly under the hood of the U.S. economy to figure out what was really going on.

As it turned out—and painfully so for many in society—the special economic and financial era promoted by central banks was outpacing the institutions' ability to analytically understand it. Consequently, rather than lead a new parade of durable economic prosperity and financial liberalization, central bankers were in fact losing control of complicatedly leveraged bubblish economies that were fueling ever-excessive credit entitlement, irresponsible lending, and extremely lax risk management. They were consistently and meaningfully falling behind a debt parade that would require a massive cleanup operation in its wake.

In effect, and as I discussed in my first book, written in the fall of 2007,[2] central banks were failing to adequately evolve their understanding of economic and financial developments. Like many others, they had been lulled into a sense of complacency that, at least in their minds, was robustly underpinned by the notion of a "great moderation." They also believed that the financial sector was dominated by sophisticated private sector participants who were armed with better risk mitigation instruments and therefore it was enabled to do more good than before in its two key areas of societal responsibilities: allocating resources to productive uses in a cost-effective manner, and the good management of risks associated with this.

From former Fed chair Alan Greenspan to Tim Geithner, who served both as Treasury secretary and as president of the New York Fed, several officials have subsequently acknowledged that they underestimated not just the fragility of the banking system but also the looming mortgage crisis, the failure of risk management approaches, and the degree of interconnectedness of all this.

It is now crystal clear that central banks ended up taking an overly relaxed approach to the deregulation of financial activities. They sat largely idle as whole chunks of complex financial activities migrated to shadow banking sectors that lacked proper supervision and were subject to little external regulation and insufficient internal discipline. Even though banks benefited from safety nets funded by the taxpayer, regulators and supervisors became oblivious to the complicated risks that banks were adding to balance sheets.[3]

This slippage was shared by many. In a frank interview with *Business Insider* on the "big things" he had misread in his career, the Nobel Prize–winning economist Paul Krugman stated that he had had "no idea of the fragility of the banking system."[4] And he was certainly not alone.

This was a generalized phenomenon among the majority of economists and financial commentators. It was aggravated by a failure that persists even today: the inability of conventional economic approaches to integrate well the financial service industry along with important insights from behavioral science.

As William Dudley, the president and chief executive officer of the New York Federal Reserve, stated in his thoughtful January 2014 speech, which included an assessment of the current state of knowledge at the Fed: "We still don't have well developed macro-models that incorporate a realistic financial sector."[5]

With the benefits of hindsight, this was an era that distorted central banks' understanding not just of what banks were doing but also of general economic developments, creditworthiness, regulation, and supervision. As a result, instead of seeing and treating the financial service industry for what it is—subservient to the real economy—they stood by as the industry was elevated to a stand-alone position that proved unrealistic, unsustainable, and very damaging to the general economic well-being.

Thanks to lax supervision and regulation, a significant part of the banking sector was no longer focused on its traditional role of serving the real economy—by mobilizing savings and channeling them in a cost-effective fashion to the most productive investment opportunities, and by managing associated risks. Instead, banks sought to develop an independent and separate status that would deliver lots of dollars to the bottom line. But it was one that far outpaced—if not ignored—realities, and that was undermined by misaligned incentives, comprehensive failures, and excessively short-term motivations and behaviors.

Even the common labeling of the industry itself changed—from "financial services" to just "finance." To make things worse, the industry was elevated in some quarters as constituting a superior phase in the historical evolution of capitalism, and one that any self-respecting mature economy should aspire to.

No longer was the historic process of economic development characterized as just involving the various value-added stages of agriculture, industry, manufacturing, and services. Suddenly, the highest level of capitalistic achievement involved "finance." And an increasing number of countries competed to establish "the world's financial center" or smaller offshore centers. And some of those who couldn't do so directly felt comfortable renting out segments of their domestic financial sector or leveraging that of others.

Enabled and empowered by this new approach, and helped by financial innovations such as securitization, banks embarked on a whole new range of activities (many of which involved trading ever more complexly structured pieces of paper among themselves, as well as placing them with others that had an even weaker understanding). With hindsight, it is now clear, including to banks themselves, that too many of these activities involved risk taking that they only partially understood but that seemingly appeared too lucrative to pass up. More generally, their operational focus became increasingly divorced from basic economic functions.

Banks were not the only ones caught in this feast of leverage, credit, and debt entitlement. Indeed, as detailed by Atif Mian and Amir Sufi in their recent book, *House of Debt,* the phenomenon was a much broader one, with households (and, I would add, companies) also falling victim to it.[6]

Having access to new "exotic" lending vehicles that dismantled traditional barriers to expensive and, for some, hard-to-get credit—such exotic instruments as home mortgage loans and refinancing that required no income verification, involved no up-front fees or down payments, and whose repayment conditions could be structured in a very back-loaded manner—too many households embarked on financial activities that they could not pay for, taking risks that they really did not understand. In the process, they did more than mortgage future income that they would have difficulty generating. To capture a piece of what appeared as a housing market that could only go up in value, too many took on mortgage debt that they could not afford, fueling an unusual combination of subsequent foreclosures, bankruptcies, and poverty.

Governments were not immune to this societal phenomenon. Many, including the least creditworthy ones that could ill afford commercial borrowing terms, were tempted by the easy availability of debt financing as creditors rushed to provide financing at ever more lenient terms. With the private sector credit factories working at feverish levels of activity, the notion of proper creditworthiness analysis gave way to an emphasis on driving lending volumes ever higher. As such, a crazy culture of risk tolerance and spread convergence took hold. Even the worst-managed countries found themselves able

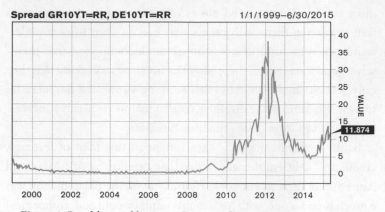

Figure 1. Bonds' spread between Greece and Germany
(Data from Thomson Reuters)

to access large loans on terms (interest rate and maturity) that no longer diverged materially from those offered to the best-managed ones (Figure 1, illustrating the extent to which the spread on Greek bonds relative to German ones was compressed for many years).

The result was a generation that mistakenly fell in love with the notion that credit rather than income could underpin a growing standard of living and national prosperity. Debt became an entitlement rather than a bridge to be used cautiously. One financial bubble after the other emerged and remained unaddressed. Central banks essentially sat on the sidelines, comforted by the notion that banks and institutional investors were mature and responsible enough to mitigate risks in a timely manner. They believed in the self-regulation of these influential market participants, and they were confident that markets had the ability to self-correct in a timely and orderly fashion.

Drawing lessons from this extraordinary period, Bank of England governor Mark Carney presented this important insight to the conference on "Inclusive Capitalism" in 2014: "The answers start from recognizing that financial capitalism is not an end in itself, but a means to promote investment, innovation, growth and prosperity. Banking is fundamentally about intermediation—connecting borrowers and savers in the real economy. In the run-up to the crisis, banking became about banks and not businesses; transactions not relations; counterparties not clients. New instruments originally designed to meet the credit and hedging needs of businesses quickly morphed into ways to amplify bets on financial outcomes."[7]

It became a matter of time until all this illustrated Herbert Stein's famously simple yet elegant formulation about the unsustainable: "If something cannot go on forever, it will stop." And when it stopped, it did so in an abrupt and incredibly damaging manner.

CHAPTER 6

CASCADING FAILURES

"Everyone has a plan until they get punched in the mouth."

—MIKE TYSON

"These are days when the improbable can become the inevitable."

—JIM DWYER

Rather than mark a decisive victory over the vagaries of the business cycle, the golden age of central banking ended up underpinning an historic period of excessive and irresponsible risk taking. The economic and financial chaos that followed was so intense as to totally discredit the concept of the great economic moderation and of sophisticated risk management by the private sector. In the process, it dismantled the notion of central bank dominance, along with their sterling reputation.

By 2007, it started to become clear that finance-dependent economies had gone too far in trusting and enabling banks, and in regulating them just with a "light touch" that assumed adequate "self-regulation." This was not just the case in the United States and the United Kingdom, which had engaged in a vigorous battle that pitched New York versus London as the dominant global financial center. It was also the case for places such as Dubai, Iceland, Ireland, Switzerland, and elsewhere, which sought to use finance to escape the domestic limitations of small economic size by leveraging and internationalizing their financial institutions.

It also started to become clear, albeit only very slowly at first and then in a frighteningly accelerating fashion, that national authorities had been pushed into an awful catch-22: either bail out financial miscreants using taxpayers' funds, or allow a financial debacle to cause even greater havoc to an already struggling real economy.

The first public sign of problems surfaced in the first week of August 2007, when Paribas, a sizeable French bank, announced losses and restricted investors' ability to withdraw their capital from some investment funds. The shock was notable because it involved two of the elements that market participants fear the most, and, understandably so. In fact, they fear them much more than large adverse price movements: First, access to funds was restricted as the bank could no longer provide the liquidity that its clients desired, expected, and had assumed was automatic; second, the disruptions sent broader tremors as they undermined the normal functioning of markets.

Recognizing the threat at hand, the ECB under its experienced president Jean-Claude Trichet responded quickly and decisively. In doing so, it managed to deal with the immediate threat. That was the good news. The less good news is that neither the ECB nor the central banking community as a whole seemed to fully grasp the notion that the Paribas shock, rather than being isolated and institution-specific, was indicative of something that was much bigger and much more consequential—that is, the formation of a potentially catastrophic tsunami.

If anything, the central banks' reaction function ended up being too gradual and way too piecemeal. Its design was a tactical one, lacking both the sufficient analytical foundation and the more comprehensive follow-through of a well-thought-out strategic approach. With hindsight, it was yet another illustration of the extent to which they (and much of society) still lacked sufficient understanding of realities on the ground—and not only in areas that had migrated outside their formal supervisory purview but also for activities that were taking place right under their regulatory noses.

Increasingly, central banks found themselves caught between conflicting internal/external narratives. To the outside world, they displayed a sense of calm, highlighted by the often-quoted remarks by Chairman Bernanke reassuring the world on the soundness of the U.S. housing market and of its heavily exposed banks and specialized institutions. Internally, they had started to play a game of catch-up with dangerous circumstances that gradually became increasingly obvious over the next year, culminating in cascading failures that very few policymakers and market participants will ever forget.

The second big visible tremor hit in March 2008. Bear Stearns, once one of America's most established and reputable investment banks, found itself on the verge of a total collapse. Once again, complex financial engineering and extremely leveraged positioning were at the heart of the problem, together with inadequate understanding, sloppy supervision, and lax accounting given the extreme risk taking that all this entailed. And once again, dramatic central bank action—this time quarterbacked by the Federal Reserve under Chairman Bernanke—was needed to restore calm before things got really out of hand.

Unlike the ECB's emergency response seven months earlier involving liquidity injections, the Fed's intervention made broader use of the public balance sheet. Importantly, it provided financial (loss-protected) backing for a shotgun wedding between failing Bear Stearns and solid-standing JPMorgan Chase.

Central banks' hope was that these two very sudden and disturbing shocks, together with the exceptional nature of the policy response, would entice banks to de-risk in an orderly manner. Instead, banks seemed beholden to what economists call "moral hazard"— that is, the inclination to take more risk because of the perceived backing of an effective and decisive insurance mechanism.

There is perhaps no better example of this phenomenon than what

Chuck Prince, the then CEO of Citigroup, one of the biggest and most closely followed banks in the world, told the *Financial Times* in a front-page interview. Commenting on the prospects for problems down the road, he stated: "When the music stops, in terms of liquidity things will be complicated. But as long as the music is playing, you've got to get up and dance. We're still dancing."[1] And when the music did indeed end, Chuck Prince lost his job and Citi almost went bankrupt.

In effect, good old-fashioned human blind spots, rigid mindsets, cognitive narrowness, hubris, and institutional rigidities were in play. Their potentially disastrous impact was amplified by irresponsible risk taking associated with misaligned financial incentives, classic principal-agent problems, and excessive short-termism. And the results were cumulative deteriorations on the ground that had already far outpaced the ability of the whole system to adequately understand the problem and play catch-up. As such, it wasn't long before the consequences became scarily obvious to all.

By the summer of 2008, it was no longer a question of crisis prevention; the world was thrown into full crisis management mode—and on a scale and scope that few had ever thought possible in our modern global economy.

This type of potential economic calamity had not been seen since the Great Depression. It ran counter to deeply held beliefs about the efficiency and self-regulatory nature of modern capitalism. It placed huge demands on crisis managers who still had not fully grasped the enormity of the issues. And it involved some private sector leaders who were either too blind or too proud to realize the extent of reckless business that had taken place under their noses during their leadership tenures.

With multiplying banking disruptions and some spectacular bankruptcies, including the disorderly collapse of investment bank

Lehman Brothers in September 2008, it quickly became blatantly and horribly apparent to all that finance had brought the world to the edge of a multi-year great depression. In the process, the popular perception of central banks went from enabler of sustainable prosperity to inadvertent accomplice in allowing irresponsible financiers to gamble with the fate of current and future generations.

The sudden popular dismay, including accusations that financial authorities had been on the receiving end of a massive "regulatory capture,"[2] was accompanied by panic among central bankers that, in addition to lacking sufficient first responder tools to deal with the emergency, they also had only partial information on critical economic and financial linkages.

Noting that the transcripts of the Fed's 2008 meetings (a 1,865-page document released to the public in 2014) presented "one of the most detailed portrayals of the fear and confusion that reigned in the autumn of 2008," Robin Harding wrote in the *Financial Times,* "When Lehman Brothers collapsed, the U.S. Federal Reserve struggled to comprehend the danger facing the global economy."[3]

The battle to understand the full extent of the calamity was combined with the need to mentally pivot on a number of issues—a pivot that challenged many established and entrenched mindsets.

The transcripts of the 2009 meetings that were released in March 2015 show Federal Reserve officials intensely worried and quite pessimistic as they scramble to come to grips with an economy "spiralling into Japanese-style economic crises."[4] Chair Yellen, who then sat on the FOMC in her capacity as president of the San Francisco Fed, remarked that a quick, V-like rebound was implausible and that "even a gradual U-shaped recovery was unlikely." She added that, in applying aggressive policy measures, "we are desperately trying to power a bicycle uphill rather than pressing an accelerator on a high-powered sports car."

Coming into the crisis, quite a few Fed officials were caught looking at the wrong set of risks. As the transcripts show, they were much more concerned about the threat of inflation than the possibility of a financial "sudden stop" that would bring the world to the edge of something really sinister.

Commenting on this, Matthew O'Brien of *The Washington Post* undertook a simple yet illuminating word count in a blog post for the Brussels-based Bruegel think tank. He found that, in the run-up to the Lehman collapse, the mentions of "inflation" in the transcripts vastly outnumbered those for "systemic risks/crises": 468 versus 35 at the June 2008 FOMC meeting and 322 versus 19 at the August meeting. Even more notable: "At the September 16, 2008 meeting [that is the day after Lehman failed] there were 129 mentions of inflation . . . and only 4 of systemic risks/crises."[5]

This was in turn related to a massive historical underestimation of the extent to which a once much-admired and sophisticated financial network could go from being an efficiency creator/risk mitigator to a complex disseminator/amplifier of financial and economic chaos.

As such, central bankers—acting both nationally and in a coordinated global fashion—struggled to trip whatever circuit breakers they could come up with. As failures cascaded from one place to another, however, they struggled to find enough to trip, and they were nowhere near finding the major switch.

By the fall of 2008, Ben Bernanke, the chair of the Federal Reserve, the world's most powerful central bank, had no choice but to go to Congress and warn of a massive economic calamity that was hitting America and the world. Accompanied by Treasury Secretary Hank Paulson, they essentially begged lawmakers to approve, in record time no less, previously unthinkable amounts of funding to stabilize a financial system that had lost all of its anchors and was now spreading damage far and wide. There are even stories of Secretary Paulson going down on one knee to urge congressional leader Nancy Pelosi to back his controversial and expensive rescue plan.[6]

A shocked and scared global citizenry started wondering how central banks had allowed the situation to get so out of hand, so desperate, and so dangerous. Many routine economic and financial activities were now subject to disruptive sudden stops. People like me started receiving multiple calls, not only from bewildered lawmakers and policymakers around the world, but also from everyday individuals and family members—including requests to speak at schools, libraries, and other venues to explain what was going on and why.

Facing a potential chaos that had been deemed by so many to be unlikely if not unimaginable, some central bankers were seemingly "flapping around like fish on a slab." Even the more qualified ones were "bewildered by the speed and novelty of the events unfolding before them."[7] And this was before they were able to fully comprehend the scope and scale of the calamity.

The fourth quarter of 2008 turned out to constitute one of the most dramatic modern collapses in output and trade. Unemployment shot up, with the United States alone losing 8 million jobs (Figure 2). Cross-border trade came to almost a virtual stop (Figure 3), adding to the collapse in economic activity. Letters of credit were virtually impossible to open. Even successful companies with robust balance sheets found themselves cut off from working capital.

Prices across a very broad set of financial assets hit huge air pockets. And many of those that were able to deploy cash quickly to take advantage of striking bargains lost their willingness to do so, even when confronted with what a few weeks earlier they would have regarded as dirt-cheap prices and historic bargains.

As catastrophic as things seemed at the time, it was only later that many realized how really bad things actually were. And all this paled in comparison to what would have occurred had the "sudden stop" continued. For well beyond the visible economic and financial disruption lay a much less visible weakness that nonetheless constitutes one of the greatest Achilles' heels of market economies and an interlinked global economy—the erosion of trust in the payments and settlement system.

Living in California, a car-oriented culture with a soft spot for drive-through fast-food joints (and now drive-through Starbucks, too), I have used a simple analogy to illustrate what happened during those dramatic few days. This was the period when Lehman's disor-

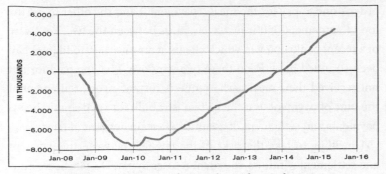

Figure 2. Job losses in the United States due to financial crisis
(Data from Bureau of Labor Statistics [2015])

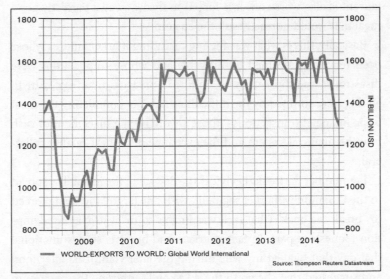

Figure 3. Cross-border trade collapses
(Data from Thomson Reuters)

derly bankruptcy and its aftermath brought the whole leverage edifice down, taking the world to the edge of a disastrous multi-year depression. It was a situation that no country in the world could have escaped unscathed.

Imagine a customer ordering a Big Mac meal at her local McDonald's drive-through. She is directed to two windows after placing the order—one to pay for the meal ("payment") and the other to get the food ("settlement"). It is just a few yards between the two. Yet aware of a recent bankruptcy in which clients at another fast-food joint had been stranded in between these two windows—having paid for but not received their meals—she requests instantaneous settlement at the time of payment. But the system isn't built for such simultaneous payments and settlement. It assumes a certain amount of trust.

Unwilling to take the risks of the few feet between the payment and settlement windows, the client refuses to pay. Despite being hungry, she ends up driving away with no food. And, remember, she has both access to food and the means to pay for it. Meanwhile, the restaurant is also worse off. It is forced to throw away a perfectly good meal that would normally suit the customer.

Basically, this is what was fueling cascading market failures whose occurrence was deemed unthinkable and whose implications were disastrous. And those of us on trading floors with direct exposure to all this were stunned by the difficulties faced in completing the most basic financial transactions—those involving the placement of cash into the financial system and the exchange of highest-quality collateral.

I remember particularly vividly the day when the instability spread to the U.S. money market segment, with one large fund being forced to "break the buck" (that is, it was unable to meet its client redemption requests at par). In fact, markets had become so dysfunctional that day that I called my wife during the later California afternoon and suggested that she go to the ATM and withdraw the maximum allowed for us per day ($500 I think it was). When she asked me why, I responded that I felt there was some chance that the banks would not open the next day.

I doubt many would have believed me at that time. After all, the United States was no fragile developing country with immature financial institutions and a badly managed central bank. We were living in a mature capitalistic country with a sophisticated financial system, a powerful central bank, and crisis circuit breakers.

It was only many months later that my worries were validated by the public recollections of Chairman Bernanke and Treasury Secretary Paulson, including Bernanke's characterization of those "very, very dark hours."[8] Yes, the United States and therefore much of the rest of the world had come very close to declaring a "bank holiday" that would have shut down the financial system in order to subsequently reset it in a sustainable fashion.

Moreover, as Secretary Geithner noted in his book on the crisis, members of the economic team "talked openly" about nationalizing major banks. And this was but one of several issues over which they found themselves "at odds," though the message from his book is that these "disagreements did not turn out to be consequential."[9]

With the world suffering significant damage and dangerously standing on the edge of an even greater calamity as a result of financial irresponsibility, it was only a matter of time until the blame game started in earnest. Banks would find themselves in the direct line of fire, of course, and understandably so. Central banks would also be targeted, if only because they had evolved—inadvertently—into naïve enablers of malfeasance.

CHAPTER 7

CENTRAL BANK RESURRECTION

DURABLE OR A DEAD CAT BOUNCE?

"The best way to predict the future is to invent it."

—ALAN KAY

"In the last three years plus, central banks have had little choice but to do the unsustainable in order to sustain the unsustainable until others do the sustainable in order to restore sustainability."

—MOHAMED A. EL-ERIAN

Faced with all this chaos, and the possibility of even worse things to come, central banks shifted from a laissez-faire mode to a highly interventionist "whatever it takes" (WIT) mode. It was a dramatic change.

Working with their counterparts in fiscal agencies—a phenomenon that was anticipated by that dramatic joint visit by Chairman Bernanke and Secretary Paulson to the leadership on Capitol Hill—they threw everything they had, and could think of, into stabilizing an enormously dysfunctional financial system.

The money-printing presses went into overdrive. A myriad of emergency funding windows were opened to enable cash to be injected into the financial system, and from virtually any and all directions. Sovereign borrowing and credit guarantees were issued left, right, and center. Direct public funding was placed into all the major American banks and many of the smaller ones.

It was the equivalent of desperately throwing at the wall whatever you could come up with, and hoping that something would stick. After a perilous phase, things started to stick.

The unprecedented deployment of liquidity and direct involvement in markets played a critical role in reconnecting the wires of the market system and restoring trust. It started with the payments and settlement system and spread to fixing other sources of dysfunction. Credit lines were gradually restored and, as more people were willing to reengage, the system slowly but surely normalized and healed. With that, the spiraling-down economic activity found and established the floor necessary for a rebound, though a frustratingly slow and sluggish one.

Central bankers' bold and innovative interventions saved the world from a truly terrible outcome—one that would have devastated the current generation and severely undermined the welfare of future ones. So after the central banks had been thrashed for overseeing an acutely irresponsible banking system, their standing and reputation slowly recovered. After all, they had saved the world from a horrid catastrophe.

The central banks had also bought time for the politicians to get their act together. Driven by the enormous stakes, world leaders came together in London in April 2009 at a G20 Summit that, I am willing to bet, will be characterized by the history books as an excellent example of—sadly, too rare a case—effective global policy coordination. Together the G20 committed to supporting central bank policies with reinforcing fiscal measures and expanded multilateral funding.

With the imminent danger of a multi-year world depression averted, the global economy started to heal. In a pattern that had not been seen before, this recovery process was led by the systemically important emerging economies. Rather than be totally derailed by the collapse in the Western world—indeed, it was often said that when the West caught a cold, the emerging world would end up in the hospital, and with some countries in the ICU—they led the way. Unexpectedly for many, they—with China at the front—became a robust locomotive for a global economy that was still structurally impaired by the overleveraged advanced economies.

Acting boldly in the dark months that followed the Lehman collapse in September 2008, central banks did more than avert total economic, financial, and social devastation. They also wrote a playbook that, later, in July 2012, would be deployed again to avert the collapse of the Eurozone, a central component of Europe's historic regional integration project.

This time around, it was ECB president Mario Draghi declaring that the central bank stood "ready to do whatever it takes to preserve the euro."[1] For emphasis, and to remove any possible doubt as to his steadfast "WIT" commitment and expectations, he quickly added, "and believe me, it will be enough."

Perhaps because financial markets remembered the implications of the Fed's "whatever it takes" mode, President Draghi's words were magical. By themselves, they sufficed to restore order and pull the Eurozone back from the brink of a messy and costly fragmentation. The central bank did not have to deploy any funds at that time. Instead, private market participants did all the heavy lifting.

This magic trick did a lot more than restore calm to financial markets that were on the verge of dismantling the Eurozone's monetary union. It realigned the power hierarchy within the Eurozone, propelling the ECB to a leading, if not dominant, position. Indeed, as noted by Jack Ewing and Binyamin Appelbaum, two respected financial journalists at *The New York Times,* "By some measures, Mr. Draghi is at the peak of his powers. Wielding the moral authority he acquired after calming the markets and pulling the Eurozone from the brink with his 'whatever it takes' promise, he has overseen an expansion of the European Central Bank's jurisdiction."[2]

Undoubtedly, central banks established themselves as potent crisis managers. Moreover, with politicians seeming to lose their focus after the London Summit as the most extreme aspects of the crisis receded, these monetary institutions emerged not just as effective but also as the sole policy-making entities. They were, as Governor Noyer noted, the "only game in town." But rather than warrant limitless celebration, this dominance policy would become a cause for concern (for me and others) over time.

What was meant as a temporary intervention ended up lasting much, much longer than anyone had envisioned, including central bankers themselves. The economic recovery continuously undershot their expectations, compounding concerns not only about effectiveness but also about the eventual exit process itself—including the management of market expectations, the persistence of large central bank balance sheets, and how to coordinate all this with other government agencies (particularly the fiscal agencies).[3]

These concerns were summarized bluntly in the 2014 Annual Report of the Bank for International Settlements (known as the central bank of central banks) when it referred to prospects for a "bumpy exit" as central banks found it "difficult to ensure a smooth normalization."[4] And it was confirmed a few months later with the messy exit in January 2015 of the Swiss National Bank from a currency peg arrangement designed to reduce the exposure of Switzerland to the Eurozone crisis and by the decision by the ECB and others to opt for negative interest rates.

Rather than pivot from financial normalization to full recovery, the Eurozone stalled in a multiple 1 percent zone—a low economic growth of 1 percent, "low-flation" of 1 percent, and the more generalized problem within the advanced world of the top 1 percent of the population capturing the vast majority of the income and wealth gains.

For those recognizing how close the region had gotten to severe financial fragmentation and economic implosion, this 1 percent zone did not seem that bad. Yet the longer the European economy stayed there, the greater the downside risks threatening a new recession, large structural unemployment, deflation, political extremism, and risks to the social fabric.

With other policy-making entities persistently slow to respond, the ECB had no choice but to venture deeper into experimental policies. In June 2014 it made history by doing what no central bank has done outside a major financial crisis—that is, pushed the rate on bank deposits to a negative level. In January 2015, the central bank went even further, committing to large-scale purchases of market securities that would expand its balance sheet by 1 trillion euros.

In what *The Wall Street Journal* loudly proclaimed on its January 23 front page was a "new era" (Figure 4), the ECB had embarked on a large and relatively open-ended quantitative easing (QE). It reaffirmed the use of the asset channel as a means of countering deflationary expectations and low growth. And to stress its seriousness, President Draghi indicated in the ECB press conference that the central bank stood ready to buy bonds at negative yields (yes, negative), and it did.

This was quite a statement from a central bank known historically for its reluctance to venture even an inch away from orthodoxy, and for an institution whose decision-making Governing Council has to strike difficult political compromises while retaining the support of the famously conservative Germans.[5]

Throughout all this, markets have rejoiced at the continuing engagement of central banks, institutions that became investors' best friends. They have repeatedly done so in the context of what Tracy Alloway, a *Financial Times* reporter at the time, labeled "the cult of central banks."[6]

Due to repeated conditioning, investors had come to expect central bank intervention whenever asset prices hit a notable air pocket or economic conditions faltered anew. As such, even sensible market price corrections were artificially curtailed by the demonstrable notion that, supported by central banks, investors should always buy the dip. And in doing so, they were handsomely rewarded.

Repeated and therefore reliable (at least in the eyes of most investors) central bank activism rekindled two of the most powerful terms in the markets' lexicon: "goldilocks" and the "great moderation." Their reappearance was fueled by a long period of rock-bottom interest rates—so much so that the highly respected Fed vice chair Stanley Fischer remarked in December 2014 at *The Wall Street Journal*'s CEO Council, "We have almost got used to thinking that zero is the natural place for the interest rate. It is far from it."

Markets had also gotten used to a prolonged period of unusually low volatility, a gradually improving U.S. economy, and a central

Figure 4. *WSJ*—New Era
(Credit: *The Wall Street Journal*)

bank declaring its willingness to be "patient"—all taken to signal an even longer period of relative economic and financial calm, regardless of how it is artificially sustained. Stable growth, albeit low, and repressed financial volatility translated into an environment that naturally encouraged investors to take more risk, including by borrowing and leveraging to increase market exposure across a wide range of risk factors.

With "the trend being your friend," and repeatedly so, and with asset price volatility so low, the overwhelming temptation was to "ride the market" not just up to but also beyond sensible indications of a likely "turn." After all, central banks had ensured that corrections would prove small, temporary, and quickly reversible. "Rational bubble riding" became acceptable, and the incentive to do so was turbocharged by an industry that has become more short-term focused in assessing both absolute and relative performance, and in which capital can move quite quickly given that few end investors are willing to revise down their return expectations.

To some, the behavior of financial markets once again showed insufficient heed paid to the important insights of Hyman Minsky, the American economist. Known for his "financial instability hypothesis,"[7] Minsky argued that, in capitalist economies, periods of financial stability give rise to subsequent periods of great financial instability.

The extent of underlying moral hazard became more and more notable. I remember being bemused in October 2014 by the extent to which the return of some modest market volatility caused some respected market participants to call for the Fed to come up with "QE4"—that is, yet another program of large-scale asset purchases in order to repress market volatility and artificially boost asset prices again.

To be clear, this was a period during which U.S. growth was picking up and (very slowly) becoming somewhat less skewed to favor the better-off; the economy was on an impressive run of producing 200,000-plus jobs each month (one that lasted more than twelve consecutive months). Consumer confidence was on the rise, and the Fed was in the very final stage of a well-communicated exit from QE3. Yet all it took was some volatility triggered by developments in the rest of the world for pleas to be made to the Fed to introduce yet another large-scale asset purchase program.

To render this situation even more absurd, the most direct targets of a QE4—interest rates on government bonds, new mortgages, and home refinancing—were already at very low historical levels.[8] Banks were flush with liquidity, holding large excess reserves at the Fed. There was nothing to suggest that the upcoming midterm elections would deliver a less dysfunctional Washington that would be able to come up finally with a comprehensive policy response that the Fed could bridge to. And, in any case, the vast majority of American companies and households were starting to benefit from the precipitous decline in international oil prices.

And yet quite a few people found it quite natural to advocate a QE4. The underlying behavioral conditioning spoke to a nasty reality facing many central banks around the world.

This episode served as a reminder of how several prior attempts to exit experimental components of monetary policy ended with central banks pulled in deeper instead. Now, it is not as if central bankers were not aware of the problem. They were. Indeed, during periods of market calm, several of them had warned markets about the potential for volatility down the road, including Bank of England governor Mark Carney, who in January 2015 warned during the World Economic Forum in Davos, Switzerland, that "the difference between market and policymakers' expectations could have a large impact on financial system volatility."[9]

And the longer they persisted with their experimental policy approach, the more I worried about the greater danger that they would gradually slip from being part of the solution so far—indeed, in practice, *the* only meaningful and consequential part of the solution—to being part of the problem.

Disappointing economic outcomes and heightened concerns about inequality, along with surging financial markets that have sharply decoupled from Main Street's more sluggish realities— developments that we will discuss in greater detail in the next part— naturally aggravated popular dissatisfaction with the financial sector and its regulators. This was about much more than "bailout fatigue." It involved (and still involves) deep-rooted anger and a considerable trust deficit—not only for central banks' enabling irresponsible risk taking but also for then funneling trillions of bailout dollars into the sector and engineering a huge financial recovery whose benefits, once again, accrued disproportionately to Wall Street as opposed to Main Street.

There was in fact very little understanding of the following valid observation in Secretary Timothy Geithner's book on the crisis: "The President knew he couldn't fix the broader economy without first fixing the financial system. Banks are like the economy's circulatory system, as vital to its everyday functioning as the power grid. No economy can grow without a financial system that works."[10]

But as much as banks were "fixed," the broader economy still languished at the national, regional, and global levels. The major areas of malaise, and those consequential for the well-being of current and future generations, could be grouped in the ten actionable areas discussed in the next part. The longer these forces are in play, the greater the internal tensions and contradictions that eat away at the sustainability of stable growth and low financial volatility.

PART III

FROM THE WHAT
TO THE SO WHAT

"So what do we do? Anything. Something. So long as we just don't sit there. If we screw it up, start over. Try something else. If we wait until we've satisfied all the uncertainties, it may be too late."

—LEE IACOCCA

CHAPTER 8

SETTING THE STAGE

THE TEN BIG CHALLENGES

"The virus of radical monetary intervention has entered the world's political bloodstream."

—JIM GRANT[1]

This recent roller-coaster journey by central banks has been associated with ten concerning developments that together set the stage for the book's transition from the *what* to the *how, what next, why,* and *so what*—not only of central banking, but also of what lies ahead for the global economy.

After falling asleep at the switch in the run-up to the financial crisis, these powerful institutions responded in an impressive fashion and helped the world avert a global depression. But, when other policymakers with better tools failed to step up to their responsibilities, they were forced to continue to rely for too long on partial and imperfect instruments. As such, the results have fallen short of what was both expected and needed, and the bold and impressive response of central banks can be deemed as only partially successful, and certainly not without unintended consequences and growing risks of collateral damage.

Yes, central banks managed to arrest the spread of horrendous economic and financial crises and thus averted tremendous human suffering. Yes, they helped economies establish a floor and grow from there, albeit timidly. And yes, they forced banks to restructure and get their act together while buying time for companies and households to heal.

For all that, we should all be grateful for their courage, innovation, and determination. But given "the only game in town" syndrome, it should not come as much of a surprise that central banks have failed to generate what Western economies—and the world—need most: high, durable, and inclusive growth together with genuine financial stability. As a result, central bank actions indeed ended up being a lot more helpful to Wall Street than to Main Street.

The Economist put it well in May 2014, when it stated that "low interest rates and low volatility have a bigger impact on asset prices than on real investment, and risk creating financial bubbles long before economies reach full employment."[2]

The Bank for International Settlements (BIS) went further when it warned advanced economies about "financial booms [that] sprinkle the fairy dust of illusionary riches."[3] Then there was a *Wall Street Journal* article looking at the "Investor's Dilemma" and noting that "investing these days is like shopping at Neiman Marcus: Almost everything is expensive."[4]

Both the BIS and the *Journal* were reflecting a concern shared by many others. In normalizing and sprinting ahead to break record after record, financial markets had decoupled quite a bit from the more sluggish fundamentals. Specifically, since central banks' unconventional approach has a much larger impact on financial markets than on the real economy, asset prices had surged to levels that by most measures were higher than what would be warranted by underlying economic and corporate conditions. The larger this decoupling got, the heavier the associated stress and strain on social cohesion, political coherence, and multilateral coordination.

As hard as they had tried, it remained to be seen whether central banks would succeed in firmly placing the economies back on a sustainable path of high inclusive growth and durable financial stability, or be able to exit their hyperactive mode without that in itself creating economic problems and financial instability.

Today, it also remains unclear how the world will deal with growing "divergence" in policy prospects among the most systematically important central banks. (Some central banks, such as the ECB and the Bank of Japan, are likely to press even harder on the stimulus accelerator; others, such as the Federal Reserve, will be gradually easing their foot off the pedal.) Moreover, because it can be argued that they have acted less and less as monetary institutions and more and more as "quasi-fiscal" agencies, it remains to be seen how much political risk they have incurred for their hard-won independence from governments, together with the critical operational autonomy that that allows.

As much as we should all wish otherwise, more than eight years after the big eruption of the global financial crisis, the advanced economies are saddled with ten key issues whose detrimental consequences are multifaceted and worrisomely self-feeding. The consequences are not limited to these countries. Even the most successful emerging countries and companies find it hard to navigate the new environment characterized by these ten key challenges. And because of all the moving pieces and the complex interconnections in the global economy, we need to understand and pay even greater heed to Chairman Bernanke's 2010 reminder that central banks' experimental policies involve a mix of "benefits, costs, and risks" that entail a truly "unusually uncertain outlook."

The longer it takes for other policy-making entities to join central banks in meeting their economic management responsibilities, the greater the risk that the benefits of our prolonged reliance on unconventional monetary policies will be outweighed by collateral damage and unintended consequences. The concern is less the traditional one—connected to an inflationary surge—and more the trade-off between immediate growth and financial instability down the road, as well as political ramifications of insufficient and noninclusive growth. As Larry Summers put it in his contribution to an important CEPR ebook on secular stagnation, "There is likely to be a price paid in terms of financial stability."[5]

As we will see shortly, the challenges are not limited to growth, price formation, and financial stability. They extend well beyond—to issues of inequality, global imbalances, and joblessness. In the process, already challenging economic and financial dimensions are amplified by even more tricky geopolitical, national political, institutional, and social aspects.

CHAPTER 9

THE QUEST OF A GENERATION

SUSTAINING INCLUSIVE GROWTH

"We choose to go to the moon not because it is easy, but because it is hard."

—JOHN F. KENNEDY

Issue 1: Repeatedly inadequate and unbalanced economic expansion, reflecting cyclical/secular/structural headwinds, highlights the extent to which many advanced economies still lack proper growth models.

As shown in Figure 5, advanced economies have had enormous difficulties growing since the global financial crisis, and without growth, it has been hard for them to improve living standards, reduce poverty, and invest in the future.

Gross domestic product (GDP) levels in the Eurozone and Japan have struggled mightily to regain their pre-2008-crisis growth levels. The United Kingdom and the United States have done better, growing more robustly as they have taken advantage of more favorable national and geopolitical circumstances—be it, for example, the entrepreneurial nature of America's more flexible and optimistic system, the ability of Britain to attract disproportionately large investments

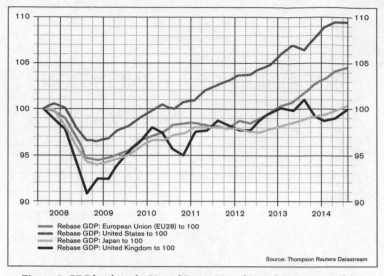

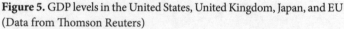

Figure 5. GDP levels in the United States, United Kingdom, Japan, and EU (Data from Thomson Reuters)

from certain parts of the world (though the Brexit process is raising questions on this), or lower exposure to the effects of geopolitical tensions over Ukraine and parts of the Middle East. Yet even their growth rates have fallen far short of what is both desirable and achievable.

This generally disappointing outcome speaks to an unfortunate reality: Too many advanced economies lack proper growth engines—though it's not surprising, since they had gotten deeply hooked on an unsustainable approach that substituted financial engineering and credit entitlement for proper drivers of growth. To make things worse, rather than spur efforts to do better, the persistent recent underperformance has made it harder to secure the political consensus needed to revamp growth engines in a fundamental and durable fashion.

As I argued in 2013, quite a long list of countries emerged from the crisis saddled with the legacy of ill-designed, inadequate, and sputtering growth engines: "Some countries (for example, Greece and Portugal) relied on debt-financed government spending to fuel economic activity. Others (think Cyprus, Iceland, Ireland, the U.K., and the U.S.) resorted to unsustainable surges in leverage among financial institutions to fund certain private-sector activities (e.g., housing), sometimes almost irrespective of underlying fundamentals. Still others (China and Korea) exploited seemingly limitless globalization and buoyant international trade to capture growing market shares. And a final group rode China's coattails."[1]

It takes time to reset and recalibrate all these growth impulses in ways consistent with today's global realities. In the easier cases, this involves a period of healing and mere tweaks to the current growth model. In many other cases, however, it is about a fundamental restructuring of the model, or a transition to a new one altogether. The latter includes countries like Greece, where prosperity has little chance of returning without a deep-rooted redefinition of how growth will be attained and shared, and that assumes a significantly eased debt burden.

The longer our global economy lacks sufficient individual growth engines, the greater the temptation (and the higher the likelihood) that individual countries will seek to capture growth from others rather than create incremental expansion. So, like the old days, quite a few will resort to exchange rates as the primary means to do so; and some could be tempted by trade protectionism.

By depreciating their currency, countries seek to take market shares from others by making their exports cheaper and their imports more expensive. Indeed, with the notable exception of the United States and (until August 2015) China, that is the course that the vast majority of the world's economies, big and small, have embarked on recently—some consciously and some unconsciously. And, until now, because it is a relatively closed economy where trade accounts for a rather small (albeit growing) share of GDP, the United States has been the only major economy willing to see its currency appreciate significantly, and able to afford a transfer of growth impetus to other countries. But even here there is a limit, especially as companies find it harder to compete and as political anger grows.

Given that this currency approach is (under most conditions) a zero-sum game—indeed, some have called it a stealth currency war—

and given the limited successes that the advanced world has had (individually and collectively) in engineering an economic "liftoff," adjustment and reform fatigue has tended to set in. This is the case for parts of the Eurozone and among certain segments of Japanese society as well as in the emerging world. As a result, and understandably, some governments have been tempted to go back to old, exhausted growth approaches (like Brazil before the 2016 impeachment of the president), notwithstanding their limited effectiveness and their potential collateral damage and unintended consequences.

This is a particularly acute problem for countries that are still trying to overcome enormous debt burdens. Think of Greece, where, as noted above, countering the dramatic collapse in GDP (Figure 6) requires a complete renovation of the growth model. It is a country where the struggles of the last eight years have wiped out all of the progress that its poor had achieved in the previous twenty-eight.[2] Not surprisingly, therefore, the majority of Greek citizens have not felt much relief from the policies pursued in 2012–14 by the Antonis Samaras government to narrow the budget deficit, improve tax administration, reduce spending inefficiencies, lower the trade deficit, strengthen the banking system, and increase the transparency and accountability of government operation.

Most of these measures involved important sacrifices on the part of a population that already had been hard hit by unemployment and wage reductions. Because they find it hard to protect themselves—and though they could least afford to do so—the country's poor carried the largest burden. Not surprisingly, citizens opted in the 2015 national elections for what they believed would be a completely different approach under a new government led by Syriza, the Coalition for the Radical Left. But even this new, energetic government, led by the charismatic and skilled prime minister Alexis Tsipras, found it hard to buck the system and deliver the needed policy pivot. After months of tortuous negotiations, capital controls, a national referendum, repeated games of chicken, and a three-week closure of Greek banks, the government was forced to do more of the same—the so-called extend-and-pretend approach.

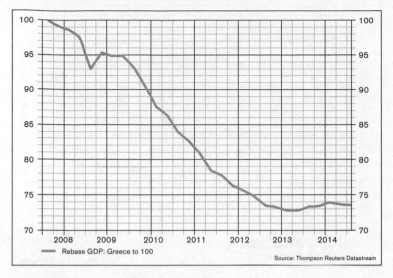

Figure 6. Greece GDP (2008 = 100)
(Data from Thomson Reuters)

Inadequate growth has also been a persistent problem for Italy and, of course, Japan (Figure 7). It is such a generalized problem that even countries that managed to implement reforms and avoid the lure of finance—such as Germany—are finding it hard not to be adversely affected by what is going on around them.

Having initially been fixated on just cyclical restraints to a proper post-crisis recovery, the economics profession has played analytical catch-up to this reality. It has been interesting to observe how the consensus has evolved—something that my former colleagues at PIMCO and I have been able to do from a rather unique position.

As many of you may know, PIMCO first rolled out the concept of the "new normal" in May 2009 after several rounds of discussion among the firm's investment professionals.[3] The idea was a simple one and reflected our assessment of the aftermath of the massive financial and economic imbalances that had led to the global financial crisis.[4]

Simply put, we did not believe that, coming out of the financial crisis, the advanced economies would reset in the traditional cyclical

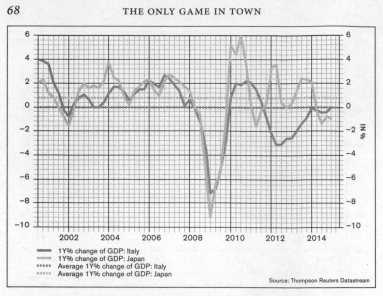

Figure 7. Growth in Italy and Japan over the last fifteen years
(Data from Thomson Reuters)

manner.[5] Indeed, as I reminisced in March 2014 about the formulation of the concept of the new normal, "adapting an old Monty Python sketch, the crisis would prove much more than a 'flesh wound.' Rather than a quick bounce back in growth (the rubber band 'V' shaped recovery), economic activity would remain persistently sluggish and unemployment unusually high."[6]

Having come up in January 2009 with the term the "new normal," I proposed it to my colleagues in an Investment Committee meeting. We then played around with various permutations of the words "new" and "normal," as well as related concepts (such as a "stable disequilibrium"), to see if there was a better phrase to powerfully convey the notion that this would not be a conventional recovery. After trying various combinations, such as "the new abnormal," we coalesced on the original "new normal" as a way of signaling that this unusual state of affairs would likely last for a while—for at least five years, in fact (which, by the way, is an eternity when it comes to predictions in the investment management world).

As it turned out later, we were not the first one to use the term. Unbeknownst to me at the time, Rich Miller, the highly respected economic reporter at Bloomberg News, had used the term earlier— something that he alerted me to sometime later in his wonderfully constructive and gentle manner.

The new-normal concept had difficulty gaining traction. Indeed it went through the classic stages: first ridiculed, then resisted, and finally accepted. I particularly remember being bemused when someone from the official sector dismissed it as "idiotic" back in 2009.

Despite the enormity of the ongoing economic dislocations, many were still hostage to the conventional cyclical mindsets that had served policy making well for many decades—that is, the notion that advanced economies follow business cycles around a rather robust and stable path. As such, they wrongly believed that the sharp downturn in 2008–09 would be followed by an elastic-band-like rebound.

The reaction I received in official circles to the concept of the new normal in the advanced world grew even more skeptical when I suggested that, in formulating their policy responses, these countries would be well advised to study and learn from the experience of emerging countries. After all, this latter group of economies had spent a lot of their time living in secular and structural space, rather than a cyclical one.

What I did not realize at the time is that all this in fact reflected the difficulties that the policy-making apparatus, as well as other components of society, was having in adapting to new circumstances. Even when it started to become clear that the advanced economies were indeed facing an unusual challenge, the concept was called "too fatalistic." It wasn't. It simply argued that policymakers needed to think differently and develop more open mindsets if they were to help their economies recover properly.

And so the initial policy response fell well short of what was required. Valuable time was lost. By the time more policymakers really started to get it in 2012–13, the political context was no longer conducive for enabling the type of bold holistic response that was desperately needed. In the process, many opinion leaders continued to brush aside insights from other parts of the world, and not only from emerging economies.

Heading into the crisis, many economists and policymakers in the West had confidently proclaimed that "Japan could not happen here."[7] Indeed, quite a few of them had assertively lectured the Japanese government on what it should have done and could still do to avoid lost decades. However, in the process of doing so, and as I wrote back in 2011 when I suggested that Japan was owed an apology, they severely underappreciated the challenges of post-bubble recoveries.[8] Given the extent to which Europe's and America's inadequate post-crisis recoveries have surprised to the downside, quite a few feel considerably chastened now.

Having said all this, there was ultimately quite a broad transformation in 2014. Reacting to overwhelming evidence of post-crisis economic mediocrity, the insights of the new normal went mainstream and, in the process, acquired at least two alternative names—one more sophisticated, and the other more catchy.

In a powerful February 2014 speech, Larry Summers popularized the notion of a "secular stagnation,"[9] suggesting that the disappointing underperformance of recent years had important structural components that could make it last even longer. First limited to economists and policymakers, its popularity spread in April 2015 thanks to an unusual blog exchange between Professor Summers and former Fed chair Bernanke—again centered on the balance between secular/structural drivers and cyclical ones.

Six months earlier, Christine Lagarde, the head of the International Monetary Fund and former French finance minister, decided to use a more down-to-earth label. During presentations to the annual meetings of the IMF and World Bank in Washington, D.C., she referred to the new-normal phenomenon as the "new mediocre."[10]

However one labels it, various explanations have been put forward for this unusual and worrisome phenomenon—from the difficulties of escaping a liquidity trap and the challenging aspects of balance sheet recessions to a change in productivity trends, lack of infrastructure investment, the effects of debt overhangs, demography, and "the race against the machines." These are all factors that, first, hold actual growth below the potential of the economy, and second, act to pull down future potential growth. There have also been attempts to formalize some of these drivers via comprehensive analytical models of secular stagnation, including by Gauti Eggertsson and Neil Mehrota, who have proposed an insightful New Keynesian overlapping-generations model.[11]

Drawing on the insights of Alvin Hansen, the distinguished American economist, these two economists illustrate why conventional self-correcting mechanisms can fail in driving a proper recovery.[12] It essentially has to do with an oversupply of savings that results from a permanent deleveraging shock, slower population, and an increase in inequality. As such, growth is held back repeatedly, and economies can end up in a "long slump . . . in which usual economic rules are stood on their heads." With that, Gauti Eggertsson and Neil Mehrota show why "a permanent slump is possible."

The difficulties that individual economies faced domestically were accentuated by global interactions, including difficulties in reconciling different national circumstances and approaches. Writing in the *Financial Times* back in October 2010, shortly after then-chairman Bernanke had signaled the new stage in Fed activism, Martin Wolf observed that "the U.S. is seeking to impose its will, via the printing press. The U.S. is going to win this war, one way or the other: it will either inflate the rest of the world or force their nominal exchange rates up against the dollar."[13] Either the Fed's experimental stimulus policy would serve as an example for other countries to follow immediately, or it would be the exception, thereby forcing the dollar to weaken against other currencies and allowing the United States to steal growth from elsewhere.

Martin Wolf was right, though both issues transpired, in a sequential fashion. Initially, only the Bank of England accompanied the Fed, while the Bank of Japan and the ECB held back. As a result, the dollar initially weakened significantly against the euro and the yen. This put pressure on other countries, one of the factors that prompted the Bank of Japan and then the ECB to act unconventionally.

Overall, the United States did succeed in surging ahead of most of the rest of the world. But its breakout was not sufficient to act as a locomotive for the global economy as a whole. Subsequently, with other countries trying to do to the United States what the United States did to them (that is, de facto use of the exchange rate as a policy instrument), the growth gap narrowed. All along, however, the world's economic system did not resolve in a way that could restore global prosperity and financial stability.

These developments and insights point to the unusual risk of an even more prolonged slump in advanced economies. Importantly in terms of actionable outcomes, their insights can (and should) be translated—albeit not without some risk of oversimplification—into the four broad policy implications discussed earlier—namely, addressing simultaneously 1) lagging structural reforms to revamp growth engines; 2) the mismatch in aggregate demand between the ability and willingness to spend; 3) persistent debt overhangs that undermine existing and new productive capacity; and 4) Europe's incomplete regional integration project, as well as other multilateral bottlenecks that frustrate sufficient cross-border policy coordination.

I believe that if we were to bring together in one room a large number of economists, we would find the vast majority agreeing that each of these four policy implications is valid—even though they would disagree on the exact relative weight of each. But this lack of unanimity on the specific individual weights would certainly not justify the absence of comprehensive policy actions, especially with the real and disturbing example of Japan's two "lost decades" looming over all this.

The need for better analytical understanding is not limited to the dynamics of real growth. Economists are also playing catch-up to explain price dynamics—specifically, the persistent disinflationary forces that, at low initial levels of inflation (or "low-flation"), aggravate the deleterious impact of excessive indebtedness and low growth. The more people expect prices to fall in the future, the greater the possibility that they will delay their spending, thus also undermining companies' appetite for expanding productive capacity and investing in new ones.

Economists are also trying to figure out where "neutral" interest rates (that is, the steady-state policy rates consistent with stable inflation) are likely to settle once advanced economies finally overcome the liquidity trap and migrate up to a higher-equilibrium growth rate. There is general agreement that the new-equilibrium interest rate structure is likely to be below historical averages. But there is still quite a bit of disagreement on how far below, especially given the difficulties in explaining unusually sluggish productivity growth.

This frantic catch-up process is not limited to economists. Central banks are also scrambling—and not only in Europe and Japan, where detrimental disinflation is either a reality or a high risk. The Fed is in a similar position. In an April 2014 speech, Chair Yellen worried that the traditional approaches used by central banks may be inadequate to understand and predict inflationary forces[14]—and this when inflation is at the core of these banks' objectives, be it in a single-mandate approach (such as the ECB) or a dual one (the Fed). If officials do not adequately comprehend the price formation process, it is hard for them to be confident about delivering on their mandates.

This was but one of the many complicated issues facing Chair Yellen when she assumed her position at the beginning of 2014. And while all three of her immediate predecessors—Paul Volcker with high inflation, Alan Greenspan with the "Black Monday" crash in the stock market (October 19, 1987), and Ben Bernanke with the global financial crisis—were tested early on during their new tenure, none faced the breadth of issues that she did (and still does).

Commenting on what she was about to inherit as Fed chair, I noted at the time that while "not quite a poisoned chalice, . . . Yellen is taking over a Federal Reserve that has ended up, mostly inadvertently, underwriting a series of consequential and unusual disconnects."[15] And the consequences extend well beyond the welfare of the United States and of advanced countries.

The advanced economies' failure to grow nominal GDP, and so in a sufficiently inclusive manner, has made life a lot more difficult for emerging countries—a phenomenon that accentuates not only their internal challenges but also the trials of navigating a global financial system that is inevitably distorted by the pursuit of unconventional policies and is periodically subject to discomforting bouts of financial instability. Examples include the "taper tantrum" of May–June 2013, the U.S. Treasury "flash crash" in October 2014, the Swiss currency shock of January 2015, the volatility in German bond rates in May–June 2015, the surprise China currency move in August 2015, and the recession scare of January 2016—all of which highlighted the combined impact of disorderly unwinds by levered traders, limited appetite for risk taking among broker-dealers and other intermediaries, and a tendency for some end investors to head quickly to the door at the first sign of trouble.

Brazilian and Indian officials have been particularly outspoken on this issue, and understandably so. In the context of sluggish growth in the advanced world and only partial policy responses, their economies have been on the receiving end of volatile and disruptive capital flows whose major drivers have had a lot more to do with developments abroad than what is going on in these two economies. It's the issue of the "tourist dollar," and it is an important and persistent one. So let me explain it as I did in a presentation at the Peterson Institute for International Economics.

During periods of large capital flows induced by a combination of sluggish advanced economies, robust risk appetites, and highly stimulative central bank policies, emerging markets serve as destination for a huge pool of crossover funds, or what I refer to as tourist dollars. Because these crossover funds have such large total assets under management, the flows they devote to emerging markets—while small for them—tend to be a multiple of those invested by more knowledgeable dedicated funds (what I refer to as the "locals"). And their drivers have a different and more volatile mix.

Rather than "pulled" by a relatively deep understanding of country fundamentals, this type of capital is typically "pushed" there by the prospects of low returns in their more traditional habitats in the advanced world.

Instead of being associated with specialized vehicles, they tend to come from more general accounts typically managed against benchmarks dominated by advanced-country securities. Searching for higher yields and/or greater possible price appreciation, their investment managers are "crossing over" into smaller (and typically off-benchmark) market segments.

Once they are invested, it doesn't take long to observe that crossover flows lack the conviction and staying power of the dedicated funds. As such, they often act as tourists rather than locals.

At the first sign of instability, they essentially tend to rush to the airport, looking to get out quickly; this can even occur when the initial source of instability has little to do with the emerging markets themselves (as was the case, for example, during the May–June 2013 "taper tantrum," when financial markets in advanced countries were disrupted by a statement from Fed Chairman Bernanke indicating that the central bank could start reducing the support it was providing via QE programs).

Crossover tourist investors are usually inclined to stay in emerging market investments for only a limited amount of time. They have a decisive home bias, and they tend to overreact to unanticipated news.

The resulting fluctuations in capital inflows and outflows have tended to overwhelm financial markets in the emerging world. Remember, the flows are not driven primarily by individual country fundamentals. Rather, they are more the product of credit factories in the advanced world and central bank policies there. And they are large relative to the absorptive capacity of the local financial system.

To my knowledge, no emerging economy has as yet found a robust policy approach for dealing with this challenge—but it is not for lack of trying. As such, their growth performance has been subject to sizable headwinds.

Perhaps no one has been more vocal and lucid about these issues than Raghuram "Raghu" Rajan, the highly respected and insightful former governor of India's central bank. With an impressive résumé that includes a professorship at the University of Chicago, heading the IMF's Research Department, and putting out an early warning about the financial crisis (and at the 2006 Jackson Hole conference, no less), he introduced a breath of fresh air into the highest levels of the global policy dialogue.

Two episodes are particularly notable, as they also illustrate how Governor Rajan's peers in the central banking world responded to remarks that put them on the defensive.

At a Brookings Institution conference in April 2014—one of the many that are organized around the Spring Meetings of the IMF and World Bank in Washington, D.C.—Governor Rajan warned about the adverse spillover effects on emerging countries of experimental advanced-country policies.[16] In doing so, he was not being especially outlandish, and he certainly was not the first to make these points.

Yet his remarks were enough to trigger quite a reaction from Chairman Bernanke, who was sitting in the audience, having left his position at the Fed earlier in the year and joined Brookings as a Distinguished Fellow in Residence.

Governor Rajan responded and, with the panel being broadcast via the Internet, the world had access to a rather unusual occurrence in the polite world of central banking: something close to a public argument between two highly regarded heads of central banks from different countries.

Chairman Bernanke reiterated the arguments advanced earlier by other advanced-country officials, which emphasize that the policies being pursued reflect the use of "domestic measures" to attain "domestic objectives," that success in meeting these objectives would translate into higher growth that is good for everyone, and to the extent that there are negative spillovers on emerging economies, that it is up to the authorities there to deal with them through timely policy adjustments (something that we will come back to shortly).

The second episode was at the October 2014 Banque de France symposium mentioned at the start of this book. Again on a panel, Governor Rajan made some remarkably thoughtful comments about the structural questions facing central banks and, more generally, the economies of the advanced world. But rather than his comments serving as the basis of a much-needed discussion, he was politely sidestepped and labeled by the moderator of his panel as belonging to the "BIS brigade"—a reference to the work of the Bank for International Settlement, whose emphasis in recent years has been on the worrisome side effects of unconventional monetary policy, including distorting the link between markets and fundamentals while failing to provide a cure for inadequate growth.[17]

Whether it is because the impact of large and volatile tourist flows is simply too big, or whether emerging economies are unable or unwilling to sufficiently adjust domestic policies, the effect has been to slow growth in the emerging world overall, so much so that this important part of the global economy is no longer a robust growth locomotive for the rest of the world—a role that it performed well after the 2008 financial crisis and that was instrumental in helping to lower the downside facing the advanced world. Indeed, with most of the systemically important countries slowing (including China, India, and Turkey) or already in recession (such as Brazil and Russia), the emerging world has transitioned to become a drag on global growth.

In sum, the elusive advanced-economy quest for growth has morphed into a generalized growth deficit for the world as a whole. In the process, the search for new growth engines has become harder, the stakes have gotten bigger, and the consequences have extended beyond economic and financial. As we will see later in this book, they now also have important social, political, institutional, and geopolitical dimensions.

The overall reduction in emerging markets growth is not the only issue to note. It has been accompanied by yet another complication—that of a growing gap in prospects, both among countries and across the populations of individual nations.

A few better-managed economies, such as India, are working hard to unleash pent-up growth drivers and surging ahead. Other traditionally well-managed economies, like China, are trying to soft-land at lower growth rates while deepening their developmental maturation process. Notwithstanding both internal and external headwinds, growth will become more inclusive in both these cases as it continues to pull people out of poverty, though not enough to avoid striking income and wealth inequalities.

Others, such as Brazil, have found themselves facing the old-fashioned and troubling problem of stagflation, or that awful combination of low income growth and high inflation. The application of the wrong policy mix to the challenges at hand was not only failing to promote growth, but was also leading to higher price increases that place even greater pressure on the population, and especially the poor. Their ability to reverse this situation was constrained by how this stagflationary situation fuels social discontent, and the resulting rise in the "misery index" (that is, the sum of the unemployment and inflation rates) complicates an already difficult political environment.

The next group, including countries such as Russia and especially Venezuela, have been dealing with economic recession, even greater currency instability, and spreading financial disruptions—all of which damage business activity in a very basic sense. As a simple but insightful example, witness Apple's decision in December 2014 to suspend its sales in Russia as, according to the company, "extreme fluctuations in the value of the ruble" prompted a review of pricing policy and practices.

The generalized slowdown in growth has been happening at a time when several economies have already used up some of the considerable resilience they had gained in the run-up to the 2008 global financial crisis—resilience that had served them and the global economy as well.

Having gone through their own internally generated debt and financial crises—and multiple times, including during Latin America's lost decade of the 1980s, the 1994–95 Mexican tequila crisis, the 1997

Asian crisis, the 1998 Russian default, the 2001 Argentine default, and the 2002 Brazilian crisis—many emerging economies embarked on comprehensive "self-insurance" programs. They involved various combinations of five key items that remain relevant today:

- Building up large financial buffers in the form of ample international reserves;
- Adopting more flexible exchange rates;
- Reducing the currency mismatch between debt issuance and assets/revenues (or what is known by economists as the "original sin");
- Paying off some debt obligations and refinancing others on more favorable terms, including via longer maturities and lower interest rates; and
- Embarking on institutional changes that render domestic economic management more responsible and responsive.

In other words, having suffered a series of small heart attacks, most emerging economies had embarked on a regime of more exercise, a healthier diet, and more regular checkups. As such, when the big heart attack came—that associated with the 2008 global financial crisis, which originated in the United States—they were in a much better place to survive it. And they did more than just survive it. They recovered quite quickly (and certainly faster than most people expected, and a lot better than their counterparts in the industrial world).

Since then, however, emerging markets have eaten into their resilience. To use another analogy, this time from the auto world, they have found themselves on an unexpectedly long and bumpy journey, having to weather the potholes created both by the West and by their own actions, but doing so after using their spare tire and with many miles between service stations.

Financial cushions in the emerging world today are less robust due to lower international reserves and higher corporate debt, a significant portion of which is subject to currency mismatches, according to research by BIS staff.[18] Meanwhile, policymakers in too many economies seem distracted, either underestimating the challenges ahead or engaging in rather pointless blame games.

In addition to lower resilience, too many emerging economies have also become less agile, failing to transition to the next stages of responsible economic management, ones that involve more micro reforms—so-called second-generation structural reforms, which are technically more difficult to implement and tend to face stronger pockets of vested interests, yet are critical for sustaining growth and advancing the development process.

As a result, absent a strong recovery in the advanced world the lower growth performance of the emerging countries is unlikely to be corrected anytime soon. Meanwhile, the more challenged the growth in the emerging world, the trickier the recovery among advanced economies. All of which risks lowering future growth potential and rendering the global economy less dynamic and much more vulnerable to policy mistakes and market accidents.

CHAPTER 10

REDUCING THE RISK
OF THE UNEMPLOY*ED*
BECOMING UNEMPLOY*ABLE*

"Unfortunately, very few governments think about youth unemployment when they are drawing up their national plans."

—KOFI ANNAN

*I*ssue 2: Unemployment remains too high in too many advanced countries; and has been getting more deeply embedded in the structure of these economies and, therefore, will become that much harder to solve.

Inadequate and noninclusive growth makes it harder for countries to overcome their unemployment problems. This is particularly the case in certain parts of Europe where high levels of unemployment are associated with alarming joblessness among the young (Figure 8).

The numbers are horrific in too many places. In early 2015, Greece was still struggling with a 25 percent unemployment rate, with joblessness among the youth above 50 percent. Excessively high unemployment in other Eurozone economies—including France, Italy, and Spain, for example—kept the region's average for the population as a whole above 10 percent—and this despite record low unemployment in Germany, the region's largest economy.

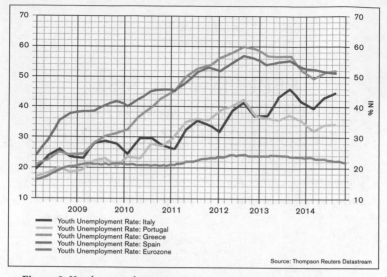

Figure 8. Youth unemployment rates in some European countries (Data from Thomson Reuters)

While the United States has done a lot better in reducing unemployment, this proved to be an unusually protracted process. It took the economy quite a few years to develop the momentum that ultimately turned it into the West's most dynamic employment creator, with over 15 million jobs created under President Obama. Yet a low labor participation rate, high long-term unemployment, excessive youth joblessness, and notable education and race disparities persist to varying extents. It is hard to overstress the dangers involved.

Remember, simple demographics produce new entrants into the labor force every year. As such, if worrisomely high youth joblessness persists, this group of young people risk going from being unemploy*ed* to becoming unemploy*able*. This is a consequential and disastrous transition. It increases the threat that Europe may not be looking at just a "lost decade" but also at the even more alarming prospect of a "lost generation," which in turn threatens not only social cohesion but the ability of democracies to function well.

Let's start with the economic effects. Undoubtedly, persistently high unemployment translates into lost production capabilities, amplifies pressures on the budget, and deepens problems of inadequate aggregate demand. It strains social safety nets, which, in many cases, are already quite stretched.

These are not problems just for the here and now. They also speak to the future given the adverse feedback loops between inadequate growth and high unemployment.

Inadequate growth, especially when it is also noninclusive, makes it much harder to create jobs and to maintain good pay for those who are lucky enough to be employed. Meanwhile, insufficient job creation and stymied wages eat away at both actual and potential growth, making it even harder to grow in the future. As noted by Fed vice chair Stanley Fischer in his August 2014 speech in Stockholm on "The Great Recession," a sluggish labor market accentuates concerns about the longer-run output potential of the economy—and this even when there continues to be "considerable uncertainty" as to the balance between structural and secular impediments to job and wage growth.[1]

These economic problems are compounded by financial, geopolitical, political, and social factors.

Long-term unemployment makes it harder for individuals, and society as a whole, to overcome debt burdens—thus the persistent debt overhangs in parts of Europe and the increasing worries about student loans in the United States, among other things. Together with growing inequality (see the next issue), it is a factor that badly eats away at social integrity and the well-being of society. As we will also discuss, it also complicates the geopolitical and national political landscapes, giving rise to alienation and the "politics of anger," thus fueling extreme and single-item political platforms whose likelihood to disrupt societies can tend to be greater than their potential to responsibly govern them, at least initially. Indeed, this very phenomenon has been spreading throughout Europe—be it the Syriza victory in Greece, the UKIP-led Brexit vote in the United Kingdom, or the growth of extremist parties in Denmark, France, and Spain, to name just a few—and all this poses real and immediate challenges to national and regional policy making.

CHAPTER 11

THE INEQUALITY TRIFECTA

"Poverty perpetuates poverty, generation after generation, by acting on the brain."

—MADELINE OSTRANDER

"Because the use of these new instruments can have different consequences than conventional monetary policy, in particular with respect to the distribution of wealth and the allocation of resources, it has become more important that those consequences are identified, weighed, and where necessary mitigated."

—MARIO DRAGHI

*I*ssue 3: *Fueled by an unusual combination of cyclical, secular, and structural factors, the worsening of income and wealth inequality has been so pronounced within countries that it now also undermines opportunities.*

This brings us naturally to the third issue, or the extent to which individual countries have experienced a rise in what I call the inequality trifecta—inequality of income, wealth, and opportunity.

Worsening inequality is not new. It has been a feature of a number of countries for decades, including the United States. But it has gotten a lot worse. Indeed, according to data compiled by the Organisation for Economic Co-operation and Development, "income inequality . . . is at the highest for the past half century," with "the average income of the richest 10% of the population [now] about nine times that of the poorest 10% across the OECD, up from seven times 25 years ago."[1]

This already considerable gap widens substantially if the richest group is redefined to be the top 5 percent and 3 percent, and it flies off the page if it's the top 1 percent or 0.1 percent.

As an illustration, just consider the following data for the United States, starting with wealth data.

By 2013, the top 0.1 percent owned 22 percent of the country's wealth, or three times the share that they had forty years ago. The top 3 percent owned 54 percent of the total. Adding the share secured by the remaining segment of the top 10 percent left the bottom 90 percent with only 25 percent.[2]

The income side has also seen a dramatic worsening in recent years. Since the crisis, the top 1 percent of the nation's earners have received 95 percent of the income growth (compared to the multi-decade average of 54 percent for 1979–2007). In nineteen states, they secured 100 percent or more[3] (meaning that, in some cases, they have gained while others have experienced stagnant or declining income).

This phenomenon of worsening inequality of both income and wealth within individual countries comes at a time when global inequality, that is, the gap between rich and poor countries, has narrowed. It is evident in both advanced and developing economies. And this domestic phenomenon has been associated with more than increasing shares for the rich and especially for the richest of the rich. It has also been accompanied by a striking hollowing out of the middle class. As the editors at *The Atlantic* observed: "The growing gulf in earnings between America's richest and everyone else means that the group that's historically fallen in the middle, living a life of neither luxury nor poverty, is shrinking."[4]

What has rendered changes in inequality more notable in recent years is on the one hand the stunning contrast between sluggishness on Main Street, and on the other the notable post-crisis recovery on Wall Street, as well as the continued historic surge in corporate profits' record share of GDP. In the process, popular discussions have shifted, from seeing inequality as an inevitable outcome of a market-based system and one that plays an important role in incentivizing and rewarding hard work and entrepreneurship, to worrying that excessive inequality can harm society in several reinforcing ways.

We have talked previously of the recovery in Wall Street's fortunes, and of the upward march in financial asset prices that has benefited the rich. Concurrently, it didn't take long for the GDP share of corporate profits to reach one record high after the other. By contrast, wages have languished in most of the advanced world, especially in countries where unemployment has remained high. Even in the United States, which, as noted in the previous chapter, finally experienced a notable fall in the unemployment rate on the back of an impressive run of job creation, the recovery in wages has been frustratingly slow.

Research by the Federal Reserve, including its data-rich survey of consumer finance, is just one of the many sources confirming what has been an unusual and material increase in inequality. It details how "between 2010 and 2013, overall average family income rose 4 percent in real terms, but median income fell 5 percent, consistent with increasing income concentration during this period." Moreover, the notable increase in the income of the most affluent households came at a time when "families at the bottom of the income distribution saw continued declines in average real incomes."[5]

This reality of widening inequality is also seen in the gap between white and minority households. Federal Reserve data show that the median income of minority households declined by 9 percent between 2010 and 2013. This compares to an almost unchanged level for non-Hispanic white households.

In a 2014 compositional study using Fed data, Rakesh Kochhar and Richard Fry of the Pew Research Center shed further light on the extent to which this inequality "has widened along racial, ethnic lines since the end of the great recession."[6] According to their findings, the gap in wealth between white households and African American households is the largest since 1989, with the former having risen from eight times that of the median African American wealth in 2010 to thirteen times in 2013. There has also been a deterioration in the gap relative to Hispanics, albeit not as large: from nine times to ten times, or the highest level since 2001.

There are secular, structural, and cyclical factors that accentuate inequalities of income, wealth, and opportunity.

Structural drivers range from the changing nature of technological advances that favor higher-skill individuals to the rise of "winner-take-all" investment characteristics and a political system that tends to favor the wealthy (indeed, some would say it has been captured by them). Meanwhile, conventional cyclical redistribution policies have been notably absent. With active budget policy making heavily constrained by political polarization, there has been a reduced emphasis on transfer payments and other support for the poor. (As an illustration, the U.S. Congress did not actively pass a new comprehensive annual budget for six years up to now, even though that is one of the most basic components of the legislative arm's economic governance responsibilities.) In Europe, both a real and perceived need to be fiscally austere has hit spending on social sectors particularly hard, further undermining the legitimate redistributive function of government.

These limits on cyclical responses to secular inequality forces have been accentuated—albeit inadvertently—by the unconventional policies pursued by central banks. As noted earlier, the expansion of their balance sheets has tended to support the wealthy since the latter hold a disproportionately large share of the financial assets being targeted for support by central bank action.

Given all this, it should come as no surprise that there is now quite a bit of general interest in the matter. Recall how in 2014 a big economic tome (almost seven hundred pages, including research analysis and historical insights) on inequality by French economist Thomas Piketty shot up to the top of bestseller lists, triggering lots of discussions, panels, and interviews in the process.[7] At the 2014 IMF–World Bank Annual Meeting in Washington, D.C., inequality was the most common topic in seminars organized by the official sector, industry groups, and think tanks. It also featured prominently in the U.S. presidential election campaign and its aftermath.

There is also a growing realization that the effects of inequality may well have evolved beyond questions of fairness, and beyond the threats it poses to social, geopolitical, and political well-being: Inequality also creates adverse economic feedback loops that make it much harder for the advanced countries to emerge from their generalized economic malaise.

As I argued in a column in October 2014,[8] the economic implications of inequality can no longer be couched in comforting notions of enhancing incentives for hard work, innovation, and entrepreneurship. It appears to me that, beyond a certain threshold, inequality begins to undermine economic dynamism and therefore also investment, employment, and prosperity. The reasons come back to the basic macroeconomics associated with the data mentioned above.

Affluent households tend to spend less of their incremental income (what economists call the "marginal propensity to consume"). As such, with the bulk of the gains going to this group, income growth does not translate into anything like the historical increase in demand. This aggravates the broader problem of inadequate aggregate demand, which itself hinders the structural reforms that are key to increasing productivity over time. That is to say, income and wealth inequality go from being part of a dynamic capitalistic system to undermining it.

In relation to opportunity, the emerging evidence is also very concerning. From persistent youth unemployment to health and educational attainment, family circumstances have been playing a larger role in determining the income and wealth configuration of the next generation. The greater the inequality, the larger the gap in access to education opportunities and health services, both important determinants of employment prospects and earnings. Add to that the recent neuroscience research on how poverty can adversely impact the brain functions of children[9] and what you get is a real threat of longer-term tragedies.

Central banks have been inserted into this complicated and emotional debate not out of choice but because of their forced reliance on a relatively narrow set of policy tools that have inadvertently aggravated inequality. Indeed, the serious debate is not whether central banks' unconventional policies have contributed to inequality (they have, especially when it comes to wealth disparities); it is whether this unfortunate outcome will be more than offset by the overall economic benefits that accrue in the future.

So far, our discussion here has focused on the effects of a central bank policy approach that boosts asset prices as a way of generating growth and employment. The effect was to amplify the already notable contrast between the rapidly improving circumstances of Wall Street and Main Street's stagnation. Indeed, QE became reminiscent of what Frank Bruni, the *New York Times* columnist, said of colleges in his review of the documentary *Ivory Tower:* "The top colleges, shinier than ever, are Porsches. They can take you far and fast, but it's a lucky few who get behind the wheel."[10]

There is a second set of effects also worth mentioning. They involve the direct income effects on borrowers and lenders of persistent highly repressed interest rates, a key component of central banks' unconventional approach.

Clearly, low interest rates—and, especially, artificially low interest rates—benefit large net borrowers and debtors at the expense of net lenders and creditors. As such, the largest beneficiaries have tended to be governments, followed by nonfinancial companies. And the amounts are not immaterial. In a paper published at the end of 2013, researchers at the McKinsey Global Institute estimated $1.6 trillion of savings between 2007 and 2012 for governments in the Eurozone, the United Kingdom, and the United States, and $710 billion of savings for nonfinancial companies there.[11]

Households have done less well in those countries. The hardest-hit segment has been savers—typically, older households—relying on income from short-dated fixed-income securities (such as certificates of deposit) and those looking to purchase new annuities from insurance companies to protect their retirement. Indeed, the drop in interest rates—to ultralow and, in some cases, negative levels—has driven insurance companies to do more than lower their guaranteed payouts; some have abandoned the annuity business altogether.

All in all, inequality has become a deeply entrenched problem whose adverse consequences can easily tip into a self-feeding, vicious cycle. No wonder central banks find themselves in a particularly uncomfortable position, forced to implement policies that aggravate aspects of inequality in the short term. All this would not matter greatly in the long term were it not for two disturbing facts: The policy approach has yet to lead to durable income and wage growth that would offset the unfavorable short-term effects, and a widespread (and understandable) backlash against inequality is on the rise, threatening to engulf central banks in the future.

CHAPTER 12

THE PERSISTENT TRUST DEFICIT

"Trust, like the soul, never returns once it goes."

—PUBLILIUS SYRUS

*I*ssue 4: *The loss of institutional credibility is part of a more generalized erosion of trust in politicians in the "establishment," in "expert opinion," and the "system" as a whole.*

Institutional credibility is crucial to generating and maintaining economic prosperity. Indeed, it is often the most important factor that differentiates stable mature economies from volatile and unpredictable ones. And the credibility of many institutions has come under significant attack in recent years.

It is difficult to explain to the general public how governments and central banks stood by and allowed reckless financial risk taking to tip into a crisis and subsequent prolonged mediocrity. It is even harder to explain why they then bailed out the banks with trillions of dollars; these were the very entities that many regard as the perpetrators of the crisis. And it is virtually impossible to defend the fact that so few bankers have been punished for their irresponsible behaviors.

Accentuating all this are stories still coming out about bank malfeasance. Almost a decade after the onset of the global financial crisis, legal fines are still being imposed, including for manipulating foreign exchange markets and LIBOR, a key commercial interest rate set by banks. Meanwhile, new research is shedding light on the extent to which some banks went around the rules while others disregarded even the most basic elements of client service and risk management.[1]

Former chairman Bernanke was among those commenting on this phenomenon. Shortly after leaving the Fed at the beginning of 2014 he observed that "the natural reaction from the guy on Main Street is 'how come you're bailing them out and not bailing me out?' By preventing the system from collapsing we're protecting the economy, we're protecting you. But it's a complicated argument to make and I don't think we always made it as well as we could have."[2]

Former secretary Geithner went further. Recognizing the difficulty of selling to the public the case for bailouts, he reacted quite sharply to those who suggested that such assistance to banks would encourage renewed irresponsible behavior down the road. He saw little merit for the claims of those he labeled in his book "moral hazard fundamentalists."[3]

Recognizing the continued anger in the country, an active group of politicians is interested not only in de-risking the banks further but also in gaining greater insights into how their de facto main supervisor, the Federal Reserve, operates—so much so as to push an inherently nonconfrontational Chair Yellen to warn in July 2014 congressional testimony that greater Fed oversight could be a "grave mistake."[4]

Yet this phenomenon will not dissipate anytime soon, especially as it unites lawmakers on both sides of the political aisle, albeit for different reasons.

Republicans tend to be concerned about the Fed's involvement in markets, including a balance sheet that had grown to $4 trillion in 2015. Moreover, as the former Fed vice chairman Donald Kohn stated in December 2013 when commenting on "the portfolio [that] could grow almost without limit," "there's some legitimacy in these discomforts [regarding] the potential financial stability effects"[5]—a concern echoed by Jeremy Stein when he served as a member of the Fed's Board of Governors. It is these sorts of issues that lead lawmakers, such as Texan Republican Jeb Hensarling, who chaired the House Financial Services Committee, to threaten "the most rigorous examination and oversight of the Federal Reserve in its history."[6]

On the other side of the aisle, Democrats remain worried about the Fed being too close to financial markets and especially way too friendly with banks. In a November 2014 hearing of the Senate Banking Committee, Senator Elizabeth Warren of Massachusetts told Bill Dudley, the president of the New York Fed, "you need to fix it, Mr. Dudley, or we need to get someone who will." The comment was particularly notable since Congress has no say over appointments at the New York Fed.[7]

Other countries have looked for additional ways to rein in irresponsible risk taking by banks. In December 2014, the Netherlands opted for making bankers take an oath that "they will endeavor to maintain and promote confidence in the financial sector, so help me God." As Liz Alderman, the *New York Times*'s chief European business correspondent, wrote, "The sinners of the banking system seem so uncowed by regulators and prosecutors that one country is trying a higher deterrent: the fear of God."[8]

All this constitutes a threat to the "branding" of modern central banking that started to take hold in the United States in the 1980s under then–Fed chairman Paul Volcker.[9] Publicly declaring a war against high and debilitating inflation, he delivered a secular victory over price instability, restored the standing of the Fed, and gave its brand quite a mystique. The mystique was augmented under the long tenure of Chairman Greenspan, when, as noted earlier in the book, the Fed and its "maestro" were celebrated for having brought about a seemingly permanent period of economic prosperity, low inflation, and financial stability.

Just like in business, central banks' strong brand standing is intricately interlinked to their operational effectiveness.

Strong brands are known around the world for reliability in delivering on quality and on their promise of good outcomes. The stronger the brand, the more likely that consumers may even act just on announcements alone—say, thousands of people willing to stand in line to purchase a newly released product despite having relatively limited information about it. Moreover, in some very limited cases, a brand (like Apple) can also create consumer "enchantment," which makes the company even more effective in selling innovations and fending off competitors.[10]

Central banks have essentially put their hard-earned brand in play: first by failing to convince the public at large of the reasons for bailing out irresponsible banks; and then by taking on massive policy responsibilities and struggling to deliver fully, given limited tools and the lack of support from other government agencies. They have done this not by choice but rather by necessity because of other policy-making entities failing to step up to their responsibilities.

In the case of the ECB, the situation has been complicated by a few other factors. One is the difficulty of maintaining unanimity on a governing council representing many countries (with different interpretations of the past, present, and future); another is recurrent questions about the legality of certain measures. It also has not helped that, like other members of this specially formed crisis management grouping for the Eurozone, the central bank has had to operate under a rather clumsy, complex, and at times troubled "troika" arrangement—one that brings together three institutions (the ECB, the European Commission, and the IMF) that are subject to varying degrees of economic influence, have different mandates, and tend to differ in their operational modalities and even their mindsets.

The list of institutional worries does not stop here. Having been subjected to a prolonged period of financial repression, savers have started to realize that, due to partial policy responses on both sides of the Atlantic, they are being sacrificed in attempts to rehabilitate banks and the economy. It is not just about nonexistent and in some cases negative interest rates on the main low-risk saving instruments, be they government bonds, savings accounts, or certificates of deposit. It is also about the challenges facing a growing number of institutions that provide long-term protection, such as life insurers and pensions. Some are already having to reduce their offerings as they are gradually pushed toward losses by the ultra-low-yield environment.

All this comes together to a boil because of the visible difficulties of political systems to respond. As noted earlier, try explaining how for six straight years up to now, the U.S. Congress was unable to deliver a new budget. How silly political bickering shut the government down for almost three weeks and, on different occasions, brought the supplier of global public goods to the verge of a technical default. Meanwhile, at a time of policy needs, measures of congressional productivity, including bills passed, have reached record lows.

It should therefore come as no surprise that in the General Social Survey for 2014, conducted by NORC, the independent research organization at the University of Chicago, the number of surveyed Americans having "a great deal of confidence" in Congress was only 5 percent; it stood at 11 percent for the executive branch. It should also come as no surprise that antiestablishment forces had a significant impact on the 2016 elections.

This all underscores a broader phenomenon, one that has gotten a lot worse in recent years and radically inhibits proper economic and financial management—an erosion in the standing of "expert opinion," the credibility of economic institutions and the politicians that oversee them. And all of this fuels the "politics of anger."

This is not just a domestic issue for the United States. Travel outside the country and try to explain the bizarre 2016 elections. Or try responding to criticisms of how Congress blocked for years reforms to the IMF that virtually every other country in the world has approved—and lawmakers did so even though these reforms do not erode the voting power of America, involve no incremental financial appropriation, and in fact were initially spearheaded by the United States itself. Indeed, these reforms serve the U.S. national interest. Yet rather than being judged on merit, they were delayed by petty political bickering, paralyzing polarization, and undue stubbornness.

Other countries have had their share of trust issues and near misses. Witness how in 2014 London almost bungled a referendum that came very close to seeing Scotland exit the United Kingdom, a development that would have entailed considerable uncertainty for both nations, as well as the European Union. And see how a small party that secured only a single seat in the UK general elections enticed the Conservative Party to hold a referendum in which voters opted to exit the European Union. Meanwhile, throughout continental Europe there has been a surge in support for nontraditional and antiestablishment parties, an issue we address in the next chapter.

CHAPTER 13

NATIONAL POLITICAL DYSFUNCTION

"Political insurgency—from Syriza in Greece to the Tea Party in America—is a feature of many western democracies."[1]

—THE ECONOMIST

*I*ssue 5: National political dysfunction is still a headwind to overcoming economic malaise and restoring genuine and durable financial stability.

The good news is that, in all likelihood and despite the very strange 2016 presidential campaign, the worst of the very harmful Congressional dysfunction we've seen in recent years is behind us in the United States. After the experiences of 2012–13,[2] few politicians seem eager to play Russian roulette again with the country's economic well-being by pursuing a prolonged government shutdown or triggering a technical debt default by refusing to lift the debt ceiling. But there isn't much good news beyond that at present, unfortunately.

In America, political parties find it very hard to agree on policies to move the country forward. Even measures that can command quite broad bipartisan support, such as basic infrastructure development, move at a glacial pace. The reason for this sad state of affairs is simple: Many moderate politicians fear that their willingness to compromise politically will cost them in their next primary—after all, in many cases these days, their electoral success depends less on defeating opponents from the other party and more on surviving friendly fire from the more extreme factions of their own.

A sense of political despair has been accentuated by a recognition that elections are unlikely to make things better unless the outcome involves a broad sweep by one party of both the executive and legislative functions. As an illustration, consider what happened in the November 2014 midterm elections.

In their "shellacking" of Democrats, Republicans gained control of the Senate and took their majority in the House of Representatives to a level not seen in many decades. Yet few believed that this was enough for a constructive "cohabitation" with Democratic president Barack Obama. Instead, within just days of this election, the already vitriolic rhetoric went up quite a few more notches as the parties accused each other of being even more uncooperative and abusing their powers. Thereafter, the gap widened, typified by something quite unprecedented—Republican senators sent a letter to a foreign country (Iran) warning leaders there that the agreement they were about to sign with President Obama to limit Iran's nuclear proliferation capability could be subsequently overturned—a clear overstepping of bounds, and a move that, more generally, could complicate U.S. foreign policy in the future.

Such messy gridlock will likely persist until the main political parties become a lot less beholden to the more extreme segments of their bases; until leaders of one party trusting that the others will be willing and able to abide by negotiated agreements; and until a genuine recognition that many of the interests of the two are roughly aligned over time, especially when the parties focus intently on better serving the national interest. All of this is to say that productive collaboration is unlikely to happen anytime soon.

In Europe, the problems are both within countries and among them.

Across a region committed to ever-closer political union, there has been a failure to agree on the difficulties besetting the implementation of a common integration vision and the resolution of periodic country problems. Countries still jealously guard their own narratives, treating them as elucidations of some absolute truth rather than part of a collective evolutionary process that inevitably involves compromises. They repeatedly present them to citizens, making it really difficult for the Eurozone to agree on a common road map for the future. So its architecture remains partial and fragile. The underlying tensions get aggravated by shocks, such as the tragic migration crisis.

Evidence of voter dissatisfaction has been widespread throughout the region. With the surge of more extreme parties, the 2014 elections for the European Parliament produced an outcome that Manuel Valls, France's prime minister, described as "a shock, an earthquake that all responsible leaders must respond to." And by "responsible leaders" he was alluding to mainstream politicians who had just seen their parties lose a significant number of supporters to nontraditional, antiestablishment parties. The success of the National Front in France is an example, as is the surge of support for the Alternative for Germany (AFD) in Germany and the Danish People's Party in Denmark, to name just a few.

Then there is the decisive win by Syriza in Greece's 2015 national elections. This was a particularly loud wake-up call for mainstream parties because it challenged the notion that the surge of support for antiestablishment parties occurs only in less consequential elections (such as those for the European Parliament, as opposed to the national ballot box) and reflects mainly negative voting (or a reversible behavior that, in addition to being too weak to win elections, is driven only by negative factors and therefore is neither firmly anchored nor durable).

Finally—and as if I needed to convince you further of the challenges—politics around the world also needs to play catch-up with a number of consequential secular and structural transformations in society; these meaningful challenges face governments that find it inherently hard to disrupt themselves for the better (it is difficult enough for business and individuals to do so; for governments it is infinitely more so). These include wide-scale urbanization and the emergence of megacities, which render even more important the effective devolution of some power to cities and municipalities. Meanwhile, and perhaps more important, rapid technological innovations have enabled and empowered individuals like never before (something that we will return to later in the book).

Today, so many more people in so many more places are enabled to connect and participate, and, soon, they will also be able to make a lot more things. It is the "sharing economy" in which so many more citizens can be productive entrepreneurs and collaborators, including by deploying existing (underutilized) assets. But it is a world that displaces existing workers in established sectors, and that makes the political center weaker. More concerning, it is a world that makes cyberterrorism and nonstate terrorism more meaningful threats.[3]

Governments that look to the technological revolution to materially improve the welfare of both current and future generations while also countering its dark side need to understand the dual nature of these transformative innovations. Think of the following tug-of-war on some of the youth at risk: On the one hand, access to the Khan Academy, an impressive online learning platform, brings academic knowledge, self-improvement, and skill acquisition to them in a highly engaging and cost-effective manner; on the other hand is the relatively easy circulation of impressionable ISIS videos that seek to recruit them for a life of violence and uprooting. And all this still occurs largely outside the reach of governments.

We need to be clear about the risks ahead. If politicians continue to dither in dealing with the economy and with the already appreciable list of secular and structural issues confronting us, perceptions will spread even more among voters that it is time to exchange seemingly exhausted and unimaginative leaders for more charismatic nontraditional ones, and they would likely do so notwithstanding the latter's general lack of comprehensive positive agendas and of governing experience. Some of the newly empowered nontraditional players may succeed in coming up with new approaches; but the majority will struggle. And while some will falter and fizzle out, others will leave lasting damage in resorting to the politics of fear and prejudice, amplifying divisions and eroding social cohesion further.[4]

CHAPTER 14

THE "G-0" SLIDE INTO THE "INTERNATIONAL ECONOMIC NON-SYSTEM"

"We are now living in a G-Zero world, one in which no single country or bloc of countries has the political and economic leverage—or the will—to drive a truly international agenda."

—IAN BREMMER

"Currently we have an international monetary non-system. Nobody has to follow any rules. Everybody does what they consider is in their own short-term best interest. The real difficulty is: What is in their short-term interest—for example, following ultra-easy monetary policy—could well backfire somewhere. It might be not in their long-term best interest. And as the easy monetary policy influences the exchange rates, it influences other countries. Almost every country in the world is in easing mode, following the Fed, and we have absolutely no idea how it will end up. We are in absolutely uncharted territory here."

—WILLIAM R. WHITE

*I*ssue 6: As national dysfunction undermines global policy coordination, traditional core/periphery relations fail and geopolitical tensions escalate.

It is not hard to see how political gridlock, challenged governments, and constant bickering among regional partners end up undermining proper economic management and cross-country policy coordination. In the process, more and more countries go from being victims of persistent economic malaise to also becoming contributors to it, thus not only undermining quick recoveries but also increasing the frightening probability of unfavorable path dependency and damaging "multiple equilibria"—that is, an increasing likelihood that, rather than revert to historical norms, a single bad outcome increases the probability of even worse outcomes down the road.

With both Europe and the United States dealing with internal issues, and with the emerging world having lost quite a bit of faith in the credibility and fairness of the multilateral system, it should come as no surprise that global policy coordination has fallen well short of what is required. But before we dig further into this, it is important to recognize that this is not to say the global system has been totally ineffective. Indeed, one notably positive post-crisis development is on the trade side—namely, the extent to which the rule-based system of international trade absorbed for several years the stress and strains of low growth and high unemployment.

Unlike in the past, trade protectionism has not been a real threat to economic prosperity, at least not until the U.S. presidential elections when anti-trade rhetoric got a lot louder. A lot of this has to do with the way in which international trade has evolved and grown, and how national and corporate incentives have changed with it.

Most if not all of the systemically important countries (and many of the less systemically important ones) interact with one another as *both* consumers and producers. The broader set of interlinkages is also true for the private sector. Many companies have registered significant growth in international sales, and quite a few now have established parts of their production chains abroad.

All this speaks to the modern-day spaghetti bowl nature of the benefits of trade and therefore the costs of protectionism. With so many entities on both sides of the equation, including households, the lure of protectionism is lessened. And with that it had proven much harder to organize political alliances to promote protectionism until very recently.

This, along with ongoing efforts under the auspices of the Financial Stability Board (FSB) to strengthen global coordination of financial regulations, is about all the good that can be said today about the functioning of cross-border coordination on economic and financial matters. And it is certainly not enough to offset the pressures that emanate from the weakness at the core of the system. And it does not mean the system is immune from a bout of politically induced protectionism.

The current architecture of the world's economic and financial system still places the advanced economies at its center. It assumes that these economies will be relatively well and responsibly managed over time. They have lots of influence and retain their historical entitlements. And they have huge influence and veto power over multilateral institutions. In return, they underpin global economic and financial stability.

With the advanced economies not able to deliver well on this implicit contract, an increasing number of countries in the periphery of the global system have naturally felt frustration and anxiety. And with repeated attempts at global architecture reform, including very modest ones, getting us essentially nowhere, this has been mixed with anger and resentment—all of which, in game theory language, has turned global policy into an uncoordinated game in which the players lack incentive alignments, mutual trust, accountability, monitoring, and enforcement mechanisms. As such, outcomes are bound to fall short—and do fall short—of what is both desirable and feasible under a reformed and modernized architecture.

Unable to improve the design of the global system, and unwilling to stand passively by, a set of countries has been gradually building small pipes that explicitly seek to bypass the core. This is particularly true for the BRICS,[1] a grouping of countries that on paper have very little in common, culturally, politically, geographically, or linguistically. Yet it is a group that has been energized into action by dissatisfaction over the way the advanced countries are managing what is still a Western-dominated international monetary system.[2]

What started out as a relatively small effort—focused on bilateral payment arrangements and, in Asia, some regional swap arrangements—has been slowly morphing into something bigger.

From the "new development bank" and the related swap lines pushed by the BRICS at their summits to the China-powered Asian Infrastructure Investment Bank (AIIB), we now see multiple attempts to replicate (albeit on a much smaller scale) what institutions like the IMF and World Bank are meant to do—and it is far from automatic that the ultimate destination of these initiatives is an eventually better-managed global system. Instead they could end up being part of broader efforts to build a parallel system that takes some power away from the West in general, and the United States in particular.

This is one of the reasons why the United States and some other countries have opposed the new institutional initiatives pushed by these emerging economies. Yet their opposition has not been as decisive as in the past. Indeed, in strongly opposing the establishment of the AIIB, a China-led initiative seeking to mobilize and allocate greater funding to infrastructure projects in Asia, the United States has suffered the unfortunate experience of seeing one ally after the other ignore its opposition to this new institution—and so much so as to potentially change the calculus for America itself,[3] from trying to stop it to finding a face-saving way to influence and shape it.

This is not the first time that the United States has strongly opposed an Asian initiative. In the midst of its 1997–98 crisis, Asia sought to form an institution—the "Asian Monetary Fund"—to better respond to the needs of the region. This came on the heels of deep disappointments with the IMF and World Bank—multilaterals that were seen by many Asian leaders as insufficiently sensitive to conditions on the ground in their countries, too eager to implement inappropriate conditions, and too influenced by the ideology, mindsets, and experience of the West.

Fearing that such a new institution would undermine the functioning of the global system, the United States led a successful campaign to squash the initiative. To appease the region, a collection of much less ambitious and partial initiatives was pursued, including the Chiang Mai currency swap. But as far as the major Western economies were concerned, there was no room for a new institution at that time; and they got their way.

Fast-forward some sixteen years and neither the United States nor Europe has the ability to squash new initiatives, including some that bring together a more disparate and less cohesive set of countries. Thus the mounting concerns among international economists about the risk of growing global fragmentation—fueling tensions, conflicts, and inefficiencies. And these worries are unlikely to dissipate quickly given the role and influence of China, including its willingness to lead by example by committing large financial resources to the endeavor.

It is important to note that the ongoing global realignment is not just about countries. We are also witnessing significant changes in the corporate landscape. In an insightful study of the "four great disruptive forces" impacting society, three authors from McKinsey note that "as recently as 2000, 95 percent of the Fortune Global 500 . . . were headquartered in developed economies. By 2025, when China will be home to more large companies than either the United States or Europe, we expect that nearly half of the world's large companies . . . will come from the emerging markets."[4]

The jury is still out on the impact and effectiveness of the young BRICS's initiatives, including the AIIB and the new development bank. As I argued in July 2014,[5] a lot depends on their ability to meet six inherent challenges that, too often, can be underestimated by these kinds of institutions—namely:

- Letting meritocracy, rather than politics and national entitlements, determine key appointments and decisions;
- Being able to strike the right balance between developmental and commercial objectives;
- Promoting the replicable use of public-private partnerships;
- Ensuring that projects are environmentally and socially sustainable;

- Comprehensively putting in place supportive institutional, regulatory, and legal structures; and
- Deploying and applying well a more modern set of evidence-based analytical and financing tools.

If these conditions are not met, the outcome of the BRICS's initiatives risks being a lose-lose-lose: a loss for the institutions themselves as they get tarnished by political disagreements, low effectiveness, and high expenses; a loss for the specific objectives that the BRICS would like to meet in terms of compensating for existing institutional shortfalls; and a loss for the efficient functioning of the multilateral system as a whole. As such, the political statement would end up being disappointing, expensive, and short-lived, in addition to potentially harming more promising initiatives in the future. On the other hand, should these conditions be met, the BRICS could end up providing a catalyst for revamping multilateralism in a manner that promotes global economic cooperation and prosperity.

CHAPTER 15

THE MIGRATION AND MORPHING OF FINANCIAL RISKS

"Quantitative easing has been a bold and innovative experiment. Its outcomes were always uncertain, and some may have been unfortunate. But central banks have been right to do what they did."

—*FINANCIAL TIMES*

*I*ssue 7: With systemic risks migrating from banks to nonbanks, and morphing in the process, regulators are again challenged to get ahead of future problems.

Undoubtedly, the banking system in advanced economies is now safer—a lot safer. The de-risking has been led by the United States, where in 2009 the government moved forcefully in implementing a rigorous stress testing of banks. The United Kingdom followed soon after. After some false starts and notwithstanding some remaining pockets of weakness, it was the turn of the Eurozone when in October 2014, under the auspices of a more powerful and empowered ECB, banks were finally subjected to a credible stress test of their balance sheets (or "AQRs," for asset quality reviews) under a range of stressful scenarios.

Forced not just by regulatory actions but also by market pressures, the majority of banks have built considerable capital cushions to off-set the impact of possible future mistakes and adverse exogenous shocks; these cushions will be further enhanced in the years ahead as additional capital requirements ("surcharges") kick in for what are now known as the "GSIBs," or the "global systemically important banks"[1]—including those banks that are still viewed as too big to manage and/or too big to fail.

At the same time, considerable efforts have been devoted to cleaning up balance sheets, be it through the disposal of shady assets or better pricing and risk assessments. There have even been efforts to better align internal incentives and try to reduce classic principal/agent problems that result in excessive short-termism and irresponsible risk taking. And all this has been supplemented by a revised legislative framework, including Dodd-Frank in the United States, the details of which are still under implementation (and some have already been diluted by bank lobbying).

The net outcome is—undoubtedly—greater banking system soundness. To the extent that there are efficiency losses, and there are, they are viewed as an acceptable cost for pulling banks away from a culture of reckless risk taking and pushing them toward greater safety, both for them individually and for the system as a whole.

Stronger regulation is being accompanied by more intrusive supervision of banks. Supervisors spend a lot more time on bank premises these days, and, especially after leaks out of the New York Fed regarding some pockets of pressure for lenient treatment, they are subject to much greater scrutiny to guard against regulatory capture. All this is being undertaken with full recognition that there is virtually no appetite in society, and certainly not in the political system, for another round of bank bailouts.

Whichever way you look at it, the banking system is on a multi-year journey toward a "utility model." It will be consistently de-risked and scaled down. Indeed, as Jamie Dimon, the intelligent and outspoken CEO of JPMorgan Chase, put it on his company's earnings call in January 2015, the "banks are under assault" from multiple regulators.

Banks, already slimmed down, have seen their list of "allowable" activities shrink further. Bankers' compensation will remain under review, with constant pressures for a larger variable equity share in the total payout. Vesting periods, which determine when bankers actually get their hands on part of their equity compensation, will be emphasized. There will be attempts to expand the use of clawbacks under which bankers must return part of their compensation should results falter over time. And there will be the occasional calls for outright dollar caps on bankers' pay.

The sector as a whole has been made less volatile and, yes, more "boring." In the process, market valuations will evolve to reflect this new banking landscape, including the relative pricing of bonds and stocks. It is a world that involves lower returns on capital, reduced and relatively less volatile stock valuations, and higher bond creditworthiness.

Yet this is not to say that systemic risks—that is, the threat of financial accidents contaminating the real economy and thus destroying jobs and livelihoods—will be eliminated or overwhelmingly reduced. After all, the risks are morphing as they migrate out of banks and to other sectors of the financial system.

Institutional vacuums that are perceived to be profitable tend to be filled quickly in financial markets. As such, both existing and new nonbank institutions are looking to exploit the business gaps left behind by retreating banks. Thus the institutional evolution of some hedge funds and private equity firms, as well as specialized, large asset managers and new entrants.

Greg Ip, formerly of *The Economist* and now with *The Wall Street Journal*, has a good metaphor to describe what is happening. He notes that "squeezing risk out of the economy can be like pressing down on a water bed: The risk often re-emerges elsewhere. So it goes with efforts to make the financial system safer since the financial crisis."[2]

This development is accentuating a growing imbalance between the shrinking intermediaries in the marketplace (the broker-dealers) and the growing number of end users (asset managers of both the traditional and nontraditional ilk, as well as sovereign wealth funds, pension managers, insurance companies, etc.). It is a durable structural change that, in addition to the liquidity implications discussed in the next chapter, will make market volatility more common, together with prolonged price overshoots, price contagion, and then sudden and sharp reversals.

There are already quite a few reasons that contribute to the repeated emergence of asset bubbles. The impact of information failures and market imperfections is accentuated by behavioral patterns that result in recurrent errors as well as principal-agent misalignments. Asset managers' approach to business risk has also been shown to be a "strong motivator for institutional herding and rational bubble riding."[3] The Minsky financial instability hypothesis is also relevant here, reminding us that long periods of stability tend to encourage behaviors that then fuel instability.

All these shifts have been turbocharged by the low-interest-rate environment. As Jaime Caruana, the general manager of the BIS, put it in a December 2014 speech in Abu Dhabi when commenting on the migration of risks to the nonbank sector: "It is likely, though not undisputed, that the search for yield in a low interest rate environment can contribute to the build-up of financial imbalances. This so-called risk-taking channel of monetary policy could be particularly relevant when economic agents anticipate that the low rate environment will persist or that monetary policy will be eased in the case of market turmoil—a kind of central banker's put, if you will."[4]

Together, these factors add an important element of pro-cyclicality to financial market behaviors, one that will likely fuel overshoots in both directions. They point to the need to seriously expand the emphasis on financial stability outside the strict confines of the banking system, which requires more than the current macro-prudential approaches.[5]

Of course, this is not the first time that close observers of financial developments have worried about the morphing of risk and its migration from one sector to another. I, for one, expressed a similar concern back in 2007.

Having observed how new structured products were used, I noted at that time that complex derivative products were acting as a "credit risk transfer technology" that was enabling in a big way the migration of risk "to a new set of investors inexperienced in this arena and posing exposure problems for the international financial system."[6]

This time around, the assessment of risk and return is accentuated by an intriguing new type of entrant into financial markets. Similar to what has happened in the accommodation space with Airbnb, the transport sector with Uber, fashion with Rent the Runway, and retail with Amazon—just to name a few—the financial service industry is seeing interest from disruptors from "another world."[7] These nontraditional players disrupt traditional industries through the smart application of technological innovations and insights from behavioral science. In the financial world, as a *New York Times* article put it, "they are focused on transforming the economics of underwriting and the experience of consumer borrowing—and hope to make more loans available at lower cost for millions of Americans."[8]

Together with the expansion of P2P (peer-to-peer) interactions and crowdfunding, these approaches offer the possibility of improving the provision of financial services (especially to badly served segments of the population), lowering barriers to entry, reducing old-style overheads, and broadening sources and uses of loanable funds.[9] But it is also an area where regulation is lagging and modes of operation are yet to be properly tested in a general economic downturn; it is also an approach whose individual collective institutional rigor has yet to be subjected to a full market cycle.

Recognizing the ongoing shifts, regulators and supervisors are now playing catch-up, and they are looking to step up their efforts lest they end up fighting the last war. In the process, they will need to pay particular attention to the extent to which liquidity risk has been terribly underpriced, and thus to the more limited ability of the financial system to reposition should key elements of the underlying market paradigm change. Indeed, in my opinion this is such a big issue that it deserves to be looked at on a stand-alone basis (see next chapter).

In adjusting to these new realities, regulators are slowly discovering that they cannot simply apply to nonbanks the approaches developed with great care for banks. The institutional structures are different, and so are important components of risks, behaviors, culture, and balance sheet management. As such, there is a lot that regulators still need to do at the national, regional, and international levels.

As Jaime Caruana notes, "There is relatively little knowledge as to what policy measures could be taken to address the build-up of financial excesses that originate from outside the banking system. A relevant consideration here is the way in which credit intermediation is moving away from the banking sector to the debt securities market." I would add that it is moving well beyond even that.

CHAPTER 16

THE LIQUIDITY DELUSION

"Unlike other bond markets, U.S. Treasuries are viewed as being open for business for the entire global trading day. . . . Any indications that the market can suddenly shut down with little warning raises troubling questions about how the nature of trading has changed in recent years."[1]

—TRACY ALLOWAY AND MICHAEL MACKENZIE

"The impact on liquidity of ETFs, liquid alternatives and the Volcker Rule are yet to be tested in tough times. We'll see what happens in the next serious downturn."

—HOWARD MARKS

*I*ssue 8: *When the market paradigm changes, as it inevitably will, the desire to reposition portfolios will far exceed what the system can accommodate in an orderly fashion.*

In one of the scenes in *When Harry Met Sally,* the 1989 comedy starring Billy Crystal and Meg Ryan, Sally talks to Harry about her relationship with Joe. She reminisces about how, as a couple, they prided themselves on the possibility of doing things at a "moment's notice," from flying to Rome to engaging in a certain act together on the kitchen floor. But when Harry digs a little deeper, it turns out that the couple didn't do any of these things. It was more about *thinking* that they could do so, rather than actually *doing* it.

Judging from the portfolio risks accumulated in recent years—including the large amount of dollars at risk, the low compensation paid to investors for assuming such risk, and the extent to which many crowded portfolio positions can move together—investors appear to strongly believe that the markets would provide ample liquidity for them to reposition their portfolios should they ever need to. That is to say, when the time comes to sell or buy securities, there will be someone on the other side willing to transact in size and at a reasonable cost. Yet there are many reasons why this is unlikely to be the case, setting up the markets as a whole for some harrowing roller-coaster journeys.

Interestingly, this expectation of ample liquidity runs counter to what has actually transpired when consensus views have changed and investors have sought to reposition their portfolios accordingly. In May–June 2013, when Chairman Bernanke uttered that famous word—"taper"—and raised questions about the Fed's continuous support for markets, many investors were unable to complete their desired transactions for even the most vanilla-type securities. The same thing occurred again in May–June 2015, this time in the usually staid markets for German government bonds. Again prices moved violently on very little volume, with many investors feeling frustrated by their inability to reposition their portfolios fully and in a relatively cost-effective manner.

These are but two of many examples of episodes in the last few years in which broker-dealers have shown very little appetite to take on the risks that end investors were looking to dispose of. In each of these episodes, the resulting large gapping in market prices was accompanied by rather illiquid markets, and in a manner that worried the Federal Reserve and other regulators charged with overseeing the smooth functioning of markets—and rightly so.

On several occasions, I have argued that liquidity is the most underappreciated risk factor for investors today. The potential problem is a change in markets' conventional wisdom that induces a collective desire to reposition portfolios into illiquid markets. The result is a series of cascading disruptions as investors, unable to dispose of certain assets, look to liquidate other holdings to compensate. As prices overshoot and correlations spike, various tipping points are triggered, forcing the capitulation of overleveraged broker-dealers and investors.

Concerns about liquidity have also been expressed by those close to the day-to-day functioning of the markets. In his annual letter to shareholders in 2015,[2] Jamie Dimon, chairman and CEO of JPMorgan Chase, noted that "already . . . there is far less liquidity in the general marketplace." This becomes a bigger issue "in a stressed time because investors need to sell quickly and, without liquidity, prices can gap, fear can grow and illiquidity can quickly spread—even in the most liquid markets."

Liquidity was also rated as the number one concern by David Hunt, the CEO of Prudential Investment Management. In calling it a "big risk," he added that "it is one of the unintended consequences" of recent regulatory changes.[3]

The risks associated with the widespread illusion of ample market liquidity—actually, it is more accurate to call it a delusion—speak to more than the threat of sharp price movements and strains to the functioning of markets. Periodic episodes of liquidity-driven dislocations can cause longer-term market damage that undermines economic activity—a similar dynamic to when a sovereign's severe liquidity crisis risks turning into a solvency one. Using economic jargon for those of you that are so inclined, it illustrates the extent to which the velocity-adjusted quantity of "money" has been endogenized by markets, rendering central bank policy effectiveness even more vulnerable to swings in market risk appetite.

As noted earlier, there have already been quite a few liquidity frights within the overall liquidity fest led by central banks looking to suppress financial market volatility. It is what the insightful economist Nouriel Roubini has called the "liquidity paradox." These periods of liquidity stress were chilling enough to force central banks to intervene even more, illustrating once again that these powerful institutions didn't have much appetite for pronounced financial volatility. They felt compelled to rush out reassuring statements of support

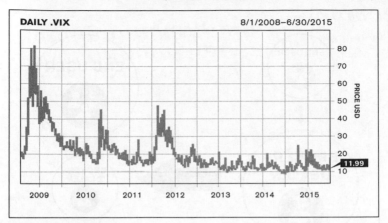

Figure 9. The VIX
(Data from Thomson Reuters)

for the markets and, in some cases, to follow up with actions. As a result, the dislocations ended up being blips rather than catalysts for a series of further disruptions and mayhem.[4]

After spiking, the VIX, or CBOE Volatility Index, which is commonly referred to as the markets' "fear gauge," returned rapidly to its unusually low level (Figure 9)—leading someone I greatly respect to take to Twitter to wonder whether the index should be renamed the "complacency" or "hubris" index.[5]

The faster markets recovered in response to additional central bank interventions, the greater the conditioning for investors to brush aside liquidity concerns and take on even more risk at inadequate historical compensation for doing so. This would not be as much of a concern to global economic and financial stability if it weren't for some consequential structural changes.

The last few years have seen a fundamental change in the structure of market intermediation, that is, the setup under which markets move inventories among different participants. Most notably, the size of the market makers and their appetite for assuming balance sheet risk have shrunk considerably relative to the universe of clients they serve (Figure 10).

Pressured both by regulators looking to de-risk finance in order to

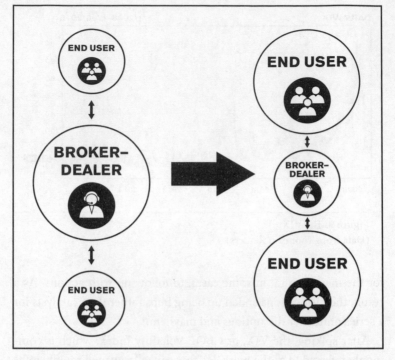

Figure 10. Intermediaries and end users

avoid another 2008 global financial crisis, and by shareholders who have diminished appetite for countercyclical adventures, dealers have been a lot less willing to take the other side of large trades. As such, the intermediation capacity that sits at the core of the established market system and lubricates its functioning has been materially shrunk. Not so for those that access it. The last few years have seen a meaningful growth in the size and complexity of end users, be they asset managers, hedge funds, pensions, insurance companies, or sovereign wealth funds. Yet, having to go through a diminished middle, the pipes that link them have done more than fail to keep up in relative terms; they have actually contracted.

Two factors amplify the consequences of this growing imbalance, which is particularly acute for certain asset classes that lack inherent depth (such as emerging-market corporates and high-yield bonds) as well as products that many investors seem to believe are always highly liquid at acceptable prices (from ETF structures to TIPs).

First, only the middle circle has access to funding windows of central banks. The end users in the outer circles do not. As such, there is no easy way to diffuse the pressure of too much flow trying to get through very narrow intermediation pipes.

Second, while there have been attempts to relieve the pressure by building new pipes that connect the end users directly—including that spearheaded by BlackRock, the world's largest asset manager—the outcome has been disappointing. It appears to be operationally difficult and legally challenging for end users to deal with one another directly and largely bypass the broker-dealers. Moreover, as much as these end users (known in the industry as the "buy side") distrust the broker-dealers (the "sell side"), they often worry even more about divulging information to one another given the intense competition between these asset managers.

Stand-alone exchanges have relieved some of the pressure, but not enough. Accordingly, the current structure has too few release valves to cope with attempts to transact in size and quickly. In fact, if anything, broker-dealers are likely to act pro-cyclically—that is, join the buy-side herd—rather than use their balance sheets in a countercyclical manner. This is particularly the case for those that are wedded to VAR-type approaches for managing their balance sheet risks, under which an increase in market illiquidity and volatility increases measured risk, forcing a commensurate deleveraging.

All this speaks to what I believe is a systemic—and potentially dangerous—underestimation of the liquidity risk facing the global financial system, one that is hard to deal with easily, given its structural underpinnings.

CHAPTER 17

BRIDGING THE GAP BETWEEN MARKETS AND FUNDAMENTALS

"Financial booms sprinkle the fairy dust of illusionary riches."

—BIS

*I*ssue 9: *Yet none of these uncertainties and fluidities seemed to disturb financial markets that, operating with unusually low volatility, went from one record to another. As such, the contrasting gap between financial risk taking (high) and economic risk taking (low) has never been so wide.*

You would expect higher financial market volatility in the face of the long list of economic, financial, institutional, geopolitical, political, and social uncertainties we've covered thus far. Yet this hasn't happened much in 2011–16, judging by the most common measures of volatility (at least as yet). Instead, volatility has been unusually low, with the very occasional spikes that have occurred proving temporary and reversible.

This post-crisis volatility regime has been reminiscent of the descriptors that the Hildon company in the United Kingdom offers its mineral water drinkers—"delightfully still" or "gently sparkling." It is an operating environment that has sucked in many market participants, reminding us of John Maynard Keynes's observations about how herd behaviors can take over markets. After all, "worldly wisdom teaches that it is better for reputation to fail conventionally than to succeed unconventionally." And the longer the herd behavior continues and builds on itself, the greater the validity of a hypothesis put forward by Hyman Minsky—that is, the risk that the resulting "stability" proves temporary as, behind the scenes, it is breeding instability.

The explanation for this unusual "vol" behavior lies in a combination of factors—from growth having been stuck in a rather stable low-level equilibrium to investors seeking "carry" income and other investment gains as a means of meeting ambitious return targets that are resistant to any meaningful downward revisions regardless of how much asset prices have already risen. The result is to live in the moment, downplaying its artificial nature and the subsequent risk of major dislocations.

This special moment has been underpinned by two huge injectors of cash into the marketplace: central banks and the deployment of unusually large cash balances held by large companies.

The determined efforts of central banks and their unquestionable influence on financial assets have translated to markets operating under the mantra that "bad economic news is good for markets." Rather than lead to a downward revision in investors' assessment of fundamentals and, therefore, what constitutes fair financial value, disappointing economic news has been interpreted as implying that central banks will be even more engaged in repressing volatility, pushing asset prices to higher artificial levels and, by making people "feel richer," getting them to spend more (also inducing companies to invest in expanding production capacity). To the extent that there are hiccups along the way, and there inevitably will be, markets have been conditioned to expect central banks to deal successfully with them.

Corporate cash has played a similar, albeit smaller, role until now.

Having been shocked and shaken by the ferocity of the global financial crisis, including a virtual shutdown in their access to credit and working capital, companies subsequently accumulated significant cash holdings for prudential reasons. Initially they were hesitant to deploy this cash. Yet the longer it sat on their balance sheets, and especially given that it earned very little interest income, the greater the pressure on corporate management and boards to release it to shareholders via share buybacks and higher dividends; part of it also ended up in defensive merger and acquisition (M&A) deals. All of which has served to push up financial asset prices.

As we noted earlier, the impact of such factors has been so pervasive as to also override historical correlations between asset classes. Rather than follow long-established historical patterns warranted by the fundamental attributes of securities within individual asset classes—be they bonds, commodities, equities, or foreign exchange— these inherently different instruments have tended to move together in strikingly anomalous fashion. Indeed, you need only look at what happened in 2014 for an illustration.

For the year as a whole, investors in U.S. equities earned a handsome return of 14 percent (as measured by the Standard & Poor's index) at a time when they also made quite a bit of money on their holdings of ultrasafe government bonds (whose prices went up as the yield on ten-year Treasuries fell by some eighty basis points and on thirty-year long bonds by about one hundred basis points). From an historical and analytical perspective, this is quite an unusual correlation: Riskless government bonds are not supposed to go up in price at the same time as risky equities; and both rose substantially.

To amplify this phenomenon of unusual covariances, the rise in stocks was accompanied by a fall rather than rise in commodities, and quite a sharp fall at that. Commodity prices fell by 18 percent during the year (as measured by the Thomson Reuters Core Commodity CRB Index), with the internals going well beyond energy, which (as will be detailed later) was impacted by a change in the supply paradigm. Again, that is not supposed to happen. Conventional wisdom is that many commodities tend to do well when equities surge.

Remember, these are highly liquid markets that are heavily trafficked by sophisticated investors. Yet one (equities) was suggesting good economic news while the other two (bonds and commodities) appeared to flash a yellow (if not red) light about what lay ahead for the economy and for financial risk takers.

Such breakdowns in correlations naturally undermined the more refined market differentiations that sophisticated investors pursue, thereby further distorting market signals and accentuating the threat of meaningful and ultimately unsustainable and damaging resource misallocations. Once again, generalized risk taking has run ahead of what would be warranted by fundamentals, thereby resurrecting the catch-22 situation that governments and central banks had hoped to decisively put behind them after the global financial crisis: tolerate excessive risk taking by those that would deal with the consequences, but at the risk of widespread financial disorder down the road, which in turn could contaminate the real economy, or stand ready to deploy expensive bailouts to again rescue offenders in the financial sector.

I suspect that none of this would come as surprising news to central banks. It is, after all, one of the unintended consequences of them being the only policy game in town that they have to use blunt instruments that are poorly suited to the tasks at hand. I also suspect that some central bankers would argue that it's a bet worth taking— and would do so in the hope that artificially high prices would end up promoting economic activity and allow economies to pivot from artificially induced growth to genuine expansion. Under their hoped-for scenario, economic risk taking would catch up and validate financial risk taking, and central banks could collectively embark on that elusive "normalization" of monetary policy.

In such (admittedly ideal) circumstances, the initial volatility associated with the policy regime change would quickly give way to underlying stability in the context of a firmer foundation for risk assets. There would be no need for a really messy correction in financial asset prices down the road.

The scarier alternative speaks to higher volatility as a result of increasing policy ineffectiveness. With genuine more inclusive growth not returning, financial risk taking would not be validated by fundamentals. Even if they were still willing to do so, central banks would be less able to counter the cumulative headwinds arising from economic, financial, geopolitical, institutional, political, and social factors discussed earlier. In such a world, they would face the risk of being criticized (and worse) for having irresponsibly manipulated asset prices and contributed to major resource misallocations over a number of years.

Answering questions in May 2014 after a speech to the Joint Economic Committee, Fed Chair Yellen acknowledged that she and her FOMC colleagues "probably do have an impact on the stock market." But she reacted sharply to the notion that they were "goosing" the stock market, stating that "I would hardly endorse the term goosing the stock market."[1] Other central bankers have been more open about what monetary policy seeks to intentionally do to asset prices.

In the beginning of 2015, Charles Plosser noted that "one of the things I've tried to argue is look, if we believe that monetary policy is doing what we say it's doing and depressing real interest rates and goosing the economy and we're in some sense distorting what might be the normal market outcomes at some point, we're going to have to stop doing it." Linking this to the risk of financial instability down the road, he went on to argue that "at some point the pressure is going to be too great. The market forces are going to overwhelm us. We're not going to be able to hold the line anymore. And then you get that rapid snapback in premiums as the market realizes that central banks can't do this forever. And that's going to cause volatility and disruption."[2]

Whether you label it "goosing" or "stimulating" markets with the hope of enhancing economic growth, this is what central banks have been doing for a number of years. It reflects the few instruments they have at their disposal and the fact that they have essentially been acting on their own. And it is a path that is difficult to alter without the risk of ending up being the cause of disruptions and dislocations, if not worse.

In speeches in the run-up to the December 2014 FOMC policy meeting, Fed officials had prepared the markets for an adjustment in the language governing the central bank's forward policy guidance— specifically the clean removal of the phrase "considerable period" (which applied to the timing of the next interest rate hike). Indeed, many seasoned market participants believed that, with such preparation, there was only a small probability of a "language tantrum" similar in consequences to the "taper tantrum" some fifteen months earlier.

Yet for reasons best known to the FOMC—and, judging from the relatively large (three) number of dissenters, this was not a straight-forward decision—officials opted for yet another language formulation that introduced the notion of a "patient" Fed, linking it to the notion of "considerable period" of ultralow interest rates for a specific number of policy meetings. This maneuver was reminiscent of how the Fed reacted back in September 2013, when, after preparing the markets for a taper of its QE3, it refrained from doing so.

Both episodes were perplexing for a central bank that has gone out of its way not to unnecessarily surprise markets. And it was particularly so at a time when the Fed was in the business of seeking to repress all risk factors. Yet something—whether internal or external— made central bankers hesitate to err too far from the prior path. It highlighted a repeated dilemma for central bankers around the world as they venture deeper in experimental policy terrain, where both the status quo and changed circumstances render policymakers uncomfortable.

Needless to say, the reactions of the markets—seeing central bankers again confirm that, whenever there is some doubt, they will opt for being more dovish—during both episodes were similar: They took off in a big way.

The December 2014 episode was particularly revealing of the nature of the codependence that had developed between the Fed and markets. Equities registered one of their largest-ever two-day gains despite a disorderly collapse of oil prices, a currency implosion in Russia, and weaker-than-anticipated data out of China and Europe—again highlighting the extent to which investors' faith in central banks gave them confidence to shrug off developments that impact more directly fundamentals that determine global economic growth and corporate earnings.

What all this speaks to is the repeated ability of central banks to decouple asset prices from fundamentals. With the related trades working well—after all, two of the most popular investment mantras over the years have been to "never fight the Fed" and "the trend is your friend"—investors have been conditioned to respond well to unexpected Fed stimulus almost regardless of the level of asset prices.

While investors as a group have benefited enormously from having central banks as their best friends, not all have been overjoyed, and some hedge fund managers in particular have been quite vocal about their displeasure. Their rhetoric got so loud that central bankers felt compelled to respond, with Richard Fisher, then president of the Dallas Fed, remarking that "big money does organize itself somewhat like feral hogs." After recalling the epic battle between billionaire hedge fund manager George Soros and the Bank of England in 1992, he added, "I don't think anyone can break the Fed."[3]

Hedge funds' loud and persistent protests reflected the difficulties of investing in markets heavily influenced—and, they would stress, manipulated and distorted—by central banks. With prices and correlations no longer following established analytical and historical patterns, such a situation constitutes a frustrating "structural break" for the models, experiences, and mindsets that have served many of these investors well.

It also drives many of these managers crazy to have central banks participating in markets not just as referees but also as competitors on the same playing field, with a lot better information and a powerful printing press, to boot. It is even more infuriating for them that these referees are willing and able to change the rules at a whim.

Possessing "permanent capital" and a highly elastic balance sheet subject to few constraints, central banks can stick with a "losing trade" much longer than most of the hedge funds can bet against it. After all, they are not commercial players in these markets. As such, extreme market mispricing and irrational correlations among asset classes can easily outlast most hedge funds' patience.[4] Realizing this, a few well-known hedge fund managers even decided to close their funds and exit the industry—at least for now.

Needless to say, this battle was driven by two very different assessments of what constitutes the right destination. End investors, including pension funds and university endowments, trust their capital to hedge fund managers with the understanding that the latters' fiduciary responsibility is to pursue profits. Not so for central banks. For them profitable market outcomes are not a destination. It could be part of the journey dedicated to achieving macroeconomic objectives, mostly focused on growth and price stability, but even then, not necessarily so.

Of course, there is some limit beyond which it becomes totally unreasonable to divorce highly elevated asset prices from sluggish fundamentals. The closer you get to this limit—and I believe we have gotten quite close—and the more elusive genuine growth is, the greater the risk of a subsequent disruptive collapse in prices that not only rapidly converge down toward levels warranted by fundamentals but also overshoot them. And the more dramatic the overshoot, the greater the risk that the resulting financial disruptions then undermine the fundamentals.

Academic support for this concern may be found in the work of Michael Feroli (formerly at the Fed and now with JPMorgan Chase), Anil Kashyap (University of Chicago), Kermit Schoenholtz (New York University), and Hyun Song Shin (Princeton University and now the BIS).

Speaking at the well-attended February 2014 U.S. Monetary Policy

Forum in New York, which included central bankers, they joined others in warning about the "trade-off between more stimulus today at the expense of a more challenging and disruptive policy exit in the future." Why? Because their "analysis does suggest that the unconventional monetary policies, including QE and forward guidance, create hazards by encouraging certain types of risk-taking that are likely to reverse at some point."[5]

Similar worries have also been expressed by the BIS, and not just on unusually low interest rates and exceptional large-scale balance sheet operations by central banks. In a March 2014 paper in the *BIS Quarterly Review*, Andrew Filardo and Boris Hofmann warned that "if financial markets become narrowly focused on certain aspects of a central bank's forward guidance, a broader interpretation or recalibration of the guidance could lead to disruptive market reactions."[6] Reacting that month to a change in forward guidance, Narayana Kocherlakota, then-president of the Minnesota Federal Reserve, lamented publicly that such an approach could not only damage the central bank's credibility but also contribute to undermining the economic recovery.[7]

These are also issues that former Fed governor Jeremy Stein took up several times, most pointedly in his powerful May 2014 speech to the Money Marketeers Club of New York University.

Respected for bringing to the Fed a comprehensive understanding of financial developments—one that I characterized as combining "practical market and theoretical economic assessments with insights from both the efficient market literature and behavioral finance"[8]—he pointed to the inherent complexities associated with three realities: "the fact that the market is not a single person, the fact that the Committee is not a single person either, and the delicate interplay between the Committee and the market." As such, there is always a risk that "efforts to overly manage the market volatility associated with our communications may ultimately be self-defeating."[9]

While acknowledging the risks inherent in a policy approach that excessively decouples financial asset prices from fundamentals, defenders of prolonged reliance on unconventional monetary measures point to three potential mitigating factors: an economic liftoff (also known as the attainment of "escape velocity"), where rapid growth would validate what previously were artificially high asset prices; effective "macro-prudential" measures that contain the spillover from excessive risk taking; and, should both fail, a stronger financial architecture and new tools to clean up the financial mess without much contamination to the real economy.

Chair Yellen eloquently spoke to these issues in several speeches, including during her presentation at the IMF in July 2014. In her remarks, followed by a conversation with Christine Lagarde, the institution's managing director, she acknowledged that low interest rates "heighten the incentives of financial market participants to reach for yield and take in risk," adding that "such risk-taking can go too far, thereby contributing to fragility in the financial system."[10]

Having said that, Chair Yellen has often reiterated a firmly held view in the official sector: that, rather than require a change in the monetary policy stance, most of the concerns about bubblish markets would be alleviated by a stronger and durable economic recovery. And to the extent that some may not, they would be mitigated by the use of more robust macro-prudential measures.

Chair Yellen noted that macro-prudential measures, rather than monetary policy, constitute "the main line of defense" against financial excesses—though she would not take "monetary policy totally off the table as a measure to be used when financial excesses are developing." After all, macro-prudential measures "have their limitations." Accordingly, she favors keeping monetary policy "actively in the mix," though "not [as] a first line of defense."[11]

Undoubtedly progress has been made in strengthening "macro-prudential" measures. Indeed you need only look at the list of accomplishments contained in the July 2014 speech by vice chair Stanley Fischer—which shows the extent to which globally coordinated measures have been supplemented by further Fed actions.[12]

Yet the overall level of effectiveness has yet to be measured properly, let alone tested, and any hope that they indeed will be effective cannot but be increasingly challenged the longer it takes for proper growth to return and the greater the reliance on central banks as the only game in town. Indeed, as then-Governor Stein noted in that February 2014 speech, "the supervisory and regulatory tools that we have, while helpful, are far from perfect."[13] It also does not help that, as noted earlier, financial risks are both migrating and morphing.

A similar point was made by Jaime Caruana in December 2014, observing that, "While we now have a sense that all the policies involved need to pull their weight, the truth is that our understanding of how they might interact is still limited." Caruana noted that especially when the situation is made more complex by macro-prudential and monetary policies pulling in opposite directions, as has been the case in recent years, "gauging the effectiveness of macroprudential policies is another big challenge, especially when more than one tool is deployed."[14]

Then there is the IMF's important reminder, which, interestingly enough, comes from a comprehensive staff guidance note that looks at design and implementation issues, including the balance of benefits and risks as well as how to take into account individual country circumstances: "For macroprudential policy to be effective it needs to look beyond banks."[15]

Finally there is the issue of how, when the time comes to do so, central banks will be able to exit from experimental policies in an orderly and calm manner. If it takes too long and/or is too messy, central banks could become not just ineffective but also counterproductive—currently a clear and present danger for the Bank of Japan.

The difficulties were illustrated well in January 2015 by the messy way in which the Swiss National Bank removed an exchange rate floor that it had implemented three years earlier to minimize the damage to Switzerland from the Eurozone crisis. The move came as a complete surprise to markets, triggering the sorts of immediate price moves (including 40 percent in the currency and 10 percent in stocks) that would be notable in developing economies, let alone a mature economy like Switzerland known for its stability and predictability.

While highlighting a range of things and leaving several questions unanswered, Switzerland's bumpy exit is indicative of something that we will develop at greater length in the next two parts of this book and that should be of interest to us all—namely, that the destiny of central banks is increasingly slipping out of their own hands.

How history books end up judging them has more to do with the prospective actions of others than with what the central banks themselves do (though that is not inconsequential). Moreover, to use a gymnastics analogy, I doubt that central banks' accomplishments will be judged with adjustment for "degree of difficulty." If they were, their scores would end up quite high. But few will make that adjustment, including politicians, who may well become even more interested in how these powerful institutions carry out their daily functions.

CHAPTER 18

IT IS HARD TO BE
A GOOD HOUSE IN A
CHALLENGED NEIGHBORHOOD

"What is needed is intelligent accommodation."

—MARTIN WOLF[1]

"When the blind lead the blind, there's little confidence in the direction of travel."

—SWAHA PATTANAIK

*I*ssue 10: *All of this adds up to considerable headwinds for the better-managed part of national, regional, and global systems.*

The difficulties of maintaining a good or improving house in a continuously challenged or deteriorating neighborhood speaks to the fundamental nature of many of the headwinds facing the bright spots of the economy—those that have the potential to contribute to higher and more inclusive growth worldwide. These bright spots—well-managed economies, centers of corporate excellence, cash-flushed companies and households, and pockets of transformational innovations—are challenged to thrive, operating in an environment that can frustrate the full realization of their potential.

Consider the extent to which the corporate sector has been hesitant to take on greater economic risk even though it has been in an unusually favorable position to do so, something that has played out in quite an educational manner in the M&A (merger and acquisition) space.

Economic textbooks would have predicted an across-the-board M&A boom given the characteristics of the last few years, namely, cheap and plentiful financing, record corporate profitability, and large cash holdings. In the real world, however, it has taken an unusually long time since the financial crisis for such activity to ramp up, and when activity did pick up, the moves being made initially were largely defensive—that is, companies sought to consolidate costs and reduce competition rather than expand aggressively.

Coming out of the financial crisis, companies opted to retain earnings and build up a cash cushion, minimizing the chance of being traumatized again by the market grinding to a halt. But with the growing reality of activist investors—that is, financial investors that use various instruments to place considerable pressure on managements and boards to change—it became only a matter of time until money started flowing back to shareholders through share buybacks and higher dividend payments. While in some cases this resulted in better outcomes, in others it forced companies to manage more intensively to short-term pressures rather than longer-term business interests. As such, "the resulting economic gains for society have paled in comparison to the financial gains that materialize for two particular groups . . . the facilitators of deal-making [and] . . . financial investors."[2]

This rather cautious approach taken by corporations flush with cash stood in stark contrast to the ever-expanding risk taking in capital markets that found financial investors willing to be active quite far away from their natural habitat, their investment "edge," and their relative advantage in analytics, information gathering, and research.

There are a number of reasons for this, and understanding them is important.

First, many financial investors feel confident that they can unwind relatively quickly their risk positioning (even though, as we noted in the discussion on the delusion of liquidity, they tend to seriously underestimate the associated risk factor). By contrast, economic risk takers, such as companies, invest in physical plants and equipment that is hard to unwind. They hire labor that may need to be trained and retooled. They have to be much more confident about their longer-term prospects.

Second, financial investors invest in areas that are much closer to the reach of hyperactive central banks, if not in their direct domain. After all, monetary policy acts directly on asset prices, especially if officials are in the business of directly buying securities in the marketplace. Not so for economic investors. They have to trust a much longer policy transmission mechanism whose effectiveness has been far from convincing in recent years. For them, central banks' demonstrated ability to manipulate asset prices has yet to be accompanied by greater assurances that this does indeed lead to higher economic activity.

Third, time assessments and related incentive structures play a role. Many financial investors are subject to daily, weekly, and monthly performance comparisons; as such, funds invested with them are deemed to be highly mobile, making the cost of standing on the sideline and earning virtually no return quite prohibitive, especially if others are doing better. Less so for economic risk takers. They are assessed on a quarterly period, and longer if they are private. And the opportunity cost attached to their optionality is deemed lower.

Finally, economic risk takers have no choice but to be more sensitive to potential multi-year regulatory changes. For example, by changing expected net returns, corporate tax reforms can meaningfully alter projects' future profitability, both in absolute terms and relative to one another. As such, uncertainty about the structure of the future tax system can act as a disincentive to economic risk taking today.

For all these reasons—and I suspect others—the post-2008 world has been characterized by too much risk taking in financial markets but insufficient economic risk taking when it comes to companies investing in plant, equipment, and people. Importantly, for companies it has been less an issue of the wallet (or ability) to spend and more a question of will (desire). And the longer they have held on to their cash, the bigger the pressure on them to deploy it via share buybacks and higher dividends—a phenomenon that has been accentuated by the emergence of greater shareholder activism.

The growing pressure on companies to release cash to shareholders was highlighted by an attention-grabbing letter sent in March 2015 to CEOs by Larry Fink, the chairman and CEO of BlackRock (the largest investment management firm in the world, with more than $4 trillion of assets under management).

Quoting the S&P estimate of more than $900 billion in U.S. dividends and buybacks for 2014, the letter acknowledges that companies face a "business ecosystem [that] has evolved significantly and presents a daunting challenge for companies working to resist short-term market pressures"—this at a time when S&P expected further increases in both dividends and buybacks. Specifically, dividends were projected to maintain their double-digit growth of the last four years, with a similar growth rate for buybacks.[3]

Larry Fink correctly noted that pressures on companies come from many directions, including "the proliferation of activist shareholders seeking immediate returns, the ever increasing velocity of capital, a media landscape defined by the 24/7 news cycle and a shrinking attention span, and public policy that fails to encourage truly long-term investment."

Notwithstanding this rather daunting list, Larry Fink urges corporate leaders to reverse the resulting "underinvesting in innovation, skilled workforces or essential capital expenditures necessary to sustain long-term growth." Labeling this as "corporate leaders' duty of care and loyalty . . . to the company and its long-term owners," he urges them to "resist the pressure of short-term shareholders to extract value from the company if it would compromise value creation for long-term owners." He stresses that those who do can expect support from BlackRock's large pool of money.

The overall result of all this—namely, large corporate cash hoarding that has been meaningfully disturbed only by shareholder activism favoring short-term deployment—has been to add to the headwinds holding back the global economy from realizing a significant upside potential, something that we will come back to shortly. And it is a private-sector issue that has multiple dimensions.

There are many pockets of excellence, and quite a few well-managed companies and governments. Corporations and banks are better capitalized today than ever in my thirty-plus years of academic and professional observation. Indeed, if this is not enough to get you excited about the upside potential, let me name one more: truly transformative innovations, be they in the energy field or that powerfully combine mobility, Internet access, big data, computational power, artificial intelligence, information-gathering capabilities, and the seemingly never-ending string of imaginative applications.

Individuals today have access to mobile productivity tools that not so long ago were deemed unlikely if not unthinkable. Agile innovators can disrupt whole sectors using core competencies that come from "another world" to the one being disrupted, and do so with amazing impact.

From the ability of farmers to better time crop rotation, to cost-effectively customizing uses of productive capital, this is also a notably productivity-enabling world. It is also one that facilitates more timely price discovery and technological leapfrogging, particularly in some developing countries. It enhances "winner-take-all" tendencies and is inseparable from rapidly changing consumer behaviors that seek more self-directed lives.

It is a phenomenon that has been visibly conducive for companies like Airbnb and Uber to enhance consumer access to services that for too long have been deemed too expensive and/or unpleasant. They do so using a powerful combination of technology, mobility, artificial intelligence, and superior customer interfaces. And they take advantage of underutilized assets.

Just think, Airbnb is now a major supplier of "hotel" rooms. Yet the company has not built a single building. Uber is expanding aggressively in cities around the world, capturing a growing share of the urban transportation system. Yet it has not bought a single cab or limo. Both "share" the substantial stock of underutilized assets.

We are living through an exciting transformational period, which, by encouraging a shift from narrow product orientations to more holistic solution mindsets, places an increasing premium on companies' and governments' ability to respond anytime and anywhere, and to do so in a manner that meets individuals' expectations for more frequent and broader engagement.

So far, quite a bit of the impact of such disruptive innovations has been limited to the spectacular emergence of certain new companies, the redeployment of existing assets, and the disruption of specific sectors. But, as we will see in detail shortly, it is just a matter of time before the impact goes macro, fueling the transformation of the broader economic landscape.

When the PC was introduced, it revolutionized the technology industry, radically altered the workplace, and transformed the ways we go about our daily lives. Equally profound changes are on the horizon.

Yet the enormous scale and scope of the potential gains for society as a whole on the horizon also risk being held up by a system that holds back long-term economic risk taking and limits the upside of individual empowerment.

The frustrating (and avoidable) headwinds to new-growth drivers add to the factors discussed earlier that undermine the effectiveness and credibility of central banks. Remember, the policy bet is underpinned by the expectation (I would call it hope) that growth will come roaring back despite the repeated failure of governments to promote a more conducive productive environment, and that this will also help contain and manage the risk of future financial instability, reduce inequality, restore institutional credibility, relieve political dysfunction, and alleviate social tensions.

The whether, how, and when of all this are the focus of the remainder of this book. And the approach taken speaks to the importance of being quite open-minded about what lies ahead, taking a multidisciplinary approach to specifying what is needed to navigate well an inherently "unusually uncertain" outlook—and doing so conscious of the global interlinkages.

PART IV

THE DESIRABLE WAY FORWARD

"You don't have to see the whole staircase, just take the first step."

—MARTIN LUTHER KING, JR.

CHAPTER 19

ADDRESSING THE
TEN BIG CHALLENGES

DEALING WITH WILLING CENTRAL
BANKS THAT LACK SUFFICIENT TOOLS

"We have all heard that 'central banks printing money leads to hyperinflations' so often that it must just be true. A simple, short narrative—exactly the kind that produces false memories."

—JAMES MONTIER

The well-being of current and future generations depends on successfully addressing the ten big issues just outlined. By now, I suspect or at least hope that they are on the radar screens of every major central bank around the world. If they had the tools, they would be addressing them more effectively, conscious of how much is at stake. I would even venture that central bankers would willingly embark on a reinvigorated policy path even if they were initially incapable of identifying the entirety of the required response and its consequences.

I also suspect that central banks agree that time is of the essence. The longer these issues persist, the more entrenched they become in the structure of the global economy, the greater the adverse feedback loops, and, consequently, the harder the solutions become. The longer we wait, the harder it gets.

Self-interest also plays a role here. Being "the only game in town" for too long already means that central banks are especially vulnerable to the winds of political backlash should economic mediocrity continue and financial instability return. This is particularly important in a world in which unconventional monetary policy is also altering the configuration of financial services, actively taxing one segment of the population to subsidize another, and visibly inserting public-sector institutions in the pricing of financial markets and the resulting allocation of resources. Rather than just act as referees, central banks have also taken the field in quite a range of sports.

In the United States, there are already mounting legislative attempts—unsuccessful so far—to subject the Federal Reserve to greater scrutiny, auditing, and accountability. The Fed and its chair, Janet Yellen, were the subjects of criticism during the primaries and the general election campaign. And a week following the election of Donald Trump, Chair Yellen was asked at a regularly scheduled congressional testimony whether she envisaged stepping down before the end of her tenure.

Should any of these attempts gain traction, the institution's operational autonomy and policy responsiveness would almost certainly be undermined. With that, yet another important component of policy management would be unduly constrained, limiting the ability of the system to address challenges to its economic and financial well-being. It would be the equivalent of a boxer competing with both hands tied behind his back.

Across the Atlantic, an even greater sense of irritation is visible and growing, fueled by economic underperformance and the continuation of the horrid crisis in Greece. In Germany, for instance, politicians increasingly feel that the ECB has gone too far in constantly trying to support governments that delay reforms and instead are enabled to act on their inclination to overspend. They also do not like the way that the ECB is perceived to be following the Fed in taxing savers in order to subsidize borrowers. Being inherent savers, they lament the extent to which artificially repressed interest rates are undermining institutions that provide longer-term financial services, be it life insurance or pensions. And all this was amplified when interest rates went negative.

Rumblings are also evident within the halls of monetary institutions themselves. Already, some "hawkish" central bankers on both sides of the Atlantic have publicly expressed concerns about institutional mission creep. For them it is not just about the extent to which central banks have had to venture into experimental policy space, using untested instruments and doubling down on them. It is also about what they perceive as a tendency by the central banks to expand beyond their traditional policy purview, taking on too many responsibilities and for too long.

Before stepping down in March 2015 as president of the Philadelphia Fed, Charles Plosser stated that he worries about "the longer-term implications for the institution. Part of my criticism has been that we have pushed the boundaries into fiscal rather than monetary policy.... What happens to our independence? What happens to our ability to do things effectively?"[1] Other figures, including some not already known for hawkish tendencies, stated similar opinions.

Speaking in London on March 23, 2015, James Bullard, the thoughtful president of the St. Louis Fed, warned of the risk of artificially low interest rates causing damaging financial bubbles. "Zero is too low in that kind of environment."[2] In saying so, he was reinforcing one of the messages that Fed vice chair Stanley Fischer had delivered on several occasions; indeed, Stanley Fischer had just reiterated it that week in his speech to the Economic Club of New York, warning that markets would be ill-advised to behave as if zero rates were anything other than an anomaly that needs to be corrected.[3]

Yet none of this has been decisive in stopping central banks from being the only game in town—so much so that it has become quite common for them to be even more dovish than what they have conditioned financial markets to expect. Just look at how, to the surprise of many given the controversial nature of the policy step and the divided setup in the governing council, the ECB opted in January 2015 for a new large-scale asset purchase program that was larger and more open-ended than consensus market expectations. And look at how, in removing the word "patient" from its policy statement in March 2015, the Fed went out of its way to remind markets that this did not mean it would be impatient!

At every occasion until now, central banks have erred on the side of short-term caution, almost irrespective of the longer-term consequences. And this is unlikely to change anytime soon, even as the U.S. looks to embark on more active fiscal policy under a Trump administration. Indeed, even when they embark on removing all the exceptional monetary policy stimulus—a process that the Federal Reserve will lead given the more advanced stage of economic healing in the United States—the result will be what I have called the "loosest tightening" in the history of modern central banking.

Whichever way you look at it, there should be little doubt about central banks' *motivation* and therefore *willingness* to take action to generally maintain the current path until reinvigorated growth helps address the ten issues discussed in the previous part. Both are huge. But central banks also know well that these are not just their issues— the global system as a whole is in play and multiple policies are required, including crucial ones that go beyond central banks. And it is just a matter of time before the realization sinks in that motivation and willingness, no matter how strong, may not be sufficient to deliver effectiveness and, therefore, the desired outcomes.

It needs to be stressed over and over again that the fundamental problem confronting central banks is not their willingness but their *ability* to effect systemic and lasting change. And here there are grave uncertainties. To understand why, we need only go back in greater detail to the critical four sets of necessary measures we introduced before—pro-growth structural reforms, better composition and level of aggregate demand, lifting of debt overhangs, and progress in completing Europe's regional integration project and improving global policy coordination. We will turn to these after a brief specification of the analytical approach.

CHAPTER 20

THE REDUCED-FORM APPROACH TO A GRAND POLICY DESIGN

"Wouldn't that be nice, Professor? One simple elegant equation to explain everything."

—THE THEORY OF EVERYTHING

Certainly at first, the ten challenges facing the global economy may appear big but not overwhelming.[1] But the ways that they interact with one another can threaten large and durable damage to economic, institutional, social, and political stability, increasing the risk of complete policy paralysis. To manage such a risk, the natural inclination on the part of policymakers and other decision makers, including in households and the corporate world, is to formulate a laundry list of solutions.

Such an approach certainly has its appeal. But a long list of required policy areas will not fly in the current political environment, which has inhibited agreement and action on even the simplest of things. What is needed instead is a handful that can provide anchors—or, if you prefer battle analogies, air cover—for progressing successfully on design and implementation of a medium-term corrective vision. After all, if you have to undertake a difficult journey, it is virtually impossible to navigate it without a good notion of the destination.

To help us think through what's required, we will use a rather neat approach that econometricians resort to when dealing with particularly complex problems—the "reduced-form equation." Rather than seek a full solution—and, in the process, risk analytical paralysis and/or implementation hell—this approach solves for a smaller set of actionable variables. We are not seeking to speak to every element of the problem. Instead, we attempt to encompass enough of them—say, 75–90 percent—to find a solution that is both actionable and desirable.

Applying such an approach, it is clear (at least to this author) that advanced economies are in desperate need of the four major policy initiatives mentioned above, though some may well disagree on the exact weights of each. To be truly effective the four would need to be pursued simultaneously; moreover, given the structural fluidity of today's global economy and the related quest for new growth models, implementation would need to be undertaken with an open mindset— one that is responsive to incoming information and midcourse corrections should they be warranted.

A simple analogy will clarify the point. Imagine a patient who has been released from the hospital after being in the intensive care unit and having undergone emergency surgery. The good news is that she is out of immediate danger. But she has yet to fully heal. She can walk, slowly and tentatively, but cannot run as yet.

Full recovery is hindered by such factors as the legacy of an inadequate diet and the lack of exercise. Medicine and time help, but they are not enough. Changes in behavior are also needed.

So it is for the global economy—and advanced countries in particular. While time will continue to heal many (but not all) balance sheets, this is unlikely to prove sufficient to produce high growth let alone enhance potential, and while cyclical rebounds will please many, they will prove frustratingly insufficient if they do not hand off to longer-term inclusive growth momentum (a point that the Economic Report of the President, prepared by the White House Council of Economic Advisers, led by Jason Furman, made in February 2015).[2]

With that, here are four key outputs of a reduced-form approach to the ten major challenges facing the global economy.

1. GETTING SERIOUS ABOUT
INCLUSIVE ECONOMIC GROWTH

The first component of a comprehensive solution involves rejecting financial engineering as a growth strategy and instead returning to the basic building blocks of economic prosperity. It entails a decisive exit from a global monetary configuration, public and private, that has depended for more than a decade now on injection after injection of artificial liquidity to mask the real, structural and cyclical impediments to growth. And this must succeed in an overall context that has gotten more complicated due to the unusual worsening in income inequality within nations, political polarization, and institutional degradation.

From revamping the education system to strengthening infrastructure, and from removing antigrowth fiscal distortions to improving labor competitiveness and flexibility, this First Policy Component involves a host of structural reforms that are often classified as "supply-side measures"—that is, they influence the ability of the economy to supply goods and services that are consumed domestically and traded internationally. The pursuit of such policies can be successful only if underpinned by a medium-term program that is also subject to annual review and tweaking. It also requires consistent communication and broad-based buy-in from key segments of society.

Just as has been the case for the more narrow policy response by central banks, this approach will require an uncommon degree of experimenting by governments on the way forward, and for a simple reason: It is too analytically complicated and historically challenging to know in advance all the answers on policy effects. As such, governments—as well as financial investors and some companies—will need to overcome the current excessive degree of short-termism.

For some countries, it is a mindset change that cannot be achieved without also reforming economic institutions. And it is not just about breaking down the influence of vested interests and the paralyzing power of bureaucratic turf battles. As we will see later, it is also about modernizing operational approaches, updating data and analytical tools, improving inter-agency coordination, and making decision makers more accountable. It is also about escaping the trap of overly ideological debates that inhibit the dynamism needed to overcome the challenges we face. Without that, the much-needed policy initiatives—from higher public infrastructure investment and more leverageable public-private partnerships to greater emphasis on human productivity, labor retooling, and pro-growth tax reforms—will prove hard to sustain and expand on. We will have more to consider on these specific issues shortly.

One of the most insightful thinkers on the perplexing issues of what creates and sustains economic growth is Professor Michael Spence of New York University, Nobel laureate in economics and a wonderful friend who has taught me a lot over the years. Marrying solid theoretical underpinnings with empirical observations, his work shows that for any given set of labor/capital/natural endowments, structural flexibility plays a key role in facilitating economic recovery and helping countries "adapt to long-term" technological change and global market forces."[3] Such flexibility normally requires a good "quality of government" as it inevitably involves lifting economic rigidities that favor specific interest groups.

2. MATCHING ABILITY
AND WILLINGNESS TO SPEND

A renewed emphasis on pro-growth structural reforms needs to be accompanied by steps to resolve the mismatch on the demand side between the will to spend and the wallet—the Second Policy Component. Otherwise a chronic deficiency of aggregate demand will continue to hold back consumption and corporate investment in new plants, equipment, and hiring.

Fiscal policy has a key role to play here, and it is high time to break the paralysis that has taken hold of this critical instrument of economic management—one that Mark Blyth of Brown University has labeled the "can't, won't, and shouldn't" syndrome. In large part due to concerns about slipping back into old habits of overspending, the political approach to fiscal policy has been reduced to silly extreme discussions—so much so that, in a country as advanced and sophisticated as the United States, it proved impossible for Congress to deliver on the most basic of all economic functions, that of actively agreeing to an annual budget for the nation. As noted earlier, lawmakers have resorted essentially to simply rolling over last year's budget—though this may quickly change in the United States now that, under President Trump, the Republican party controls the White House and has majorities in both houses of Congress.

This is not just about revisiting approaches and mindsets that result in excessive rigidity and austerity, and do so by chronically underestimating the size of the negative fiscal multipliers and the need for greater policy responsiveness—that is, the extent to which fiscal cuts unleash a dynamic that causes a disproportionately large reduction in overall aggregate demand. It is also about using tax and expenditure measures more actively to improve the quality of spending without unduly impacting the incentives that fuel innovation and entrepreneurship.

In the United States, for example, this would include—going from the least to the most controversial—closing tax loopholes and cascading exemptions, increasing the taxation of carried interest earned by private equity firms and hedge funds, reforming inheritance taxation, streamlining home mortgage subsidies, and a higher marginal tax rate for the highest-income earners combined with higher transfers to the most vulnerable segments of society. It would also involve decisive steps to modernize a system of corporate taxation that is littered with anomalies, distortions, and misaligned incentives that undermine rather than promote economic growth—including by encouraging firms to spend a lot of money on "inversions," that is, the purchase of foreign entities in order to geographically shift and reduce tax burdens while keeping productive operations as is. And it would involve improving the impact of fiscal spending in promoting productivity and better unleashing human potential, including, as noted earlier, through greater emphasis on investments, infrastructure, education reform, and health.

Such measures would also serve to temper the worsening in the inequality trifecta that accentuates challenges to both supply and demand drivers of prosperity. By helping to alleviate excessive growth in income and wealth inequalities, the first two components of the trifecta, they can also arrest the deterioration in the third crucial one, which speaks directly to future generations as well: the inequality of opportunities.

The more that incremental income accrues to the rich, and it has done so in a pronounced fashion in recent years, the lower the increase to consumption at the margin, given that rich households spend a smaller portion of their income than middle- and lower-class households. As such, a small increase in the top marginal tax rate and cuts/transfers elsewhere would help alleviate this issue, and in the vast majority of cases it would do so without seriously disincentivizing work. But its broad-based acceptance by society, along with that for the other individual and corporate tax measures, would need to be accompanied by credible commitments that the incremental receipts would be spent on sectors that are key to long-term productivity growth.

There is also scope for greater use of modern approaches that better match the ability to spend with important national priorities. Despite analytical progress, the focus on enlarging the scope of private-public partnerships continues to lag. The potential is definitely there. As an example, just think of, on one hand, severely underfunded infrastructure investment needs and, on the other hand, the large pool of long-term capital looking for long-dated opportunities (be they sovereign wealth funds, insurance companies, or pensions). It is a gap that is especially glaring given that a part of this pool is also seeking to have socially beneficial impacts. Yet too little has been done by governments to offer a matching menu of partnership options, and this despite the fact that, from roads to city parking facilities, there are encouraging operational examples.

The demand mismatches are even more visible at the regional level, especially within the Eurozone. Countries such as Greece had (and have) the willingness but not the ability to spend. Meanwhile, others like Germany had (and have) the wallet but not the will.

Moving forward on the fiscal component of European regional integration would also have gone a long way in addressing such issues, including avoiding unfortunate hiccups in the historical process of regional political integration. But, once again, there was a strong need to ensure that the implied fiscal transfers would not be wasted. And the challenge for making the case at the regional level is a lot harder than at the national level. At the minimum, it requires early confidence-building measures to signal that funds are being used to support structural reforms rather than substitute for them; it also needs evidence-based verification processes. Neither challenge is overwhelming, but they both require greater mutual trust and active adherence to the overall goal of regional integration. With that, it is important to have a common understanding of the past and a shared vision for a prosperous future together.

Then there is the global mismatch, which is even harder to solve. It is illustrated in a pattern of national surpluses and deficits that are frustratingly stubborn to change, and in an insufficiently productive recycling of surpluses. In sum, we remain very far from what the founding fathers of the Bretton Woods Agreement envisaged in terms of symmetrical adjustments of imbalances among surplus and deficit economies in a manner that promotes global prosperity and reduces bilateral tensions and forgone opportunities.

As it is wired and operates today, the global economy consistently solves at a level of aggregate demand that is lower than what is both feasible and desirable. And as much as one is tempted to propose grand architectural solutions, they involve such a fundamental restructuring to the system and its multilateral institutions as to make them unrealistic from the get-go. Indeed, they make the national and regional solutions look easy—and that is far from the case. But this is not to say that it is worth abandoning the topic altogether. After all, a clear G20 diagnosis of the problems could be combined with some progress on the deployment of underutilized pools of capital. And this is yet another reason that, if they are serious about their common endeavor, G20 members would be much better off creating a small permanent secretariat for the group rather than experience the inevitable interruption in continuity associated with annual handoffs among countries in both chairmanship and secretariat.

3. REMOVING DEBT OVERHANGS

The Third Policy Component involves intelligently dealing with residual pockets of excessive and persistent indebtedness that sap productive energies and discourage new investments. We need to recognize that crushing debt burdens don't just frustrate the existing potential for economic dynamism today—they prevent new entrants from joining in with fresh capital that can act as oxygen for economic entities gasping for productive breath. Fresh air cannot make a meaningful difference if it is immediately overwhelmed by what has become extremely stale and toxic air. In fact, if left to its own devices, the fresh air would choose not to come in and be contaminated! As such, new investment simply avoids being part of what can often be a productive rehabilitation process.

On paper, there are four ways to overcome debt overhangs. The best is through high economic growth, which allows debtors—be they countries, companies, or households—to service and pay off existing debt while also maintaining living standards and investing in their future. But, having let the situation fester for so long, the West does not have this option readily available. Instead, as illustrated by the (albeit extreme) case of Greece, situations of excessive indebtedness can slowly slip into a vicious cycle in which inadequate growth aggravates debt overhangs, while at the same time the expanding overhangs themselves undermine growth further. To make things worse, the liquidity and solvency challenges become deeply intertwined and even harder to solve.

By taxing creditors and subsidizing debtors through artificially low and repressed interest rates, the financial repression regime that central banks have been imposing can help alleviate debt overhangs. But it takes a long time—a very long time—for such a strategy to make a decisive breakthrough. In the meantime, it risks significant collateral damage and unintended consequences that, among other things, distort growth engines, as we have discussed earlier.

A third way to deal with debt overhangs is through unilateral default. This has been tried many times, including by Russia in 1998 and Argentina in 2001. But this approach does not by any stretch of the imagination constitute a silver bullet.

The inevitable disruptions and adverse consequences of unilateral default add to growth challenges in the short run, severely limiting access to credit and making it very expensive. It slows the reengagement of fresh capital and induces lenders to charge a much higher risk premium, at least initially. It can also encourage the sort of moral hazard that undermines responsible economic management over time.

All of this leads to the fourth way—that involving orderly debt and debt service reduction (DDSR).

DDSR is needed to overcome debt overhangs in situations where sufficient growth is not forthcoming, default would be too disruptive, and financial repression is not enough. Fortunately, history provides a guide on fruitful approaches. An example is the Brady Plan at the end of the 1980s/early 1990s, an issue that I worked on as an economist at the International Monetary Fund.

Having spent many years arranging both public and private debt-creating financing to highly indebted Latin American countries so that they could pay their creditors, including banks that would have faced severe difficulties otherwise, the international community came to the realization that bolder steps were needed if the continent were to resume growing properly. Specifically, it was time to bite the bullet and engineer an orderly reduction in both debt and debt service. Otherwise, new capital would not sufficiently engage, thereby risking a prolongation of Latin America's "lost decade."

Work undertaken in both public and private institutions (including the IMF, which had active programs with several Latin American countries at the time) made it apparent that the private sector component of excessive indebtedness could be handled through market-based menu solutions that reconciled the need to reduce the debt burden with some of the constraints that creditors had, be they accounting or regulatory. They typically involved a menu of exchanges that grant present-value reductions to debtors while increasing creditors' probability of repayment on the remaining (albeit reduced) contractual claim. They were enhanced where appropriate by various addendums, such as GDP warrants that made an incremental part of future debt servicing a function of how well the country recovers economically.

Generally speaking, design has become much less of a binding constraint over the years for orderly DDSRs. However, the second component—timely implementation—has remained a lot trickier given the ability of a small set of creditors to hold up an overall agreement. Accordingly, recognizing the usefulness of orderly DDSR within the toolbox for crisis management and crisis prevention, officialdom (spearheaded by the IMF) has been working on ways to limit the ability of uncooperative minorities to unreasonably derail what the debtor and the majority of creditors are willing to agree to.[4]

The public component of DDSR essentially involves debt forgiveness. It was most clearly illustrated by the international community's powerful adoption in 1996 of the "HIPC" Initiative[5]—a comprehensive approach to reduce the debt burden of "highly-indebted poor countries" and simultaneously redirect resources toward growth, poverty alleviation, and the social sectors in those countries. This effort proved instrumental in unleashing the growth potential of several low-income countries in Africa. Because of that, and despite enormous economic and non-economic challenges, Africa has maintained a better growth performance that for quite a few years included outper-forming many other areas of the developing and developed worlds.

Going back to when I first started working on debt-restructuring issues back in the mid-1980s at the IMF, the traditional focus was on covering balance-of-payments funding gaps, usually annually but sometimes for a slightly longer period. But as the reality of Latin America's "lost decade" sank in, it became increasingly clear that the existence of excessive debt spoke to a lot more than just the numerator of debt sustainability (that is, debt and debt servicing). It also spoke to the prospects for the denominator (that is, economic growth). As such, the focus also shifted to "debt sustainability analyses," including how to overcome the legacy of persistent debt problems. Some of these involved large stocks of debt; others spoke to onerous terms, be they maturity, interest rates, or currency denomination. The result was a rich new analytical tool set that focused on the need to resolve the problem of excessive indebtedness that, almost irrespective of the reform efforts of the populations involved, made a return to financial viability and debt sustainability doubly hard—it imposed an excessive debt payment burden on the economy up front, and it discouraged new investment, which is the key to growth over time. With that, the economics profession produced the solid theoretical and operational underpinnings for a change in practical approaches.

Today there is a much broader agreement about the economic im-portance of dealing comprehensively with pockets of excessive pub-lic indebtedness. This hasn't solved the problem, but the hang-up is now much more political than theoretical or operational: First, how do you allocate the losses among different groups of creditors (not just between the public and private sectors, but also within each of these sectors). Second, how do you explain to taxpayers in creditor countries that they have ended up subsidizing foreigners? Third, how do you minimize the risk of setting a bad example that encourages excessive indebtedness by others in the future?

Take the painful example of Greece. To their credit, the country's Eu-ropean partners provided hundreds of billions of euros' worth of loans at extremely low interest rates and with maturity payments far into the future. But they resisted bold outright debt reduction, fearing both the precedent and the popular reaction at home. As such, Greece continued to struggle under the stifling weight of a large debt overhang. Human costs cascaded. And the problems became even more deeply and stubbornly entrenched, dividing creditors and making the solution harder and more expensive.

Looking at the Eurozone situation, one cannot but regret the extent to which advanced countries resisted internalizing lessons from the history of emerging market crises—and this despite the recent insistence of the IMF. They remained too focused for too long on cyclical solutions when the answer also involved structural and secular components. They emphasized flows when stocks also mattered. They avoided talking about debt reduction despite the fact that their emergency liquidity support to highly indebted countries was associated with growth rates that consistently undershot their own expectations and projections. And they underestimated the societal and political implications of a prolonged period of economic underperformance and financial insecurity.

The harmful consequences have been material. As Carmen Reinhart and Kenneth Rogoff have noted, because the advanced economies have not been able to also use other options, such as debt restructuring and conversions, which were used in the 1930s, they have been undermined by a "forgotten lesson."[6]

It is high time to change this.

4. GETTING THE ARCHITECTURE RIGHT (OR, AT LEAST, LESS WRONG) AND IMPROVING CROSS-BORDER POLICY COORDINATION

A. EUROPE

Finally, there is the issue of the regional and global architecture and how it relates to the important need for effective cross-border policy coordination.

The challenges are most urgent in Europe, where, according to the former Italian prime minister Matteo Renzi, the European Union (EU) has behaved like a "boring old aunt"—having failed to convert the restoration of market calm into a more durable economic state of affairs. Now he faces a potentially defining referendum, for him and for his country. And its inability to be more imaginative and decisive is massively undermined by the incomplete regional architecture.

Most agree that if Europe is to successfully pursue its historic economic integration project, governments will have to work much harder to complete the four legs of the regional stool. Otherwise, prolonged prosperity and durable financial stability will continue to elude the biggest economic bloc in the world.

As currently constructed, the Eurozone's stool stands on one and a half legs. The full leg is that of regional monetary integration, which is quite solid. Under the auspices of the ECB, it has performed a yeoman's job in maintaining regional financial cohesion and monetary/currency integration.

The half leg speaks to banking union. Having discovered the hard way the perils of banking fragmentation within a monetary and currency union, Europe has made progress in recent years in building a more robust banking system. The initiative got a major boost in 2014 with the fuller empowerment of the ECB. But it is still incomplete, requiring quite a bit more work in both national and regional jurisdictions.

The third needed—but largely missing—leg has to do with fiscal integration, and it is the one that triggers the most heated debates both within and outside the Eurozone.

There is still disagreement on what exactly is meant by fiscal integration. For some it is about a set of rules and penalties that ensure that countries abide by uniform budgetary discipline. For others it is about the principle of a common budget that, similar to how the federal system operates in the United States, facilitates transfers, along with joint and several liability (that is, members of the collective are individually liable with respect to the same liability). And the latter are right if the ultimate aim remains a cohesive and coherent economic union that fosters ever-closer political, social, and institutional integration.

Clearly there are enormous philosophical and operational differences here. Until this gap is sorted out in a mutually acceptable and durable manner, Europe stands little chance of successfully completing its historical regional integration project. With that, day-to-day policy coordination will continue to face periodic challenges that undermine effectiveness.

Political integration is the fourth leg. It too needs more work.

Shaken by the regional crisis and the near collapse of the euro in 2012, members of both the Eurozone and the EU have paid greater attention to building more robust and responsive regional institutions. Yet the delegation of responsibilities between the national and regional levels remains erratic, hindered by a huge variation in the willingness of national governments to transfer power up to the regional level. And the challenges of an unprecedented refugee crisis have amplified the shortcomings.

Many regional institutions lack the operational flexibility needed to respond. And the system of regional transfers has more to do with a series of messy historical political compromises than with the needs of the Eurozone of today and tomorrow. Indeed, even the latest (2015) effort to have a holistic look at turbocharging integration efforts ended up with rather modest proposals. Meanwhile, threats to the EU were amplified by Britain's referendum vote to leave ("Brexit"), as well as the historical challenge of refugees coming in the tens of thousands from Afghanistan, Iraq, Libya, Somalia, Syria, and other failed, failing, or fragile states.

Then there is the issue of reconciling the two very different tracks that the Eurozone and EU are on. The traditional political parties in the vast majority of the Eurozone members see themselves on a journey to complete integration. The speed and bumpiness of the journey are of course a function of prevailing conditions, including the noise created by Euroskeptic politicians and the related emergence of nontraditional parties in quite a few of those countries. But the end goal is clear.

Not so for the EU. There, a few members, including the United Kingdom pre-Brexit, have been happier to treat the existing situation as a steady state rather than a journey. Their membership has been focused much more on the EU as a super free-trade area rather than on broader integration objectives. Reconciling these two visions for Europe needs to happen if the region is to deliver more of its promised outcomes. Ironically, the UK's dramatic decision to exit its EU membership—if handled well, and that is a big if—could help this process along over the long term (and albeit at the cost of considerable short-term uncertainties).

A lot of this ultimately comes down to trust. Without it, European countries' interconnectedness and interdependencies can go at times from being strengths to weaknesses. You need only look at how bitter and acrimonious the German-Greece relationship became to get a sense of how disruptive this can be, or how the refugee crisis has polarized nations and even led to isolated border restrictions.

Game theory, which analyzes decision making under different contextual conditions, provides important insights as to the need for mutual trust. As Michael Spence once put it to me, the problem comes when you try to play a "cooperative game" in an uncooperative fashion. That is essentially what Europe has ended up doing over and over again, and inadvertently so.

Without trust, it is hard for any individual country to move forward, and the resulting difficulties are compounded by verification, monitoring, and enforceability issues. And this will continue to be the case until all parties find ways to reduce their trust deficits.

B. THE INTERNATIONAL SYSTEM

If regional issues aren't complicated enough, consider the global dimension.

To truly exploit its considerable potential, the world economy needs more effective cross-border policy coordination. This is unlikely to occur without a better global conductor. Lacking that, insufficient policy coordination will hold back the beneficial impact of better policies at the national level.

Think of it in terms of an orchestra. The world economy consists of many sections—brass, percussion, strings, woodwinds. Each can be good at what they do, and some will excel. But if they're not reading from the same score, or if they lack an able conductor, the outcome risks being pure incoherence.

The global economy lacks both that common sheet of music and that respected conductor.

Who could fix the problem? The obvious answer is the IMF, an institution that enjoys virtually universal membership, has talented staff, and possesses considerable expertise and experience. Yet, as discussed earlier, the IMF's role is constrained by its member countries' unwillingness to agree to meaningful reforms, even relatively minor ones. Instead the organization remains mired in some quite feudal practices that eat away at its effectiveness, legitimacy, and credibility.

And the "G's" aren't much better placed, either.

The G8, the grouping of seven Western countries that was expanded in 1998 to include Russia, is hampered by the unpredictability of Russia and its failure to follow international norms of behavior. In fact, after Russia's annexation of Crimea and its role in the escalation of violence in eastern Ukraine, the G8 construct may well be totally obsolete.

The return to the original G7 setup (consisting of Canada, France, Germany, Italy, Japan, the United Kingdom, and the United States) may be easy and comfortable, but it is too narrow to be effective given the complexity of today's global configuration. The G20—founded in 1999 to combine advanced and influential emerging economies such as Brazil, China, India, Indonesia, Mexico, Saudi Arabia, South Africa, South Korea, and Turkey—has broader membership. Yet its operating effectiveness is undermined by the absence of agenda continuity, policy follow-through, and proper unifying vision. Its deliberations have been made more complex by the fact that so many of the member countries suffer from what the *Financial Times* once labeled "a host of local ailments."[7] These ailments make it hard to focus in a sustained manner on global policy coordination issues. To make things worse, this is the G-grouping that was most prone to being hijacked by particular events, as was the case in Australia in November 2014 when Russian president Vladimir Putin stole the show, including leaving early to "get some sleep."

The operationally straightforward alternative of a G3 (United States, Europe, and Japan) is obviously way too narrow in its membership. Domestic considerations also hold back the G1 (United States) when it comes to playing the role of conductor on the global economic policy stage—a phenomenon that was amplified by the dysfunction on Capitol Hill during the administration of President Obama. As such, the United States seems to have risked the dominant position it once had in informing, influencing, and sometimes even imposing outcomes on other countries (as it had done repeatedly during various crises in prior decades around the world). In fact, whether in emerging economies or on the occasion of Secretary of the Treasury Geithner's visits to Europe during the height of the debt crisis there in 2012, there is something of a tendency these days to downplay the views of the United States, even when they make clear sense.

All this speaks to Ian Bremmer's notion that the world is steadily marching toward the G-0. Efforts at international coordination are undermined by the lack of a common assessment of the global environment, supplementing the problems associated with the erosion in common values and aspirations among advanced countries. And with the West no longer trusted to evolve the international architecture in a way that is consistent with the changing global configuration, emerging economies find it easier to try other things even though they are—at best—only partial solutions.

Absent a major correction, we may be marching toward a world in which global policy coordination is a mere shadow of its former self. A growing number of countries are becoming either unable or unwilling to reconcile their global role with their domestic situations. As such, global economic and policy outcomes repeatedly and frustratingly fall short of what is needed and indeed feasible.

It is a world in which summits are driven more by public relations considerations than substance. And to the extent that notable substance takes place, this occurs through bilateral negotiations. (Indeed, on the optimistic side, if there is one thing that the big "G" summits achieve it is providing country leaders with cover as they conduct delicate bilateral negotiations outside all the expectations, attention, and pressures that accompany the more traditional bilateral summits.)

This general state of affairs is a problem for what Tom Friedman rightly characterizes as our "hyperconnected" world. Despite the sophistication of its hyperconnectivity—indeed, because of it, as pointed out by Nassim Nicholas Taleb—this is a world that is subject to periodic coordination failures and vulnerable to possible catastrophic risks should finely tuned networks fail. In turn, this fuels excessive nationalism. And it's a world in which national approaches can take too little account of international spillovers and spillbacks that ultimately undermine what is being pursued at home.

This increasing isolationism among advanced countries is not limited to the economic and financial spheres. It has also played out in politics. As an illustration, consider not just the outcome of the Brexit referendum in June 2016 but also the blow the parliament of one of the United States' closest allies—the United Kingdom—inflicted in September 2013 over efforts to organize a multilateral response to the atrocities in Syria.

This was a case where it was sensible to believe that collective international action would take precedence over individual domestic responses.[8] After all, tens of thousands of civilians were losing their lives, and hundreds of thousands more were being displaced. In addition to massive human suffering, such enormous casualties and population movements risked destabilizing neighboring countries and fueling extreme and violent movements. Yet, as visible as this was to all, once again the potential for coordinated responses fell victim to a growing national isolationism. For many, it was an event that reinforced the more general concern about the extent to which national politics and policy making was downgrading the importance of global spillovers, spillbacks, and interdependence. And the cost of this was illustrated by the emergence and growth of ISIS.

To overcome these repeated slippages, the world needs to return to the wisdom of strong multilateralism. But rather than create new structures, it should get serious about modernizing existing ones. In the economic and financial sphere, this is particularly important in the case of the IMF, an institution that, when called upon, has shown an ability to deliver even in the most difficult circumstances.

Time and time again, the IMF demonstrated in the past not just its crisis-management skills but also its potential to be a "trusted adviser" to individual countries, provide technical assistance, cross-fertilize best practices, and act as a forum for multilateral discussions on key challenges facing the international economic and monetary system. Yet its ability to deliver on this potential has been undermined by avoidable hindrances, chief among them the failure to adapt the institution's governance and some of its operating modalities to the changing realities of today's world.

The comprehensive modernization and empowerment of the IMF is long overdue. Here again the required steps are not a mystery. Several working groups have looked at the issue, including ones that I have served on over the last few years at the request of the institution's managing directors. These groups have tended to come up with similar conclusions. It is implementation that has proven difficult.

If individual countries wish to improve the prospects for their current and future populations, they must supplement their national policy adaptation with serious efforts to

- Enhance the financial resources of the IMF;
- Restructure the institution's voice and representation so that it reflects the world of today and not that of decades ago;
- Dismantle once and for all remaining nationality entitlements, including a feudal "tradition" under which the head of the institution should be European, and thus fostering meritocracy at every level of the organization;

- Strengthen its ability to name and shame countries, both surplus and deficit ones, that persistently contribute to global imbalances and vulnerabilities.
- Continue to modernize its economic and financial analyses, using its flagship publication to inform and influence public opinion.

BACK TO CENTRAL BANK EFFECTIVENESS

In addition to setting out the components of a much-needed holistic political solution for a world economy that operates so frustratingly short of its potential, this marking out of four key policy prerogatives is meant to serve another purpose—to highlight again the extent to which central banks are challenged when it comes to delivering good economic outcomes. No one should doubt that if they remain "the only game in town," there is a very real chance that they will go from being part of the solution to being part of the problem. Moreover, the destiny and future standing of central banks are no longer in their own hands.

There isn't much central banks can do to improve countries' growth engines. These institutions have neither the expertise nor the mandate to pursue reforms in education and labor markets. They are not in a position to lead national and regional infrastructure drives. They simply do not have the power to influence fiscal reforms, let alone impose them.

So what can they do? A few small things, though they are limited and unlikely to prove decisive as long as other policy-making entities remain on the sidelines.

Central banks can do a little bit more when it comes to the problems of inadequate demand and debt overhangs—though, again, we need to understand that because they are just one part of the required policy response, their efforts come with unintended consequences, including increasing the risk of financial instability down the road and contributing to wealth inequality.

A few small central banks can also try to facilitate economic recovery by making their individual currencies more competitive—though you will never hear them say so. Indeed, even when some G7 member countries de facto embarked on such an approach, they found it necessary to obfuscate the issue by stating that they were not in fact pursuing such a path!

Despite some obfuscation (meant essentially to stop any talk of "currency wars"), the policy approach is quite straightforward. A weaker exchange rate is meant to boost activities of both export-oriented companies and those whose domestic sales compete with foreign-supplied goods and services. But again, effectiveness is far from complete, and, again, there are costs involved as noted above, including the risks of triggering a currency war followed by a trade war. After all, and critically, not every country can devalue at the same time. And with the United States already having carried too much of the currency appreciation burden, the risk of protectionism can be consequential.

Finally, when it comes to policy coordination, the problem is not with central banks. Of all the economic agencies across the globe, they remain the gold standard when it comes to consultation, sharing ideas, and, when needed, applying coordinated action. And what they do is greatly facilitated by one of the best-kept policy secrets in the world of policy coordination—those highly effective and regularly scheduled meetings held in Switzerland.

Having been invited as an external speaker to a few of these meetings, I have come to appreciate their effectiveness, and this despite the fact that I have been only partially exposed to what goes on in that circular building across from the train station in the Swiss city of Basel. Held away from the cameras and fanfare of the press, the BIS gatherings are said to provide for a rather candid exchange of views that in recent years has involved a larger number of systemically important countries. They have also greatly facilitated the critical emergency institutional phone calls that are required during periods of crises. Indeed, I have yet to meet a central bank official who has not praised BIS as the best gatherings for frank and effective policy exchanges.

The problem with the central banks is not lack of a venue or a conductor. It's that those present in the room lack a full orchestra—their instruments are limited. No matter how well they discuss and coordinate, they can offer only partial solutions to vast and deeply entrenched problems.

But one thing they can do, and have been doing, is to continue to try to intelligently buy time for other policy-making entities, with tools better suited to implement the four policy components discussed above to get their act together. As these entities are already quite late, and as central bank bridging is far from a costless or riskless exercise, our current circumstances will yield a rather unusual distribution of potential outcomes for the next few years, ones that will challenge our comfort zones, whether we are individuals, companies, or governments.

PART V

FROM WHAT *SHOULD HAPPEN* TO WHAT *IS LIKELY TO HAPPEN*

"Design is a constant challenge to balance comfort with luxe, the practical with the desirable."

—DONNA KARAN

"You come here to learn but you only hear what you want to know."

—*JURASSIC WORLD*

CHAPTER 21

WHEN DESIRABLE
AND FEASIBLE DIFFER

"The difficulty lies, not in the new ideas, but in escaping from the old ones, which ramify, for those brought up as most of us have been, into every corner of our minds."

—JOHN MAYNARD KEYNES

Correct predictions about the future involve what is *likely to happen* rather than what *should happen*. The difference can be quite big, as is the case today when it comes to overcoming global economic mediocrity and the risk of greater financial instability.

It is one thing to come up with a list of to-dos to address what is needed to make things better—primarily for global prosperity but also to maintain the credibility and effectiveness of central banks. It is another thing altogether to move from what is *desirable* to what is *feasible*, especially in the rather strange world we find ourselves living in these days—a world in which many unthinkables have become reality, in which economic and financial textbooks correspond even less to everyday life, in which domestic politics are influenced by antiestablishment movements, in which the politics of anger deliver unusual results, in which there is little respect for expert opinion, and in which geopolitical issues are unusually fluid, involving both nation-states and nonstate actors.

There is a significant degree of consensus on what needs to be done, particularly when it comes to the four policy priorities we have discussed (related to structural reforms, inadequate aggregate demand, debt overhangs, and incomplete regional and international architectures). Yet the probability of converting this consensus into action is quite uncertain. Decisive policy breakthroughs in advanced economies are not very likely at present, absent either endogenous or external shocks, especially as messy politics has a way of getting in the way of good economics. Old habits frustrate required change, and existing structures and vested interests hinder the emergence of better outcomes.

This is not to say that policy breakthroughs are impossible. Indeed, general awareness is picking up, as is the pressure on politicians to respond more effectively. In the United States, for example, politicians of both parties had to reframe the economic debate during the unusual 2016 elections.[1] Its outcome, with the surprise election of Donald Trump, is shaking the political environment. It has also delivered the White House and the two houses of Congress to a Republican party seeking to reconcile its own unusual circumstances.

But consequential and comprehensive policy decision making, while possible, needs more. Indeed, the best way of framing our situation analytically is that we face one of three possible outcomes: a breakthrough, additional muddling through (also known as the "extend and pretend"), or a slip back into even more disappointing growth and greater financial instability. The probability of these possible outcomes will evolve over time, and do so in a particular manner that is quite consequential and driven primarily by the response of the political class.

We should recognize up front that this unusually complex configuration could easily paralyze decision making—precisely because no one outcome is more likely than another. It is a scenario similar to that of the "rational fool" that I came across years ago during my economics studies in England, which speaks to some strange yet "rational" decision-making dynamics.[2]

A very hungry donkey is offered two bales of hay. They are identical in weight but shaped differently. One bale is tall and narrow while the other is short and wide. The donkey must choose between them, and do so under the keen observation of analysts who know that it has perfect information about the two bales.

As the donkey is perfectly rational and has full information, it understands that the preference it reveals will be assumed to contain credible information about the superiority of one bale relative to the other. And this is where the dilemma comes in.

Given that the two bales are identical in volume and content, the donkey is unable to analytically differentiate between the two. They are essentially the same. The donkey, being perfectly rational and well informed, is therefore not in a position to choose one of the two bales. Since it cannot choose both, this rational donkey ends up starving!

This simple and admittedly rather extreme story illustrates a more general point: Even under conditions of perfect information, you can end up with silly outcomes because of decision-making challenges and constraints. This risk increases significantly in the context of unusual contextual fluidity and high uncertainty. In short, the resulting complexity can end up being paralyzing.

This is one of the critical risks we face today. Indeed, virtually all of the analysis contained in this book so far can be summed up by means of the following illustration.

Think of the world we live in as solving in the intersection of four sets of factors: economics, policy, politics/geopolitics, and markets (Figure 11). Today each is fluid as a stand-alone. Now imagine how uncertain the intersection of the four is!

The resulting complexity is amplified by natural human tendencies. Most of us are wired to function well thinking about one, two, or maybe even three of the four circles. Very few of us feel comfortable operating in all four, let alone at their common and volatile intersection.

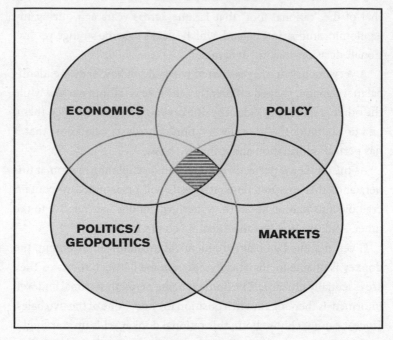

Figure 11. Solving for the world in which we live

The complexity does not stop there, as it is also quite dynamic. It is further influenced by four required global transitions that, interacting with four global experiments, end up delivering a highly unusual distribution of potential outcomes.[3] What a combination! And thus the notion of "unusual uncertainty."

The four global transitions should by now sound familiar to the readers of this book. They involve pivoting:

- From central bank–assisted growth to genuine, more inclusive growth;
- From central banks purchasing financial stability and repressing market volatility to economies developing more lasting structural stability;
- From strained relationships among systemically important countries in the global economy—including Russia

and the West over Syria and Ukraine, and within the Eurozone—to new regional and global arrangements that constructively reconcile different views, align incentives, and thus durably reduce tensions; and

- From the worsening inequality trifecta (of income, wealth, and opportunity) and political dysfunction to institutional, political, and social renewal.

Geographically, these four global transitions need to interact with four historic policy transitions:

- China, where the authorities are navigating the tricky middle-income transition in what has been an impressive multi-decade developmental process;
- Europe, where governments are trying to complete the needed components of an historical economic integration project while avoiding fragmentation and dealing with the Graccident, which has already included the economic implosion of the economy, capital controls, closed banks, and debt arrears to the IMF, one of the world's very few preferred and senior creditors;
- Japan, where, having engaged the fiscal stimulus and gone quite far along the path of unconventional monetary policy, Prime Minister Shinzo Abe's government is struggling to deploy the "third arrow" of structural reform to avoid a third consecutive lost decade; and
- the United States, where the Fed is waiting for other policy-making entities to deploy their better-suited tools to make possible a robust economic recovery.

Given the vital importance of all this, it should not come as a major surprise that so many unlikely—indeed, unthinkable—outcomes have become realities in the last few years. Indeed, we are looking at a distribution of possible outcomes that is shifting from the rather reassuring shape of a "normal bell-shaped" curve to the much less common and more anxiety-creating bimodal one (that is, a probability distribution shaped like the back of a two-hump camel, and possessing two higher-probability more extreme outcomes rather than a single one in the middle—see Figure 12). It is a transformation that will accelerate over time as central banks' ability to maintain the status quo is ever more challenged in terms of both ability and willingness.

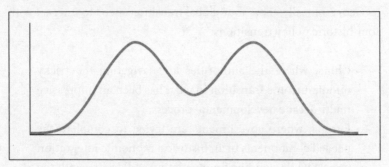

Figure 12. Bimodal distribution

CHAPTER 22

TURNING PARALYZING COMPLEXITY INTO ACTIONABLE SIMPLICITY

"Any intelligent fool can make things bigger, more complex, and more violent. It takes a touch of genius—and a lot of courage to move in the opposite direction."

—ERNST F. SCHUMACHER

"When people complain of your complexity, they fail to remember that they made fun of your simplicity."

—MICHAEL BASSEY JOHNSON

The notion of a changing distribution of outcomes adds to the unusual uncertainty—or what Mervyn King, the former governor of the Bank of England, has called "radical uncertainty"—that already risks undermining sound and timely decision making. For this reason, I would encourage you to always think of analytical frameworks that help convert potentially paralyzing complexity into actionable simplicity. This task is—at least it seems to me—very important today given that the global economy consists of so many moving pieces, and the fact that governments are struggling to step up fully to their policy responsibilities.

To illustrate the issue further, let us go back for a minute to the immediate aftermath of the global financial crisis.

Coming out of the crisis, my former PIMCO colleagues and I found the "new normal" framework particularly powerful in encour-

aging us to think beyond conventional characterizations and historical relationships—especially as we tried to parse through a deeply
shaken global landscape and the near implosion of the banking system. As outlined earlier, the approach was among the very first to
suggest that, rather than rebound in typical cyclical fashion, the advanced world faced longer-term secular and structural issues whose
consequences would surprise even the most seasoned observers of
the global economy.

How about today? What is the simple characterization?

Well, I would suggest that the global economy is approaching a
three-way junction or, to be more exact, what the British call a T
junction (Figure 13). The road that the economy is currently traveling will effectively come to an end soon. In doing so, it will yield to
one of two quite different, truly contrasting alternatives: a materially
better state of the world or a materially worse one. In one, low growth
gives way to high inclusive growth, artificial financial stability is replaced by genuine stability, and the polities of anger recede. In the
other, it's about recession, unsettling financial volatility, and even
messier politics.

As you can imagine, the consequences for you are quite different.
It really does matter, for both current and future generations, how
this T junction turns out. And there is simply not enough information today to predict the outcome with a sufficiently high degree of
confidence (that is, the required mix of both high conviction and
high foundation).

This T junction characterization is already playing out in some parts
of the world in which the economic/financial/political/social fluidity
was particularly well advanced. Greece is a case in point. Its path of
"extending and pretending" is coming to an end, forcing society—both
there and in European partner countries—to confront two very different outcomes. The United States is also coming closer to the neck of
the T as a result of political change, as is the UK with Brexit.

How about the global economy as a whole? We will get more information as we get closer to the neck of the T junction, and, fortunately, there is nothing preordained about which road it takes from

Figure 13. The T junction

the current path it is on. What corporations, governments, and households do can have an important influence on what currently are finely balanced probabilities.

Simply put, the major catalyst for taking the good road out of the T is a combination of better politics and turbochargers. More constructive politics would enable the implementation of an engineering solution that already benefits from quite a bit of professional-consensus backing. This can happen if national policy making in a few systemically important countries experiences a "Sputnik moment" that unites politicians behind a common vision and a national objective. (In the late 1950s the United States was shocked by the Soviet Union having successfully launched a satellite—Sputnik—into space. This one action provided a very loud wake-up call for the U.S. space program, galvanizing it into action. As a result, America caught up and dominated the space race.)

The trigger can come from within the political system. Here, the growing influence of antiestablishment movements raises intriguing questions. It can also come from outside in the form of an economic and/or financial crisis.

At the multilateral level, the IMF–World Bank meeting of October 2008 served as a more recent Sputnik moment.[1] With the participants coming together and sharing rather candid information about their rapidly deteriorating economic situations under a common analysis—driven no doubt by fear in the wake of the Lehman collapse—the process culminated six months later in the impressively successful G20 meeting in London.

Having gone back home and socialized the common analysis of the crisis and its potential implications, leaders from around the world reconvened in London with bold and mutually consistent policy measures. With the whole proving a lot bigger than the sum of the individual parts, the world was able to avoid a deep global depression that would have devastated both current and future generations.

What the world needs to realize today is that the road it is currently on is increasingly fragile and volatile. It is subject to a growing number of underlying tensions and contradictions. The resulting translation of improbables into realities is not just noise. It is an increasingly loud signal that the road the global economy is on—that of low and stable growth, repressed financial volatility, and contained political disruptors—will soon end.

The challenge is to ensure that the turn coming out of the neck of the T junction points to a better, and not worse, economic, financial, institutional, and political existence. Otherwise the global economy will find itself mired in even lower growth, greater inequality, market volatility, institutional instability, and political conflict, all of which would pressure social cohesion while increasing the risk of geopolitical tensions.

The path ahead is that consequential.

CHAPTER 23

THE BELLY OF
THE DISTRIBUTION
OF POTENTIAL OUTCOMES

"Rationality is not our strong suit."

—GEOFF CALVIN

As a prelude to discussing what we should do to increase the probability of the correct "turn" out of this historic and consequential T junction, let us look at the belly of a normal distribution (that is, a bell curve that involves a single high-likelihood outcome and thin two-sided tails); also, let us consider why it is getting increasingly unstable and therefore less likely to prevail. Indeed, as you run this analysis over time, the probability of the belly declines markedly in favor of higher probabilities for the two tails.

Whether you call it "secular stagnation," "the new mediocre," or the "new normal"—and all three terms have been used quite liberally—there is now a rather strong consensus out there that the global economy is looking at a rather subdued but stable economic baseline for the short and medium term. It is one in which growth remains low but stable, pockets of alarming unemployment prevail but do not result in social and political upheavals, central banks continue to successfully repress financial volatility, messy politics do not derail sensible economics, and potential growth is not only under-realized but also subject to downward drag.

Having embraced this scenario, consensus is also comfortable with the notion that you can run it for quite a bit longer without breaking something in the global economy. And here is where I differ, and I think you should, too.

It is not just that, having initially resisted it for so long, mainstream analysis now treats the new normal as the medium-term baseline. It is also striking that, eight years into this economic paradigm, consensus believes overwhelmingly that this global economic situation can (and will) remain relatively stable for many years. It is, as *The Economist* put it in its annual look-ahead for 2015, a continuation of a "world economy that has been sluggish, but relatively stable."[1] That is to say, more of the same when it comes to the new normal/secular stagnation/new mediocre.

Since 2009, as many of you know, I have been an early and consistent advocate of the new-normal paradigm as the most likely (albeit frustratingly disappointing) outcome for the advanced economies coming out of the global financial crisis. But today I am a lot less comfortable about projecting it forward for another few years. This discomfort relates to the growing difficulties that both national economies and the global system face (and will face) in reconciling in a relatively stable manner five trends that I believe will become more pronounced in the period ahead—namely:

- Multi-speed growth, with growing dispersion among influential countries;
- Multi-track central banking policies in the context of an overall decline in their effectiveness;
- Growing pricing anomalies, from negative nominal interest rates to the unusual position of having "the U.S. yield curve . . . now shaped as much by foreign monetary policy as the Fed's";[2]

- Non-economic headwinds and the greater influence of antiestablishment political movements; and
- The impact of certain disruptive innovations going macro.

Together they suggest that, as opposed to the consensus view of a relatively stable low-growth world, we are looking at increasing economic and financial volatility, which, together with prospects for national political and geopolitical disruptions, will make the belly of the distribution a lot less stable. It is a phenomenon that was already starting to become apparent at the beginning of 2015[3] and it is one that has built significant and consequential underlying momentum since.

In short, the probability of the new normal sustaining itself is declining in the face of a greater and greater probability of a tip. Let's consider why in more detail.

CHAPTER 24

A WORLD OF
GREATER DIVERGENCE (I)

MULTI-SPEED GROWTH

"The real story of the future of growth is how well the incoming generations understand our evolving interdependence, its positive and negatives, and then creatively find ways to manage and govern it."

—MICHAEL SPENCE

L et's start with economic performance in examining in more detail the points gestured at in the previous chapter. For the immediate period ahead, we should expect growing divergence in economic performance among four groups of countries that materially influence the outcome for the global economy as a whole:[1] a set of improving economies, a set of stabilizing ones, stagnating economies, and a handful of wildcards that can individually prove quite problematic for the rest of the world.

The United States is likely to lead the first group, along with India in the emerging world.

America's economy will steadily, albeit only gradually, improve as the healing broadens. Job creation will eventually be accompanied by what until now has been a rather elusive increase in wages. The labor participation rate will very slowly climb from its multi-decade lows, though not by that much.

All this is certainly good news. Yet, absent an economic policy revolution, it is far from certain that this will translate into the "escape velocity" for growth and economic "liftoff" needed to regain the full range of post-crisis lost opportunities; it won't result in a robust enough U.S. economy that restores its role as a strong global locomotive of growth; and it won't do enough in the short term to increase the country's potential growth rate. As such, growth and therefore longer-term fiscal issues will remain a concern, and there will be limited progress in reversing the worsening in the inequality trifecta of income, wealth, and opportunity. This will remain the case, unfortunately, until the political system is able to evolve more comprehensive policy solutions and the rest of the world acts as less of a drag on American growth.

For its part, India is starting to develop a momentum that, under additional policy strengthening, could well see its annual growth rates sustained in the 6–8 percent range. Absent any big policy mistake, it could well be on the cusp of a paradigm change in terms of investment, one that will allow it to compete more effectively in a larger number of sectors and economic activities, and throughout the value-added curve. The result will be a jump in the country's development process—yielding greater prosperity and less poverty for its citizens. However, it is not the kind of momentum that would allow India to do what China did a few years ago: become nothing less than an economic locomotive for the rest of the world.

The second group of countries will be led by China. They represent countries that, having experienced a notable decline in their growth rate, will be able to establish a new (relatively stable) economic equilibrium, albeit not without some hiccups.

While growth in China will stabilize in the general region of 5 to 6 percent, or well below its historical averages, the quality of this growth will continuously improve and will be accompanied by a steady maturation of economic interactions, both domestically and internationally. National priorities will clash less with international responsibilities. But it won't be a smooth process, particularly given existing pockets of financial excess. Yet it is one that China will be able to navigate thanks to a large sovereign balance sheet that allows it to afford quite a few slippages, as well as a system that limits unmanageable spillovers. The government decision-making apparatus there also has a history of quick learning and timely course correction.

Domestic demand will slowly take over exports as a stronger and more reliable engine of growth. Market discipline will be extended to more segments of the economy. The influence of state-owned enterprises will decrease, as will the risks posed by shadow banking. Regulatory frameworks will be upgraded. And as China slowly but surely navigates its tricky middle-income transition, it will behave as more of a stakeholder in the global economy.

The third group of countries is one that will essentially stagnate. To add insult to injury, the balance of risk will be on the downside.

As much as I wish otherwise, with the exception of the occasional cyclical growth spurt, it is hard to see Europe as a whole—or Japan, for that matter—decisively breaking free from a low-level-growth equilibrium. Plus, as we will shortly discuss, the region is exposed to a few particularly tricky problem cases and also has to handle Brexit and the aftermath of the 2017 elections in France and Germany. Continued hyper policy activism on the part of the ECB (and the Bank of Japan and the People's Bank of China), while notable, will simply not be enough for a meaningful growth breakout.

Notwithstanding some quite notable differences among individual countries, rather anemic growth overall will maintain the high vulnerability to shocks, do little to lift the pockets of overindebtedness, and fuel political tensions and social disenchantment (and, in the case of certain European economies, disenfranchisement that fuels the growth of nontraditional and antiestablishment parties and in some cases political extremism). Meanwhile, unemployment—and especially youth joblessness—will remain alarmingly high in some of these countries, imparting an understandable sense of quasi-permanent adjustment and reform fatigue.

The fourth group consists of what we might call "wildcards." These are regionally or systemically influential economies that could face particularly volatile futures.

The most important country in this group is Russia. Western sanctions and lower oil prices have already pushed the economy into recession, fueled capital flight, led to a currency collapse, and contributed to shortages of imported goods. Due to the resulting domestic political pressures, President Vladimir Putin faces two options, each with a radically different implication for the global economy.

President Putin could use this opportunity to reengage constructively with the West with a view to lifting sanctions. Alternatively, he could continue to resort periodically to one of the oldest political maneuvers of all time—using an external geopolitical adventure (in this case, and having already annexed Crimea and altered the dynamics in Syria, expanding Russia's involvement in eastern Ukraine, the Middle East, and perhaps even elsewhere) to distract his citizens' attention away from their increasingly dire domestic economic situation.

This second approach would be an unfortunate one for Russia, for Europe, and for the global economy.

It could trigger additional sanctions, including on Russia's energy and financial sectors, which in turn would likely trigger countersanctions that would disrupt the flow of energy to central and western Europe. Russia would face an even deeper recession, the threat of hyperinflation, dwindling reserves, an even more unstable currency regime, and credit downgrades. The resulting implosion of the economy, together with the effects of countersanctions, would tip central and western Europe into recession—and all of this would add up to strong headwinds against the global economy.

Greece is also in this category, with greater direct interconnectedness given its role in both the Eurozone and the EU. Its current economic, financial, and debt trajectory is unsustainable. The country requires a fundamental revamp of its economic policy approach and the manner in which it is being supported by its European partners and the IMF. In simple summary terms, this involves more intelligent fiscal policies, deeper pro-growth structural reforms, debt forgiveness, and more flexible liquidity support.

While quite a bit of economic logic is in Greece's favor, the new

Syriza government's ability to get things done early in 2015 was hampered by rookie mistakes in the way it handled negotiations with creditors,[2] as well as by the creditors' own intransigence. As such, the country's economy continued to languish, with unemployment stuck at around 25 percent and, very alarming, more than 50 percent of the youth without jobs. Meanwhile, deposits continued to flee the banking system, sucking even more oxygen out of the system and increasing the country's dependence on an already reluctant ECB. At one point the government was forced to close the banks for three weeks, set strict daily limits on ATM withdrawals, and impose capital controls.

In all this, the question was not whether the major players involved were interested in keeping Greece within the Eurozone. They certainly were. The problem is that none of them took the type of decisive policy actions needed, particularly when it came to the urgent need for debt relief.

To make things worse, each side had difficulties convincing the other of its seriousness. As such, the risk of a Graccident rose considerably, culminating in an economic "sudden stop" in June–July 2015—one in which a total breakdown in negotiations, amplified by acrimonious accusations and bitter personal attacks, led to a bank run that forced the disorderly closure of the banking system. Together with capital controls aimed at keeping whatever euros were left within Greece, the result was a collapse in economic activity, trade, and trust in the system. Even tourism, a key sector for Greece, was disrupted. The already alarming levels of unemployment headed even higher, already strained social safety nets were stretched even more, and poverty deepened and spread.

While Greece and its creditors were able to regain control of the situation, issues remain. Most notably, growth remains too low and insufficiently inclusive. Meanwhile, the IMF has yet to convince European creditors to grant Greece the required debt relief.

Over the last few years, the rest of Europe has worked hard to limit adverse contagion from Greece. New institutions with new crisis management tools were installed. The ECB acted to improve the health of the region's banking system and prepared additional "circuit breakers" to battle contagion. Other peripheral economies, like Ireland and Portugal, did a lot to put their houses in better order, including increasing their defenses and self-insurance. Even Italy has started to deal with its banking system issues, albeit quite tentatively, unfortunately.

Because of all this, the risk of collateral damage for the Eurozone as a whole was considerably less than what it was when the Greek crisis first erupted in 2010 and when it almost went viral in July 2012. But this is not to say there were no negative spillovers and spillbacks. There were, and their impact (particularly the political component) has yet to play out fully.

Brazil is the other wildcard to note here, although its situation is certainly not as bad as Venezuela's, Latin America's most unstable large economy. It is, after all, a relatively important and globally influential economy, and because of its size and role in Latin America, it provides important demonstration effects for other countries, both good and bad.

After an encouraging economic run under the two terms of President Luiz Inácio Lula da Silva, and under the initial years of the subsequent administration of President Dilma Rousseff, the country's growth engines sputtered badly. Rather than press forward with the needed reforms, Brazil was tempted to try to squeeze more growth from an old, outdated, exhausted, and increasingly counterproductive model. It's a model that relies in large part on inefficient credit-fueled investments by the state development bank. It is also a model that encourages corruption, which, as illustrated by the scandals at Petrobras, the country's large energy multinational, can reach quite high levels. It also contributed to the political pressures that led to the removal of President Rousseff.

In addition to failing to deliver growth, this relapse into old-style statism contributed to larger inflationary pressures, raising the specter of stagflation for a country with still-high income inequality and pockets of truly alarming poverty. With the real and present threat of returning to the bad days of high inflation and disruptive inflationary expectations, it was one of the few countries in the world where the central bank felt compelled to hike interest rates in the midst of disappointing economic growth.

Turkey also faces some rather stark choices as it deals with its own economic malaise and the aftermath of the July 2016 attempted coup d'etat. Though no Argentina, Brazil, Greece, or Venezuela, it could be added to the list of systemically important emerging countries that form a center of uncertainty for the global economy.

The aggregation of these four groups suggests a multi-speed global economy that continues to grow timidly overall while having a worsening "adding up" problem—and it is a configuration that central banks will find hard to contain because they will no longer be acting in a highly correlated manner; and they will no longer be dealing with issues just in their direct jurisdiction. Instead, divergent monetary policies will accompany a divergence in economic performance. This will contribute to even larger pricing anomalies and greater market volatility. With that, price overshoots will become more common, as will disruptive price contagion and highly unstable correlations among financial asset classes.

CHAPTER 25

A WORLD OF
GREATER DIVERGENCE (II)

MULTI-TRACK CENTRAL BANKS

"The job of the Central Bank is to worry."

—ALICE RIVLIN

The Economist put things nicely in December 2014 when it stated that "rarely have the world's big central banks pursued such divergent policies." What it was referring to of course was the extent to which the Fed and the Bank of England were trying to break away from the Bank of Japan and the European Central Bank. As it turned out, actual divergence was less as a series of factors forced central banks to remain quite stimulative. Now the pressures of divergence are growing again.

The divergence between the Fed and the ECB is the one that will matter most—and its impact and reach will assume greater importance as the extent of their divergence gradually increases (which it will). The course of economies and policies elsewhere will be altered. Global pricing power will shift and, indeed, is already shifting. The global system will work hard to "reconcile" the divergence. But in doing so it will struggle, essentially relying on just one variable to do the bulk of the heavy lifting—that is, changes in exchange rates.[1]

At one end, the Federal Reserve will take advantage of America's improved economic situation to slowly normalize its monetary policy approach. It will, very carefully and very gradually, ease its foot off the unconventional policy accelerator. The October 2014 exit from QE will be accompanied by very small and measured interest rate hikes and an evolution in forward policy guidance that will set the stage for a shallow multi-year hiking cycle that ends at a lower terminal rate than historical averages. It will thus constitute the "loosest tightening" in the history of modern central banking.

Having learned a sobering lesson during the May–June 2013 "taper tantrum," the Fed will most likely follow the example of magicians in using a diversion as they shift from one policy stance to another. The instrument will be revamped forward policy guidance, or what Jon Hilsenrath of *The Wall Street Journal* called "linguistic gymnastics."

The dynamically evolving language will not just signal the very shallow path and lower destination; it will also remind us, over and over again, that the process will be highly data dependent, and likely to involve stop-go features (especially if the economy were to prove less robust than forecasted by the Fed). In the process, the Fed will keep a very close eye on market behavior, seeking to strike a delicate balance between avoiding, on the one hand, too rapid an unwind of risk positions and, on the other hand, the fueling of even more risk taking.

To enhance the impact of such communication, Fed officials could well be tempted to consolidate all this in the impressive-sounding packaging of "optimal control." This term has the advantage of signaling two notions that central bankers hope are particularly comforting to markets: first, that the Fed is operating under an "optimal" paradigm; and second, that it has "control." In doing so, it feels that it would be well placed to continue to influence private-sector expectations and thus align both private and public actions. Indeed, as noted by Ben Bernanke, "the more guidance a central bank can provide the public about how policy is likely to evolve, the greater the chance that market participants will make appropriate inferences."[2]

Meanwhile, less hindered by concerns about subdued financial intermediation fueling economic growth, regulation and supervision will be strengthened. Specifically, it will continue to encompass a larger set of institutions (including nonbanks) and seek to take into account a greater array of risks (including, as discussed earlier, the liquidity delusion that leads to periods of patchy liquidity, especially during shifts in market consensus).

At the other end, the ECB will venture deep into unconventional policy terrain and, like the Bank of Japan, stay there for quite a while. Despite the anxiety of some of its members, it will maintain a pedal-to-the-metal approach aimed at countering damaging deflation and keeping the economy humming, albeit at a low level—all as a way of buying time for the politicians to get their act together and for the private sector to heal. Interest rates will remain exceptionally low in Europe for longer than in the United States, and rather than lighten up on QE, the ECB is more likely to expand it as part of its next policy intervention.

In terms of specifics, the ECB extends its monthly purchases of securities, expands the share of nongovernment bonds it buys, and explores other special windows to inject liquidity deeper and broader into the Eurozone economy. In the process it will grow its balance from about 2 trillion euros at the end of 2014 surpassing that of the Fed, having also pushed nominal interest rates deeper into anomalous territory for "high-quality" sovereign securities. It will have assumed additional credit risk even though some of this will also be passed on to the national central banks; and it, rather than the Fed, will have the largest impact on interest rate markets and currency values in other countries.

While there is no theoretical limit in the shorter run to the economic and policy divergence outlined above—that is, a Fed becoming less accommodative and an ECB becoming more so—orderly sustainability becomes more of an issue when exchange rate shifts are essentially the only mechanism for reconciliation. Judging from the history of sharp currency moves, the implied type of adjustment risks breaking something. It adds to the potential financial instability that is associated with the widening gap that has emerged between sluggish fundamentals and high asset prices bolstered by central banks; it also risks adverse spillovers and spillbacks—let alone the important question of how long the United States will be willing to carry the burden of currency appreciation, especially during the tenure of a Trump administration.

In the past, the breakage caused by large exchange rate movements has tended to come either from the threat of a "currency war," and the protectionist retaliation that can come with that, or from the derailment of an emerging market sovereign whose currency and economy have been taken on a roller-coaster ride due to an overly rigid link with a sharply appreciating G3 currency (usually the dollar), and whose international reserves proved insufficient to counter the worsening in the balance of trade, capital outflows, debt payments, and maturity/currency mismatches caused by large exchange rate movements.

These risks are not the only ones when it comes to triggering a deep global crisis. They are now joined by a relatively new risk—that emanating from how exchange rate instability impacts inadequately hedged corporates and imparts volatility to other financial markets, thereby undermining the policy regime that has underpinned the advanced world's economic recovery, as frustratingly sluggish as this has been.

In sum, we should not expect the exchange rate mechanism to deliver a smooth adjustment in the context of divergent monetary policy, especially if it carries the bulk of the adjustment burden. Yes, it will help, but at the risk of adding to the threat of financial and trade instability. And it certainly is not the entire answer to longer-term interest rate convergence in the highly financially interconnected world of advanced economies.

CHAPTER 26

A WORLD OF
GREATER DIVERGENCE (III)

NON-ECONOMIC, NON-POLICY HEADWINDS

"The G-Zero isn't aspirational, it's analytic. Unfortunately, it's also where we are."

—IAN BREMMER

While economists, market participants, and policymakers naturally concentrate on what is familiar, they also recognize the role that non-economic factors can (and do) play. This openness to "exogenous factors" (as economists label them) is particularly important in an interdependent world in which the scope for feedback loops and multiple equilibria is far from immaterial. Specifically, two exogenous factors warrant our attention given the impact they can have on economic prospects and central bank policy.

The first comes from national politics and, in particular, the emergence of nontraditional, antiestablishment parties. It is a phenomenon that Americans are familiar with given the rise of the Tea Party a few years ago, and the role that its members played in disrupting what they considered as harmful bipartisanship. The impact on the economy and markets included a seventeen-day government shutdown in 2013 and games of political Russian roulette with the debt ceiling that came very close to pushing the United States into a technical default.

This threat has diminished as lawmakers have recognized that the American electorate has little appetite for such political games. Yes, Congress is less likely to derail the economy via political posturing and maneuvering. And they face a new reality in the surprise election of Donald Trump to the White House. It's an event that has a catalytic potential that accelerates the journey to the neck of the T junction.

The major question facing the economy is whether this catalyst will unblock the multi-year policy gridlock in a beneficial manner or, instead, end up increasing the unusual uncertainty.

Brexit aside, Europe is at an earlier stage of this political phenomenon—one more reminiscent of the emergence of the Tea Party in the run-up to the 2010 midterm elections, with its passion to upend the established order and powered by a dedication to rewrite many of the rules of the game in Washington.

As we've noted, throughout Europe we are seeing greater popular support for nontraditional parties, on both the left and right. From Syriza, Greece's coalition of the radical left, to France's extreme right-wing Front National, these parties are intent on upsetting the status quo and established political order. It is a trend that is also visible in many other parts of Europe, including Denmark, Spain, and, yes, even Germany. Moreover, the large migration of refugees into Europe is fueling it further.

What is potentially troubling for the economy and markets is that most of these parties are clear on what they wish to dismantle and why, including exiting from the Eurozone, but much more ambiguous when it comes to their positive agenda. Most have yet to present any sort of comprehensive and coherent alternative to what they oppose. Indeed, they are reminiscent of the freedom fighters that succeed in overcoming an established order but then have difficulties pivoting to govern and build a new and better order.

As I first wrote this section for the hardcover version of the book, these dynamics were playing out in real time in Greece. As we just noted, having won a decisive national election in January 2015, Syriza struggled to come up with policies that meet its electoral promises yet are also acceptable to the external creditors that are critical for the country's financial viability. And what's happened thereafter illustrates how difficult this all is.

Despite having quite a bit of logic on its side, Syriza saw all its efforts come to very little while the Greek economy imploded further—partly a reflection of its series of rookie governing mistakes and partly due to intransigence on the part of the European establishment.

Having just come to power in January 2015, and before the new government had a chance to develop a comprehensive plan that lessens austerity in the context of deeper structural reforms and debt reduction, the ECB announced a reduction in Greece's access to its special funding windows. The Greek finance minister met a relatively frosty reception as he toured European capitals—especially in Berlin, where, after a meeting with his German counterpart in a rather unusual press conference that will stick in my mind for a very long time, they couldn't even agree on whether they had agreed to disagree! The German minister wondered aloud whether they had gotten that far.

Ultimately, and after quite a bit of internal tension, Syriza was forced to do more of what the previous government had done. With that, its European creditors resumed the much-needed flow of financial aid.

The Greek case will be monitored by other countries' traditional and nontraditional parties. It will also test the robustness of the Eurozone. But the overall phenomenon it illustrates will take time to play out throughout Europe for three reasons.

First, most of these nontraditional parties have not yet triggered political tipping points. Yes, they are having an impact on the thinking of established parties, and getting closer to being highly transformational, but these are not yet overly deterministic, with the exception of Brexit, which we will discuss shortly. This is not to say that won't happen. In fact, from the 2017 presidential race in France to the parliamentary elections in Germany later in the year, there are some important events on the horizon. But until they get nearer, markets will trade off other factors.

Second, the impact of potential national political instability has been muted by the markets' enormous faith in the power of central banks and their ability to repress volatility. As much as markets may keep an eye on political developments and their future implications, immediate portfolio positioning and volatility have been more sensitive to liquidity injections by central banks and the deployment of cash sitting on corporate balance sheets.

Third, many market participants take comfort from historical examples in which parties once deemed "extremist" became quite conventional when they assumed power. Greece seems to have undergone such a transition after an opposing start by Syriza. In some cases, such as that of Brazil starting in 2002, it was in fact the victory of such parties that enabled major progress on quite traditional economic policies.[1]

Rewind back to October 2002. Brazilian markets were in turmoil as it became clear that Luiz Inácio Lula da Silva, the firebrand leader of an untested and extreme-talking left-wing party, was on the verge of winning the presidential election. Already traumatized stock and bond prices sold off violently. The exchange rate weakened further. Depositors fled domestic banks. Both the government and companies found it difficult to roll over their credit lines and refinance maturing debt, let alone mobilize new ones.

Lula was elected in the midst of financial turmoil that was handing him the excuse to follow through on a threat he had flirted with several times in public and private—that of restructuring debt and embarking on a growth strategy heavily reliant on statism. Instead he adopted a relatively orthodox approach to economic management while reaffirming commitment to meeting all principal and interest payments on outstanding debt. And he remained steadfast on both these issues.

Calm returned to the financial markets. Growth picked up, turbo-charged by the implementation of many long-delayed reform measures. And Brazil experienced one of the strongest periods of growth and poverty reduction in its history.

While it's still early days, similar themes have played out following the surprise June 2016 referendum vote by UK citizens in favor of their country leaving the EU:

- First and foremost, this outcome was fundamentally due to a fringe political party that, as it turned out, managed to secure only one seat in a parliament of 650. In effect, UKIP has come nowhere near governing or forming a credible opposition block in the House of Commons. And yet it is responsible for an historic change in the country's economic, financial, institutional, political, and social relationships.

- Second, there would not have been a "Leave" vote on June 23 had Britain not held a referendum against the advice of many establishment figures and expert opinions. The decision to hold one was made by David Cameron, the then–sitting prime minister, ahead of the parliamentary elections that were scheduled for (and held in) May 2015. He committed to it during the election campaign because he was worried about the fragmentation of his party's base due to inroads by UKIP.

- Third, what the prime minister and many others failed to internalize was what *The Economist* labeled "the force of the rebellious tide in politics."* This force was fueled by the combination of anger and single-issue voting among a segment of the population that polls severely underestimated.

- Fourth, many warned about the implications of Brexit, including what was likely to be market chaos. In the event,

---

* *The Economist* (2016), "Uncovered: Our Misses in Last Year's Predictions," http://www.theworldin.com/article/12632/uncovered.

the selloff did not last long, and for a good reason. Rather than immediately trigger the process for exiting the EU, the British government took a slow approach. It realized that it would be highly disruptive to the economy and markets to attempt to replace something with nothing. As such, a "slow Brexit" process materialized—so much so that at the time of updating this section for the paperback edition (five months after the referendum), the government has yet to indicate whether it will pursue a "hard" or "soft" version of Brexit.

The second exogenous factor speaks to geopolitical fluidity.

It wasn't so long ago that international relations experts and others were debating whether the world was a safer place today than it was fifty to sixty years ago. Those who believed that it was would point to the lack of the superpower tensions between the Soviet Union and the United States, each with massive arsenals of nuclear weapons pointed at each other. All it would take was one small mistake to wipe out large population centers. History books suggest that the world indeed came close to this, quite close.

Those who believe that we now live in a more dangerous place would yearn for the old days of ultimately "rational" nation-states. After all, you can bring nation-states to the negotiating table, and there are structures to enhance the probability of constructive engagements, meaningful commitments, and credible verification. Not so for the world of "nonstate actors," such as ISIS (also known as ISIL and IS), which have become more prevalent today. Because they lack structure and a history of mutually enforceable engagement, it is virtually impossible to interact constructively with many of these nonstate actors, let alone ensure adherence to commitments made.

Well, it turns out that much of this debate is less relevant as both phenomena are in play today. With the Russia-West tensions over Ukraine and Syria, the world is replaying elements of the Cold War, albeit in a "lite" version when it comes to the extent of global engagement—and potential consequences. With the emergence of ISIS in the Middle East, terrorist attacks in Europe, and the threat of further attacks, governments have to play catch-up with the different types of security risks associated with nonstate actors. Even the violence in eastern Ukraine involves nonstate actors. Yes, they are influenced by Moscow, but it is not clear that the Kremlin can decisively impose its will on them at all times.

Again, it is hard to argue that markets have priced in the scale and scope of possible disruptions that come with this unfortunate combination of geopolitical risks. And, again, the reason for this is a conditioned rational one that includes enormous faith in the power of central banks to insulate markets, together with excitement about the cash sitting on corporate balance sheets. But should these influences wane, as they are bound to in the future, markets will have to play rapid catch-up with quite an uncertain and worrisome geopolitical configuration. It is not one that is easy to price in a linear and orderly fashion.

CHAPTER 27

A WORLD OF
GREATER DIVERGENCE (IV)

DISRUPTIVE INNOVATION GOES MACRO

"This gap between the potential of an innovation and its widespread adoption is one of those lessons that we learn and then we tend to forget, or we don't learn it because of inattention to history and its lessons about human and organizational behavior."

—MICHAEL SPENCE

We are in the midst of two massive technological transformations—one in the energy sector occasioned by shale, and the other due to a digital revolution that encompasses the innovations in Internet technologies, mobility, applications, and digitalization. It all adds up to rapid changes that test skills, adaptability, and, in some cases, institutional survival.

Most people are already familiar in their daily lives with what we might call the micro impact of these disruptive technologies—for example, the sharp reduction in input costs for companies and consumers using energy, especially in the United States; the manner in which the Internet has expanded the shopping universe and altered the retail experience; and how smartphones and tablets have upended access to movies, games, and information more generally.

Less familiar is the set of macro changes that are staring us in the face. Indeed, in the case of energy, they are already playing out in a visible and consequential manner, including by transforming unthinkable or unlikely outcomes into actual ones.

1. ALTERING THE ENERGY SUPPLY PARADIGM

Shale technology has already contributed to a fundamental change in the supply paradigm for oil, both directly and indirectly.

Particularly in the United States, where adoption is vastly more advanced than in any other country in the world, it has brought on sizable new sources of energy. It has altered the relative price structure within the energy complex, and it has enabled a whole host of new activities. Indeed, as Daniel Yergin, the energy expert, correctly noted in *The New York Times*, "American shale oil has become the decisive new factor in the world oil market in a way that could not have been imagined five years ago. It has proved to be a truly disruptive technology."[1]

Having said that, it is important to note that the impact of shale did not really start going fully macro until two other triggering events occurred in mid– to late 2014. The result has been an oil market upheaval that will have deep and long-lasting systemic effects.

The first was a decline in energy demand associated mainly with the reduction in Chinese growth rates. China's importance to the commodities market cannot be overemphasized given the size of its economy. The country is also a relatively inefficient user of commodities, consuming quite a high amount per unit of realized GDP. This high commodity intensity of growth is great for oil, copper, and other commodity producers when China is doing well. It becomes a real problem when China is slowing.

The second additional factor has to do with the response of the Organization of the Petroleum Exporting Countries (OPEC), a group that includes many, though not all, of the large oil producers and accounts for a sizable portion of proven oil reserves around the world.

While OPEC's importance has declined in recent years due to the emergence of other energy producers—traditional and nontraditional—it still has considerable influence on the oil markets, both real and perceived. Part of that influence comes from the fact that markets had been conditioned for many years to think of OPEC as the "swing producer"—that is, OPEC is able and willing to increase output when prices rise to excessively high levels and, conversely, to reduce output when prices fall too sharply.

The markets' conditioning was reinforced by the belief that it was in OPEC members' collective interest to play the role of swing producers. After all, the persistence of high prices would encourage the coming on stream of alternative suppliers of energy, thus undermining the longer-term value of OPEC reserves; too low prices would eat into their revenues at a rate that is not justified by the benefits of making other producers uncompetitive and pushing them out of the global energy markets.

OPEC has been able to behave in this way because of member Saudi Arabia, the world's largest producer and one with significant proven reserves and very low cost of production. In underpinning OPEC's swing producer role over time, the kingdom had shown a willingness to absorb a disproportionately large part of the output cut—not just directly through the reduction in its individual production quota but also by tolerating the inclination of some other OPEC members to consistently exceed their ceilings.

In the few historical instances where Saudi Arabia did not play the role of swing producer initially, oil prices collapsed to levels that threatened the commercial viability of even some of the lower-cost OPEC producers. And in one such episode, in the late 1990s, Saudi Arabia itself also faced a once-unthinkable speculative attack on its currency.

So imagine the market shock when, in response to an initial decline in oil prices in 2014, OPEC—under the influence of Saudi Arabia—decided *not* to reduce individual and collective output ceilings. The result was an eye-popping drop in oil prices that ended up

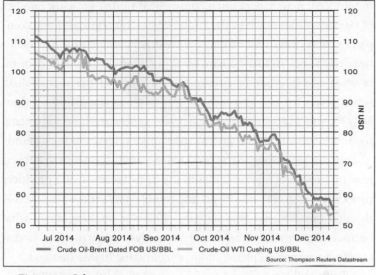

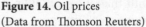

Figure 14. Oil prices
(Data from Thomson Reuters)

resulting in a halving of prices in less than a six-month period (June–December 2014, Figure 14), and after a period of some stability, they resumed their decline.

Importantly for our look-forward analysis, Saudi Arabia was not being irrational, erratic, or reckless. Instead it was applying a lesson that it had learned from past episodes.

Yes, by playing the role of swing producer, the kingdom could counter downward pressures on oil prices. But in doing so it would lose market share that in the past had proven quite difficult to regain. These days it is even more difficult now that significant nontraditional energy supplies are on the market.

Two additional considerations may have entered the Saudi calculus. First, it helped that lower oil prices put pressures on some of Saudi Arabia's political foes, including Russia and Iran, which were countering some of the kingdom's regional objectives, including in Syria and later Yemen. Second, it quickly turned some energy suppliers (both traditional and nontraditional) from profitable to loss making. Indeed, newspapers often commented on the growing number of rigs being shut down in the United States, on nontraditional companies contracting, and on cuts in investment budgets for new facilities. Yes, Saudi Arabia had incurred a significant reduction in oil revenue and international reserves as a result of the sharp fall in world prices for energy products, but this was also disproportionately slowing production and new investments elsewhere, enhancing the future value of the kingdom's substantial reserves in the ground.

This notable change in the production paradigm meant that it was now up to natural market forces in the de facto new swing producer (the United States) to restore pricing equilibrium to the oil markets— through the influence that low prices have in shutting down what become unprofitable oil fields and alternative energy supplies, in discouraging expansion plans, and in encouraging higher demand.

All this will happen and together with the return of OPEC to a more refined production agreement, will lead to a subsequent, more durable and gradual recovery in oil prices, but it will take quite a while. In the meantime, with oil prices stabilizing at lower levels, some economic (and political) behaviors have started to change in a way that will be relatively long-lasting.

On the economic front, we should look for an impact on consumption, changes in energy intensities, and the like. We should also expect altered global balances, encouraging greater consumption in oil importers (whose marginal propensity to consume is higher than in the low-absorption oil producers) and reducing the cost of production for quite a range of activities.

The likelihood of long-lasting effects is intensified when the analysis is expanded beyond economics to include geopolitical ripple effects. These low oil prices are huge problems for countries such as Venezuela. In addition to bringing their internal dynamics nearer to tipping points, they selectively reduce their real and perceived influence on other countries. Indeed, some believe that December 2014's historic Cuba-U.S. deal brokered by President Obama—one that upended a fifty-year foreign policy paradigm—would not have materialized were it not for concerns within the Cuban government that it would now be getting less support from Venezuela, an oil producer hard hit by the collapse in prices.

Few expected oil prices to fall so far, especially in such a short period of time. The surprises are unlikely to stop. What is likely to follow are economic, political, and geopolitical changes that not so long ago would have been deemed unlikely if not unthinkable. And they promise both upsides and downsides, or what we might call the good, bad, and ugly of this new energy world.[2]

Importantly for the major hypotheses of this book, the related dynamics speak to two-sided risks, and they are meaningful. It is again the notion of a distribution in which the tails are rather fat, and which, when combined with other factors, contributes to a general transformation over time from a normal bell-shaped distribution of potential outcomes to more of a bimodal one.

On the upside, low prices enhance the possibility of global economic liftoff, and since the benefits accrue more in relative terms to less-well-off households (whose energy expenses form a larger portion of their budgets relative to better-off households), they also serve to counter the forces of increasing inequality—albeit at the margin. It also encourages some oil producers to embark on comprehensive economic restructuring and diversification programs.

On the downside, the pressure on already mismanaged oil producers could tip them into playing a more disruptive regional and global role. Lower prices will also push some commodity and commodity-related companies into payments difficulties, with likely contagion for certain asset classes that are heavily dominated by them (such as high-yield bonds and emerging-market corporates). They also discourage investment in future energy capacity, including shale.

2. HARNESSING DISRUPTIVE TECHNOLOGICAL INNOVATION

The ongoing technological revolution is a second factor that contributes to a relatively unstable distribution of future potential outcomes. It, too, is shaking the world from below. It is a revolution that combines two critical elements: empowering individuals to an extent that was deemed unlikely, if not unthinkable, not so long ago; and deploying big data, artificial intelligence, and what Erik Brynjolfsson and Andrew McAfee have dubbed "the second machine age."[3] Many observers and researchers have referred to these revolutionary and transformational forces as among the most powerful in history.

In a March 2015 conference on the Future of Work, organized by WorldPost, a joint venture between Nicolas Berggruen's Institute and what was then Arianna Huffington's *Huffington Post*, Andrew McAfee added that it is "the only free lunch that economists can agree on." (He also noted that there are no economic laws that guarantee that the benefits will be shared equally or fairly.)

While opinions differ, most agree on one thing: We are still at the early stages of truly historical transformations. Innovations are becoming more numerous by the day and expanding in multiple dimensions.

At first sight, the two drivers—individual empowerment and big data—can appear contradictory. One is about enabling the individual to do more. The other is more reminiscent of movies involving the rise of machines that, by absorbing lots of data quickly and evolving accordingly, transition from supporting and enhancing individuals and individualism to displacing humankind. Indeed, just think of the simple example of playing trivia games. The amazing information-gathering power of the Internet, combined with the surge in smartphone technologies, provides you with powerful tools to answer more questions correctly, and much faster than most people ever imagined possible. Yet these are the same underlying forces that enable machines such as IBM's Watson to beat humans on game shows. They are also at the basis of work on driverless cars, remote health diagnoses, and a lot more.

But this is, in fact, far from a simple dichotomy. Yes, the phenomenon of a "race against the machines" is being felt in the labor market, the value and delivery of education, employment remuneration, and the composition of jobs in a modern economy.[4] It is also altering the risk/return configuration for new investments, amplifying "winner takes all" effects.

The more innovative the economy, the higher the turnover, and the greater the importance of safety nets. Moreover, the dual transformative forces of these innovations—enabling and displacing—come with the potential for both good and bad. It is the reason why Ian Goldin, the director of the Martin School at Oxford University, sees them as constituting a "New Renaissance," which, just like the old one, can combine great achievements with the possibility of horrible occurrences.

We have already discussed how these forces have enabled disruptions from "other worlds." From Uber to Airbnb, tech-savvy entrepreneurs are disrupting long-established segments. And rather than rely on traditional approaches, they are using core competencies that initially are mostly alien to these segments—though, obviously, not for long.

As another illustration, and a less visible one, just look at how the two forces are coming together in media and finance—two areas where disruptive technologies are having a growing influence but whose ultimate macro impact is unclear.

In media, consider how our sources of information have changed. Technological breakthroughs have fundamentally altered the landscape by changing the conditions for entry and participation, for both producers and consumers. Access is better and costs are lower. As such, what were once physical demands are converted into virtual ones, new platforms are emerging that facilitate consumption and production, and access grows exponentially. All of this in turn gives rise to "big data" that can be analyzed to make this whole combination even more potent.

It is so much easier today for lots of people to post content on the Internet, and it is a lot easier to get to it, again for a very wide range of people (mostly, though not entirely, regardless of geography, income level, and socioeconomic status). In the process, however, the number of people employed in traditional media has shrunk significantly, and technology has also at times been co-opted by extremist elements to facilitate horrible violence.

This is part of a broader historical democratization process that is reshaping social, economic, political, and geopolitical interactions around the world. You see it play out on a stand-alone basis in the growth of nonstate actors, and in the facilitation of networking, co-ordination, and self-organization. It is a broadening transformation that is enabled by the individual and the combined impact of social media and the digital revolution (including the Internet, mobility, AI, and applications). In the process, it is encouraging new entrants, who bring with them greater cognitive diversity, including a notable tilt in favor of technological disruption and behavioral science.

As powerful as these forces are, we have yet to see the full impact in media, let alone in a growing number of other sectors and activities. For one, no one seems—at least so far—to have broken the code that enables the profitable combination of new content and older, large established platforms. And it is not for lack of trying.

Several attempts have been made. Some seek to empower new content providers within traditional platforms (an example being *The New York Times* with Dealbook and the *Financial Times* with Alphaville). Others involve spin-offs from such platforms, motivated by the belief that they could not flourish otherwise (for example, VOX from *The Washington Post*). There is also the entrance into traditional platforms of those with strong and established technological prowess and virtually no classic media background (such as Amazon's Jeff Bezos's purchase of *The Washington Post*).

Then there is the case of the financial service industry, where the phenomenon of disruption is at a much earlier stage. Again, it is being driven by the combination of individual empowerment on one hand, and big data, artificial intelligence, and machine learning on the other.

Over the last two years, I have come across several cases where the forces of financial democratization are redefining the outer edges of the financial service industry. I have even gotten involved in a few, including as an investor.

The most visible is the use of increasingly-inclusive P2P and direct lending platforms to bypass costly and restrictive intermediaries. The result is to link directly borrowers and lenders in more cost-efficient ways. This is already happening on both sides of consumer credit relationships, and it will likely be a feature of asset management in the years to come. In some cases, the changes in the landscape also empower individuals by giving them access to better financial tools and information that enable them to lead less stressful lives (e.g., what Payoff is trying to do with broader access to "financial personality" and management approaches).

Given our earlier discussion about the aftermath of the global financial crisis, it should come as no surprise that outside forces are also playing a role, from the trust deficit encumbering banks to energized consumer protection approaches that rightly favor the delivery of financial services that are better aligned with client success. This is most evident in niche approaches that seek to address underserved or poorly functioning segments from a client perspective such as what Ellevate is seeking to do for women, Payoff for oppressive credit card debt, and various P2P firms for small business.

These disruptions will be embraced by some of the existing, more progressive institutions, but they will also be opposed by many more traditional incumbents, particularly those who are intimidated by the notion of "self-disruption." They are yet to be tested by an economic downturn. They will require faster regulatory catch-up, including bespoke design for burgeoning digital platforms. In the process, finance will be slowly following a path already trodden by technology and, more recently and even less deterministically, by media. And again the tendency will be to transform over time a normal bell-shaped distribution of expected outcomes into more of a bimodal one.

The upside of this financial democratization phenomenon is considerable, and it is particularly powerful because it lowers barriers to entry and better-tailored solutions. It widens the sources and uses of loanable funds, reduces overheads and other intermediation costs, and improves the financial terms offered to end users. The influx of greater cognitive diversity makes the industry more dynamic, including by encouraging providers to go beyond their traditional client acquisition and product focus to also encompass more holistic customer-centered solutions. Institutions that choose to align their products and services with their clients' long-term success become better positioned for commercial success. A more "democratized" techno-financial (or "FinTech") infrastructure has a better chance of aligning providers' priorities with consumers' genuine need for financial services and solutions.

Along with big data, through the incorporation of behavioral finance (that is, a better understanding of how cognitive and psychological factors impact financial behavior), disruptive forces are also helping gradually wean the industry off its obsession with inevitably partial FICO credit scores in favor of analytical models more finely calibrated with financial health. Though these more comprehensive models have yet to navigate a full economic cycle, a more comprehensive understanding of both financial mindset and behavior is emerging, and they are being enhanced by work on different "financial personalities."

There are also downsides. Some innovation-driven activities resemble the Wild West. Most worrisomely, badly regulated and abused P2P platforms can end up facilitating the financing of illicit activities—from drugs to terrorism.

Like many major innovations in history that significantly lowered the barriers to entry, the natural inclination of humans is to initially overproduce and overconsume the now more easily available activity. With time, this converges to a more stable equilibrium—but often only after a process involving quite a few highs and lows, along with a series of improbables and unthinkables.

CHAPTER 28

PUTTING IT ALL TOGETHER

"Advances in technology have always disrupted the status quo. But they have never done so across so many markets and at the speed and scale that is being seen today."

—RICHARD DOBBS, JAMES MANYIKA,
AND JONATHAN WOETZEL[1]

What we have seen so far can be simply summarized as a future in which the current baseline is being disrupted both *from above and from below*—that is to say, by consequential economic/geopolitical/institutional/political/social macro forces, and by disruptive micro forces. As such, I am convinced that we face a major change, of course—again, the notion of a T junction.

Top-down and bottom-up forces are threatening the consensus baseline of an even more prolonged and stable low-growth equilibrium in which central banks continue to successfully repress market volatility. This configuration will get more unstable and therefore increasingly harder to maintain over time. Being the only game in town, central banks will find it ever more difficult to keep everyone on a road that is challenged in delivering the desired economic and financial objectives. The operating environment will become trickier, more volatile, and less predictable.

Meanwhile, the probability of an outright tip gets higher, though the eventual direction of this tip is evenly balanced. The reasons for this are truly multidimensional, involving not just the range of economic, financial, geopolitical, institutional, political, social, and technological factors that we have already discussed. They also speak to the impact of innovation.

Today's innovations threaten quite a few existing industries and activities with what I have called disruptions from other worlds.[2] Going back to Airbnb and Uber as examples, both have disrupted and redefined their respective industries using approaches that had very little, if anything, to do previously with the areas they are disrupting so effectively and profoundly. Remember, Airbnb has yet to build or manage a hotel. Nevertheless in six years, it has accumulated a million rooms for rent, compared to some 700,000 for the Hilton group over a much longer time period. The result is a set of radical new game plans that fundamentally shake the target industry's rules and operating approach. And these do not come from traditional competitors.

This is a phenomenon that will spread, fueled by both demand and supply forces.

On the demand side, consumers have grown to expect a lot more from the products and services they consume. They place particular emphasis on speed, productivity, convenience, connectivity, and greater customization, and their patience for tolerating slippage in these areas is waning. All this takes place while, according to the McKinsey Institute, almost two-thirds of the value of new Internet offerings goes to the consumer.

On the supply side, long-standing entry barriers and the very definition of inventory are being altered. Just think of how Uber has adapted existing technologies to transform a long-sheltered industry that too often provided lousy and expensive service, and how long-standing hotel brands such as Four Seasons and Starwood now have to worry about Airbnb as much as if not more than they worry about their traditional competitors. Indeed, as Richard

Dobbs, James Manyika, and Jonathan Woetzel note, "With lowered barriers to entry, it is now common to see small companies take on incumbents and gain critical mass in a matter of months. The boundaries separating sectors have become blurred, and digital capabilities are often driving the shift of economic values between players and sectors."

This duality, that of disruption from both above and below, makes the existing global economic configuration harder to maintain—and especially so given the degree to which central banks have already overextended themselves. With time the duality will contribute to one of two greater extremes at the global level, and some of the more delicate areas, will confront this juncture a lot earlier.

When faced with the challenge of predicting which of the multiple future outcomes is likely to prevail, there is nothing worse than coming across as wishy-washy—as failing to be decisive about just one of the possible outcomes. Yet as much as I would like to avoid this, there simply isn't enough data at this time to predict the likely domination of one over the other of the two medium-term outcomes facing the global economy. And, to add to my frustration, the timing of the transition is not as clear and predictable as I'd like it to be. But make no mistake: We are facing a major turning point, and we need to understand this well if we are to have a good chance of navigating it properly.

This admission—that we can't determine as yet which road we will take, nor the exact timing of the shift that awaits us—is not a cop-out. Instead it is a recognition of the fluidity of Chairman Bernanke's "unusually uncertain outlook." Moreover, this state of affairs should not translate into operational paralysis and a narrowing of vision. Quite the contrary. It calls for energized thinking. In the process, it forces us to pay heed to insights from behavioral science and neuroscience, and it makes it essential that we work to enhance at every level—corporate, government, household, and multilateral—the right mix of optionality, resilience, and agility as we go forward.

The implications of all this go well beyond traditional entities having to adjust. Even the more agile disruptors will be pressed to maintain their lead, and, as Amazon, Google, and Microsoft have recently demonstrated, they will need to be willing to occasionally "self-disrupt" from a position of strength. All of this speaks to the important moment that faces us all, one that will impact not just our well-being but also that of our kids and grandkids.

PART VI

THE KEYS TO NAVIGATING A BIMODAL DISTRIBUTION

"Give me a one-handed economist! All my economists say, 'On the one hand, on the other.'"

—HARRY S. TRUMAN

CHAPTER 29

WHAT HISTORY TELLS US

"Managing a complex organization isn't easy in the best of times. It's especially difficult when the news continually reminds you that everything you thought you knew about the world seems to be wrong. Or at least a little off."

—RICHARD DOBBS, JAMES MANYIKA,
AND JONATHAN WOETZEL[1]

Let us start with an inconvenient statement: The bimodal distributions that underlie the notion of the T junctions are not easy for us all to navigate well, and there are good scientific and behavioral reasons for this. As such, history is far from reassuring about how the world is likely to handle the upcoming challenges.

The first important condition for doing a good job in this domain is to understand how most of us—as human beings—tend to react to them, whether we are functioning on a stand-alone basis or in collectives (be they households, companies, or in government service, and certainly at the multilateral level, when interacting with people from different countries and cultures). Bimodal distributions of potential outcomes run contrary to the paradigm in which we understand most of the things that happen in our lives—that based on bell-shaped distributions, which are incredibly comforting. Those "normal distributions" involve a high likelihood of a particular outcome within the belly of the distribution of outcomes. Sure, there are tails on both sides, extremely good and scary bad, but they are thin since their expected probabilities are low.

A simple illustration may help. Think of your routine preparation to catch a plane that is scheduled to leave at 2 P.M. You plan on getting to the airport in time for a 2 P.M. departure even though you know that it is not a complete certainty that departure will indeed occur at that time. It could be delayed significantly (the unfavorable, or what economists and market participants call the "left tail"); or you could end up leaving on time, not have to stand in long lines, have all the space in the world, and receive outstanding service (the "right tail"). Now, note that while you are aware of the tails, they don't determine your behavior. This is a bell-shaped distribution of possible outcomes (Figure 15).

Now imagine that, rather than 2 P.M., you are told the day before that the scheduled departure will be either at 8 A.M. or at 8 P.M. (that is, six hours on either side of 2 P.M.; Figure 16). Most of us would find this quite a disconcerting change. We would need to get our mindset around it and respond accordingly.

Here, in highly simplified summary terms, is what empirical and theoretical research tells us about our likely reactions to a pivot from a normal bell-shaped to a bimodal distribution of potential outcomes. For presentational simplicity, they may be grouped in four general categories.

For a handful of people, a change to a bimodal plane schedule would simply not register. In effect, it is excluded by "blind spots" that block modifications in the thought process and, therefore, the ability to internalize the information, compute the implications, and respond accordingly. This first group simply does not see the change in the distribution of potential outcomes. Its members continue to operate in the old paradigm, and quite confidently so.

A second group will recognize the shift away from a normal bell-shaped distribution. Yet, in processing what to do, the internal deliberation processes will be inclined to convert the uncomfortable and

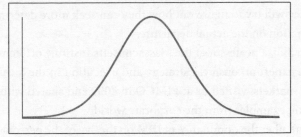

Figure 15. Bell-shaped distribution

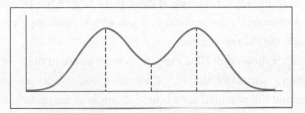

Figure 16. Bimodal distribution

unfamiliar information back into the more comforting framing of a normal distribution. Going back to the plane example, it is as if these people were to combine the two possible plane departure times (8 A.M. and 8 P.M.) and operate on the basis that the midpoint matters . . . so it is a 2 P.M. departure after all!

A third group will do better, but not fully so. They will recognize that the switch to a bimodal regime warrants a different behavior. They will discuss what that should be. Yet in going from design to implementation, they risk falling victim to "active inertia"—that is, aiming to do something different but, with all the forces of history and inertia in play, ending up doing essentially more of the same.

The fourth and most successful group will recognize that a bimodal distribution requires important behavior and strategy modifications, and, just as important, they will act on that accordingly. In some cases they will institute institutional and process changes in order to have structure help do some of the heavy lifting. They will make plans to be there for either of the two possible departures, along with the needed contingency plans, and what to do in between, and they will try to figure out how they can seek more deterministic information on the actual departure.

Don Sull, a professor at the Massachusetts Institute of Technology and an expert on business strategy and execution in the face of turbulent markets, visited us at PIMCO in 2009 and shared with us interesting examples from the corporate world.

Remember the dominance of IBM on the eve of the personal computer (PC) revolution? The company had by far the most powerful brand in technology. Each year it deployed a large R&D budget. And it was profitable. By these metrics, it was in a very strong position to dominate the PC revolution.

Research shows that IBM executives were aware of the "disruptive technology" aspect of the PC. They discussed the issues involved, recognizing the potential for a bimodal outcome for mainframe customers, their bread-and-butter clientele. Some would be lost permanently to the PC while others would be interested in mainframe upgrades to support new requirements.

The implications seemed clear, and they pointed to a strategic rebooting involving a determined shift to more of a barbelled approach. But when it came to implementation, IBM appeared to fall into the "active inertia" trap. Rather than pivot decisively to the new approach, they allowed their much more familiar historical behavior to overinfluence their future actions.

The company ended up both underappreciating the PC disruptions and overinvesting in existing mainframe initiatives. As a result, they got eaten alive, first by Compaq and then by Hewlett-Packard. Indeed, if it weren't for a corporate reinvention that transformed the company into much more of a service entity, IBM would likely not be around today. In effect, IBM identified the bimodal distribution facing it, and while they had the capabilities to manage it well, they failed to do so because they ended up overly influenced by what had worked well for them in the past (when they operated in the belly of a bell-shaped curve) rather than what would work better in the future under changed and more uncertain conditions.

Then there is the case of Pan American World Airways (Pan Am) and Trans World Airlines (TWA). They were dominant U.S. airline companies when I was growing up, as was Eastern Airlines. Their networks (and revenues) were tilted heavily in favor of cross-country U.S. routes and international ones. Along came Southwest (and others) with a disruptive technology. The company used one model of aircraft and focused initially on shorter regional routes, before shifting to a hub-and-spoke model.

While witnessing Southwest gain traction as a disruptive technology and gradually eat into their market share, the established companies failed to substantially modify their behaviors and strategies. Instead, they essentially continued to do more of the same, and it was just a matter of time before their dominance evaporated all the way into bankruptcy.

These are just a few examples, but they speak to quite a history of corporations struggling to adjust to a different distribution of potential outcomes.

Governments have a similar history.

We discussed earlier how, coming out of the global financial crisis, governments in advanced economies struggled to comprehend that they were facing quite a new distribution of potential outcomes. As such, they failed in timely supplementing their conventional cyclical mindsets with secular and structural elements, and they were blind to the need to garner insights from the experiences of countries in the emerging world (where secular/structural influences tend to dominate cyclical forces). Consequently, governments failed to exploit the political window opened by the crisis to properly retool and reinvest (thereby not adhering to the famous reminder from Rahm Emanuel, President Obama's White House chief of staff from 2009 to 2010, that you "never want a serious crisis to go to waste").

What was needed in every one of these cases was a more deliberate, holistic, and cognitively open approach. What materialized, however, was essentially more of the same.

The judgment and decision making of companies as well as governments were driven by traditional, familiar, and the comforting thought processes—the relatively easy option that involves analytical shortcuts and allows one to draw from past experiences. Unfortunately, this was not what was needed, and it didn't work well.

This phenomenon relates to the popular work of Daniel Kahneman, the psychologist who won a Nobel Prize for his contributions to behavioral economics—particularly as to how we tend to resort to two modes of thinking, and do so in quite an asymmetrical manner.[2]

A lot of the time, our automatic, intuitive mind (Daniel Kahneman calls it "System 1")[3] is in charge and for good reason, as it speaks to the characteristics of the world we normally operate in—one that is underpinned by the notion of comforting bell-shaped distribution of expected outcomes. Most of the time it serves us well.

But System 1 can lead us astray if it is not also combined with our "controlled, deliberative, analytical mind" ("or System 2"). This "slow, effortful, and deliberate" mind provides a set of checks and balances that become particularly important and valuable in a changing world—especially one in which tail events are more probable.

Daniel Kahneman warns us that we are inclined to over-rely on System 1. After all, this mode of thinking speaks to "activities [that] are largely carried out effortlessly and automatically." Contrast it to System 2, which is "clunky" (but, importantly, "capable of performing complicated actions that System 1 cannot carry out").

In contrast to System 1, which comes quite naturally to us, System 2 requires self-investment and upkeep. It is enhanced by education and analytical awareness. Only then does it "pick up cues that 'this is a situation where I'm likely to make . . . mistakes.'"[4]

The need to understand the dynamics in play here, and the importance of knowing when to deploy System 2, cannot be overstated. Additional insights can be gained by looking further into what the social sciences and behavioral and neurosciences teach us, starting with the need to recognize and deal more effectively with blind spots and biases.

CHAPTER 30

RECOGNIZING BLIND
SPOTS AND OVERCOMING BIASES

"It is not the strongest of the species that survives, nor the most intelligent that survives. It is the one that is most adaptable to change."

—CHARLES DARWIN

Whether as CEO of a global company or as a proud and happy parent, I have come across many examples of biases—both conscious (overt) and unconscious (hidden)—that hold back individuals and frustrate the collective from fulfilling its potential.[1] In the process, I have become particularly sensitive to how biases can undermine a culture of superior performance and meritocracy.

Count me among the many who firmly believe that there is a very strong business and societal case for inclusion and diversity. No company and certainly no country will be able to harvest its realizable potential if it fails to embrace and empower human talent regardless of gender, race, culture, sexual orientation, and perspectives. To do so, they need to actively and continuously encourage their people to be aware that *how* they think about challenges and *why* can be as important as *what* and *when* they think it. Otherwise they will be hostage to damaging biases, often inadvertently, and subject to harm-ful blind spots. Indeed, given all the research that has been done, there should be no doubt that it is hard to pursue inclusion and di-versity if you are unable to address these issues, both up front and over time.

These are all important considerations in a steady-state world. They become even more important when fluidity is the name of the game, as it is today. This is true for individuals, households, compa-nies, and governments. And it is particularly relevant in a world heading toward a T junction.

In my mind, there is nothing that makes one more acutely sensi-tive to the difficulties of anchoring greater inclusion and broader diversity than when you inadvertently end up being part of a performance-oriented group that is suddenly made aware of the risk of making a silly mistake. This happened to me on at least a couple of occasions in the last few years, including when I was part of a promo-tion evaluation committee.

In a meeting called to assess the suitability of names put for-ward for promotion, our group of senior management hesitated over a colleague working in Asia whose performance had been outstanding but whose internal communication skills were deemed to require some work. The group was coalescing around the deci-sion to postpone the promotion for one more year to provide this person with the opportunity to work on internal communication. Then one member of the group wisely pointed out that, by empha-sizing communication skills *in English,* we were applying a very narrow perspective to someone with exceptional performance and who conducted the vast majority of their work in a different lan-guage. After all, had we been posted to Asia, how many of us could interact well, as required, with clients there speaking the local lan-guage?

This important observation immediately made us aware that we had inadvertently adopted a narrow perspective driven by our own cultural biases. Moreover, we were unlikely to hold back the promotion of our strongly performing Anglo-American expatriate colleagues (the "majority" group) working outside the United States and United Kingdom just because they did not speak the language of the country that they were assigned to.

We had come very close to making a mistake, and not just any mistake—one that ran counter to our meritocratic culture and our own brand of "constructive paranoia." This had occurred even though the firm had been engaged in a meaningful effort to enhance awareness and minimize the probability of such events.

It was a shock to quite a few of us in the room to realize how we, as informed and committed people working earnestly in a performance-focused culture and in pursuit of superior outcomes, had almost ended up falling victim to unconscious biases and an inadvertent blind spot.

The reality is that, even with awareness training, we might not be as neutral as we'd like to think we are. Moreover, outdated but still operating societal forces can render our vulnerabilities quite deeply ingrained, thus impacting processes and decision making.

Writings and presentations by Mahzarin Banaji, professor of social ethics in the Department of Psychology at Harvard University, have had a particularly strong influence on how I think about these issues. Her work details how unconscious biases and blind spots operate, including why even the most thoughtful people and most successful companies can be tripped up by them. Fortunately, just like those modern small lights on the external rearview mirrors that now come on when there is a car in one's blind spot, Mahzarin Banaji provides tools for minimizing potential damage.

Working with Professor Anthony Greenwald of the University of Washington, Mahzarin Banaji's multi-year research demonstrates that there are well-established scientific reasons why most of us have blind spots and also fall victim to unconscious biases,[2] and they do not involve a value judgment about us. Indeed, "good people" have them. Rather they relate to the manner in which our brains are wired, how we have evolved over time, our childhood influences, how we have historically interacted, our tendency to look for analytical short-cuts, and the way we tend to frame issues.

The losses for individuals and collectives can be significant. Put another way, the forgone opportunities are not immaterial. As an illustration, in a study of 1,000 major business investments,[3] McKinsey researchers showed that returns were 7 percentage points better for corporate decision-making processes that worked hard at countering the impact of biases.

There are many anecdotal examples of biases repressing constructive dialogue within companies and the subsequent decision-making process. Writing in a *New York Times* series on "Women and Work," Sheryl Sandberg and Adam Grant discussed something that I suspect quite a few of us have witnessed in Anglo-Saxon corporate cultures—that is, often inadvertent (but sometimes quite advertent) group behaviors that inhibit women from freely expressing their views in meetings even though they have consequential things to say.

Sheryl Sandberg and Adam Grant note, "We've seen it happen again and again. When a woman speaks in a professional setting, she walks a tightrope. Either she's barely heard or she's judged as too aggressive. When a man says virtually the same thing, heads nod in appreciation for his fine idea. As a result, women often decide that saying less is more."[4]

Sheryl Sandberg and Adam Grant observe that this phenomenon is not limited to the corporate world. They point to research by Victoria Brescoll, a Yale psychologist who documented similar behaviors and outcomes in the U.S. Senate.

In both cases, remedial action includes two minimum steps: first, recognizing that this is an issue that needs to be addressed lest it continue to undermine the effectiveness of the collective; and second, making sure that very deliberate steps are taken (repeatedly) to that effect—that is, design modifications that help overcome biases. In this case, they include conducting the meeting in a way that recognizes when different people would like to contribute to the conversation and fostering a safe space for them to do so.

The household effects are also considerable. For example, research has shown that both overt and hidden biases against girls and women are positively correlated to domestic violence, teenage pregnancy, underage marriages, malnutrition, child mortality, and deep and intractable poverty. This is particularly true in developing countries.

The damage is not limited to the girls and women. The family is also worse off, thereby amplifying the costs to societies, including those that are least able to afford them.

In all these cases—whether it is to be acted on by individuals, households, companies, or governments—the solution involves understanding, education, advocacy, design changes, and determined action. Moreover, this needs to be supported by measurement, research, and openness to course corrections. Otherwise the forces of inertia are too powerful to overcome, and behaviors do not change.

A few years ago, I published a story about an experience with my daughter, who was nine years old at that time. As I noted then, "I had never thought I would be one of those parents who would slip when it comes to protecting our young daughter from gender biases and stereotypes that emerge early in a child's development. Well I was wrong."[5]

Writing back in 2013, I observed that when returning to a summer camp in which those attending pursued an academic topic, my daughter had opted for "ancient civilization" rather than continue with the science course she had enjoyed so much the prior year. Initially she told me that her choice had been motivated by interest in history and wanting to know more about Egypt (which made me happy, given my own background). Yet the explanation seemed lacking. So I asked her a few more times, and she responded that, having been the only girl in the science class previously, she had researched and opted for a subject that would have greater gender balance in the classroom.

As I admitted then, by failing to be sufficiently sensitive to how outdated forces were still playing an influential role, I had stood by and allowed a harmful stereotype to prevail.

All these slippages serve as constant reminders for me that enhanced awareness, while necessary, is not sufficient. You also need to stay constantly alert, if only to counter the recurrent influence of outmoded biases or ones that struggle to deal with unusual uncertainty, as is the case today. And there is no better way for doing so in a group setting than by engendering cognitive diversity.

CHAPTER 31

ADVANCING AND ENHANCING COGNITIVE DIVERSITY

"Strength lies in differences, not in similarities."
—STEPHEN R. COVEY

The business rationale for cognitive diversity is well established, and it is very compelling: In the vast majority of cases, more than one point of view helps to shed greater light on the issues at hand, and, through an appropriately structured process, different points of view can be brought together to underpin decision-making outcomes that are superior to those based on individual decision making.

In thinking about these issues, I have been influenced quite a bit by the work of Scott Page, professor of political science, complex systems, and economics at the University of Michigan. Combining theoretical underpinnings with practical and accessible examples, his work provides important, concrete, and actionable insights on what it takes to maximize the probability of sustainably better decision making.[1]

Scott Page argues that pursuing effective inclusion and diversity does more than improve upon individual decision making. His research suggests that "collections of individuals with diverse tools can outperform collections of 'high' ability individuals at problem solving and predictive tasks." This leads him to a simple yet powerful conclusion: "Diversity can improve the bottom line. It may even matter as much as ability."[2]

The reason for this has to do with "superadditivity," or the possibility that "combinations of tools can be more powerful than the tools themselves." A key transmission mechanism involves the different "perspectives" people use to problem solve, especially when combined with the right "heuristics."

As Scott Page notes, "Two people with different perspectives test different potential improvements and increase the probability of an innovation." They can be powerfully supplemented by operational approaches that influence how people search for solutions. Again diversity matters as diverse heuristics "identify different candidate solutions, increasing the probability of a breakthrough."[3]

This is not to say that diversity should be pursued at the expense of ability. Certainly not. Rather, it is about getting the mix right. After all, they are positively correlated. You are more likely to secure talent if you don't artificially confine your search set, especially if it is due to harmful biases and blind spots.

Like Don Sull with his powerful examples, Scott Page shares with his readers lots of everyday examples that bring these concepts to life. They illustrate the important finding that "by seeing problems differently (diverse perspectives) and by looking for solutions in different ways (diverse heuristics), teams, groups, and organizations can locate more potential innovations."[4] Moreover, when combined, the superadditivity feature means that the total impact exceeds the sum of the individual parts.

Cognitive diversity is also critical in encouraging nonlinear thinking—something that becomes even more important if the world indeed is facing a T junction, as I believe to be the case. Indeed, adapting a wonderful point first made by Pattie Sellers of *Fortune* magazine and used by Sheryl Sandberg in her book *Lean In*—both are influential thinkers, especially when it comes to career impediments facing women—one should not think of professional careers just in terms of climbing a ladder. Instead, we should also be open to the dynamics of climbing a jungle gym.

This is a very important distinction, and it is one that individuals, companies, and governments would be well advised to keep on their radar screens more broadly. A jungle gym invites greater exploration, optionality, and wider room for success. It is also a better motivator, and a stronger enabler of teamwork.[5] Indeed, as Sheryl Sandberg writes in her book, "A jungle gym provides great views for many people, not just those of the top. On a ladder, most climbers are stuck staring at the butt of the person above."[6]

Households, companies, and governments do better when they foster and leverage cognitive diversity, and a good way of doing this is by increasing individuals' understanding of how it contributes to greater success by improving awareness, problem solving, predictions, and innovation, thus aligning itself with the meritocracy culture. Through this, collectives get a lot better at identifying, mentoring, and empowering talent, thereby making both the individuals and the collective more likely to fulfill their potential.

In addition to demonstrating the power of cognitive diversity and its importance to delivering superior outcomes, Scott Page challenges the false belief that companies have to sacrifice something for the sake of diversity. They don't.

More and more companies are understanding this. Some are driven by the science. Others are motivated by the relentless desire to continuously produce superior outcomes. The more global the firm, the greater the recognition that diversity also helps serve better their set of diverse clients. And diversity has now become almost a natural for the most innovative technology firms.

Having said that, the pivot from recognition to effectiveness is not sufficiently advanced as yet, be it in the private or public sector. Indeed, as discussed earlier, we even have multilateral institutions—which, by construct and mission, should be most sensitive to inclusion and diversity—that remain stuck with outmoded mindsets and feudal practices, including when it comes to the appointment of their senior leaders.

Quite a few out there forget that leveraging cognitive diversity requires a lot more than just paying lip service to merit-based diversity that encompasses a better balance among genders, race, cultures, age, etc. There is a good (though depressing) reason for this, and it is one that everyone I have cited here, along with virtually all the others researching this field and trying to implement the findings in practice, has stressed over and over again: Effectiveness in this area requires a substantial amount of care, attention, dedication, and commitment. And this is far from an easy task.

CHAPTER 32

TRANSLATING AWARENESS INTO OPTIONALITY, RESILIENCE, AND AGILITY

"Be courageous. I have seen many depressions in business. Always America has emerged from these stronger and more prosperous. Be brave as your fathers before you. Have faith! Go forward!"

—THOMAS EDISON

Lots of researchers—including Professors Banaji, Grant, Kahneman, and Page, as well as Iris Bohnet, Sheryl Sandberg, Anne-Marie Slaughter, and other keen observers of these issues—have provided us with tools that may be used to enhance diversity and to reduce errors in judgment and decision making that come from blind spots and unconscious biases. They involve elements of behavior and design modification that speak to communication, talent development and acquisition, performance measurement, and performance evaluation. They also speak to the importance of combining the right mix of perspectives and heuristics, together with strong support systems, as demonstrated strongly by Anne-Marie Slaughter.

These tools are also important when it comes to scoring early and visible wins. This is particularly important since history suggests that many collectives have found efforts in this area hard to sustain. Progress can be slow, especially at first. Feedback can be patchy and less than timely and sufficiently open. And, with the constant need for assessing periodic midcourse corrections, the whole effort is at risk of derailment by entrenched and uninformed groups.

In addition, there is often a temptation to substitute words for action. Most often this takes the form of elegantly crafted internal (and sometimes also external) PR efforts that speak to raising awareness and signaling commitment, but actually end up replacing action.

The visible attention and dedication of the most senior levels of management, a critical condition for success, can be distracted by other corporate prerogatives, real and perceived. And when that happens repeatedly, people lower down in the firm start to be less confident about the seriousness and effectiveness of inclusion and diversity in shaping better outcomes.

Lots of these insights boil down to providing "safe zones" for people to think aloud, experiment with different approaches and processes, and interact constructively. The objective is not just to encourage various perspectives and heuristics to be applied to judgment and problem solving. It is also to break down barriers, real and perceived, to exchanging ideas and combining cognitive diversity. In the process, both individuals and groups will find it a lot easier to operate outside their individual and collective comfort zones, which can inadvertently become overly constraining and repressive of good decision making and judgment.

It is also about using structure to counter what can often become dogmatic forces of entitlement that, to make things even worse, have inadvertently been empowered to discourage change; indeed, such forces are also often afraid of change. This can be as simple as making sure that those who traditionally chair meetings are more focused on drawing out different perspectives by being more sensitive to the often invisible impact of blind spots and unconscious biases. It can (and, often, should) be more ambitious by ensuring that organizational silos and periodic performance evaluation processes are revamped to better enable, foster, and promote cognitive diversity. And, yes, some consultancy firms can add insights and value.

Throughout the process, measurement is key. As Eric Schmidt and James Rosenberg note in their fascinating book, *How Google Works,* "Managing performance should be driven by data, with the sole objective of creating a meritocracy. You cannot be gender-, race-, and color-blind by fiat; you need to create empirical, objective methods to measure people. Then the best will thrive, regardless of where they're from and what they look like."[1]

At the end of the day, it is all about empowering talent, young and old, junior and senior, and from both traditional and nontraditional backgrounds. It is about not letting the urgent always crowd out the important, especially if the urgent also happens to be unimportant, as it sometimes is.

It is about being more open to external points of view, including inviting outsiders who are valued not because of the conclusions that they have reached but because of the way they think and (even better) because they think differently. More difficult for many, it is about being willing to openly listen to dissenters, and those who like to intelligently play the role of devil's advocate. Such approaches can be particularly helpful in countering harmful groupthink and pushing collectives to evolve away from comfortable but less effective approaches.

Getting the external viewpoint becomes even more important in a world in which, as is currently the case, traditionally dominant players and structures, as well as established viewpoints, are being challenged from above and from below. At the minimum, there is a need to get help in modernizing core competencies by benchmarking beyond the narrow confines of history and preexisting ways of doing things. Without all this, timely "self-disruption" is almost impossible.

This is yet another area where multiple equilibria dynamics can be quite important. The more successful a company is at pursuing cognitive diversity and signaling it, the broader the pool of people it will have access to for hiring, mentoring, and promotion.

This has been the case for Google, a company whose hiring approach has attracted so much interest.

As executives there have stressed, what matters for Google is not those with the best grades from the best schools. Instead, because it flourishes on "insights that can't be taught," the company takes inclusion and diversity very seriously. After all, "great talent often doesn't look and act like you. When you go into that interview, check your biases at the door and focus on whether or not the person has the passion, intellect, and character to succeed and excel." This mindset, furthermore, should not be limited to the hiring process. "The same goes for managing people."[2]

Encouragingly, the interventions need not always be a big deal involving lots of resources. Specifically, "major changes can result from . . . 'nudge techniques' or small interventions that encourage people to behave in slightly different ways at critical moments. The simple act of talking openly about behavioral patterns makes the subconscious conscious."[3] And this is greatly helped by seeking feedback from a broad range of people.

When I was at PIMCO, I benefited enormously from periodic informal meetings with small, randomly selected groups of colleagues. After tentative starts, these meetings would often go long as participants, operating in a confidential setting, shared their thoughts, recommendations, and anxiety. Often it became even more insightful (and even more valuable for me as CEO) when we would end the meeting with a "tour de table" in which each person was encouraged to share whatever was on her or his mind, big or small.

I will also never forget an interaction with a particularly brilliant woman who had decided not to join PIMCO. Along with others who interviewed her, I had found her really impressive; and we were all convinced that she was very keen on coming to PIMCO. When I heard that she had rejected us, I called her. Stressing that this was not the traditional call in which I would try to change her mind, but rather one that was aimed at improving our understanding and the company's recruitment process, I asked for her reasons. She said that while she was really impressed by the firm and the people she had met, she couldn't help noting that, in the multiple interviews that PIMCO colleagues held with her, only men had sat around the table from our side. In the process, the company had signaled, albeit totally inadvertently, that it does not sufficiently value inclusion and diversity.

That statement shocked and distressed me. How could this be the case?

I called our HR department to ask about how we put together interview rosters. They responded that we choose interviewers who are best at assessing technical expertise, cultural fit, and applicable experience. We also look for a mix from different departments. I then asked whether, once we put the roster together, we check for biases and excessive homogeneity, be it gender, culture, race, and so forth. From then on, we made a point to do so.

In effectively transforming awareness into action, there is an important need to customize the approach to the particulars of the application case. In the case of PIMCO, for example, we came up with seven insights that we felt were particularly important. I just list them here, drawing from an earlier article:[4]

- Be clear about the merit-based arguments for inclusion and diversity.
- Tailor what you learn from outside research and experimentation.
- Address the unconscious biases that we all harbor.
- Guard against a "tick-the-box" mentality of excessive focus on metrics.
- Recognize that gender diversity, like other forms of diversity, is a fundamental input to cognitive diversity that is critical for navigating a fluid and increasingly complex global economy.
- Own the initiative and, as CEO, hold yourself explicitly accountable in front of colleagues.
- Finally, never let current success blind you to the greater success that is achievable in the future.

CHAPTER 33

THE POWER OF
SCENARIO ANALYSES

"The whole point was to find a way to practice nuclear war without destroying ourselves. To get the computers to learn from mistakes we couldn't afford to make."

—WAR GAMES

For those who are interested in identifying and overcoming blind spots and unconscious biases, I would encourage you to have a look at Mahzarin Banaji and Anthony Greenwald's work using IAT, or the Implicit Association Test method. It has been used in an effective manner to "explore the group-based preferences, stereotypes and identities that may not be accessible to conscious awareness."[1] They supplement in a productive manner another tool that I have found particularly useful, yet it's one that many—whether organized in households, companies, governments, or multilateral institutions—tend to chronically underuse: scenario analyses.

Scenario analyses are about the world of "what if." They extend our thinking beyond our natural inclination to focus on the one, most likely outcome. By definition, they involve devoting a lot of resources, time, and effort to working on possibilities that may never materialize. And the costs are quite high when this repeatedly involves detailing crises conditions that never occur.

I understand this point of view, but I feel that it ignores the balance between Type I and Type II errors. Yes, it is costly to think about multiple crises that never materialize (Type I). But it is even more costly not to think about a crisis that does occur (Type II). Scenario analyses help balance this better. They also facilitate asking a question that makes most people uncomfortable—that is, what can go wrong (rather than the more comforting question of what can go well).

In taking this approach, I have been heavily influenced not just by my fifteen-year tenure at the IMF, where involvement in tricky crisis management situations was quite common, but also by what I lived through during the disorderly collapse of Lehman Brothers in September 2008.

Conventional wisdom is that PIMCO must have predicted Lehman's collapse. After all, the vast majority of the firm's clients not only avoided large losses but also outperformed by making money on the funds that had been entrusted to us for investment management services.

Whenever confronted with this view, I (and others) have been quick to point out that we did not predict the failure of Lehman. We just responded better and faster than others because we had undertaken a series of robust scenario analyses, coupled with detailed action plans.

I remember that weekend very well in mid-September 2008. While government officials and bankers were meeting at the New York Federal Reserve Bank Building, a group of us at PIMCO were gathered in the Investment Committee room at the company's headquarters in Newport Beach, California. Colleagues from our overseas offices were on the three TV screens, having joined via videoconference lines. Lots of paper on the tables, and empty boxes of doughnuts and pizza along the sides. Most important, the whiteboards detailed three possible scenarios for the run-up to Monday's market open.

We had assigned the highest probability to a repeat of the March 2008 Bear Stearns experience—namely, that a fragile and failing Lehman would be taken over by a bank with a strong balance sheet. A default would be avoided, and the system would dodge a bullet that would have entailed systemic disruptions.

This was our baseline. The relatively high probability we attached to it was reinforced by news out of New York and London that Barclays was indeed considering to play the role that J.P.Morgan had played with Bear Stearns six months earlier. But we did not focus just on this possibility. We also asked ourselves the following two questions: Assuming that we made a prediction mistake, what could that mistake look like? And, if there is more than one possible mistake that could not be avoided, which one would we least be able to afford to make? This led us to the formulation of two other broad scenarios.

We assigned the second-highest probability to Lehman failing but doing so in an orderly fashion. After all, the authorities were probably as aware as we were of the interconnectivity of Lehman, together with the fragility of circuit breakers given the spaghetti bowl of interdependencies (especially when it came to crucial aspects of the payments and settlement system). Financial contagion was a real risk, as were sudden financial stops and the associated negative shocks to growth and jobs. Because of that, we looked at another possible outcome—that of a disorderly failure of Lehman—even though it commanded our lowest probability of materializing.

Well, of the three scenarios we specified, it was the lowest-probability, highest-potential-cost one that became reality. Yet despite our miscalculations of probabilities (and we were one of many who got it wrong, in both the private and the public sectors), we were able to quickly reset, get organized, and protect our clients' portfolios.

Having discussed the possibility before the worst of the storm, we had calmly specified an action plan for this scenario (as we had done for the two others), drawing on inputs from several talented colleagues. It was very detailed—from specifying who would go to Lehman to deliver the notices of failure so that we could quickly reconstitute certain positions elsewhere, to very careful cash and collateral management.

In putting this action plan in operation very early on that Monday morning, we were able to harvest many first-mover advantages to the significant benefits of our clients. We had a better mindset and were in a much better cognitive position to move forward rather than play desperate catch-up defense. In football terms, it was the equivalent of starting the second quarter just a field goal behind rather than four touchdowns back.

While we had gotten the probabilities of expected outcomes wrong, the preemptive analyses and the associated action plans had enabled us to quickly get back onside. This allowed us to do more than protect the funds that our clients had entrusted to us. It allowed us to exploit opportunities afforded to us by the more panicked responses of the late movers.

I remember being struck at the time not only by how few others had taken the time and made the effort to think about different possible scenarios earlier; seemingly too few of them shared PIMCO's culture of "constructive paranoia." I was even more surprised when, a few days after Lehman failed, I received a call from a rather distressed friend at another investment management entity that I knew well and had worked at. Having been paralyzed by the disorderly collapse of Lehman and lacking an analytical-operational framework, they were just starting trying to play catch-up. As such, their portfolio-positioning woes were being amplified by even more immediate concerns about liquidity.

Of course, not all scenario analyses are that successful. Just a few years later, we engaged on an even more detailed process because of what was happening in the Eurozone. It was analytically a lot more complex and challenging, as several of the stress scenarios dealt with the possible return to multiple national currencies, the impact of different legal contracts and jurisdiction, and, therefore, an even more complex set of interconnectedness and interdependence.

The initiative was led by impressive European colleagues who devoted a tremendous amount of time and effort—all for eventualities that never took place. Afterward some would deem it to have been a colossal waste of time. In the strictest sense of the term it was, since no substantive components of the action plan were triggered. Yet it was a needed one.

The Eurozone had gotten very close to fragmentation, especially in the final week of July 2012. But chaos was averted due to the bold response of the ECB. As such, our scenario analyses were for naught. Yet they provided us with an important analytical framework and, of course, a playbook in the event of the resurfacing of concerns (which occurred in 2015 with the return of fears about a Grexit and a Graccident).

The intuitively obvious aspect of scenario analyses—that it is better to think about possible extreme events during the prior calm periods rather than be totally surprised and have to play subsequent catch-up—is not relevant just for bad events. Even some very good surprises can be mishandled and, quite counterintuitively, end up leading to bad outcomes. Just think of the irony of lottery jackpot winners ending up bankrupt a few years later even though they won an enormous amount of money.

The beneficial use of scenario analyses finds support in psychological research, including the work of Gary Klein, a psychologist known for his work on naturalistic decision making. His insights were incorporated by the army in their command-and-control guidelines; they have also been used as an input by Daniel Kahneman in his innovative work.

Citing earlier work that had found that "prospective hindsight—imagining that an event has already occurred—increases the ability to correctly identify reasons for future outcomes by 30%," Gary Klein and his colleagues "used prospective hindsight to devise a method called a *premortem*, which helps project teams identify risks at the outset."[2]

The intuition is quite simple and powerful, and has been shown to contribute to heightened cognitive alertness, a breaking down of barriers to broader thinking, and a much greater ability to minimize failure probability.

As opposed to a postmortem, "a premortem in a business setting comes at the beginning of a project rather than the end, so that the project can be improved rather than autopsied." Its construct assumes that the tail events have occurred and looks for the reasons. The specific steps include identifying the events, generating the reasons why, revisiting the initial action plan, and conducting periodic reviews.[3]

CHAPTER 34

VALUING LIQUIDITY
AND OPTIONALITY

"Thus (a) things tend to be liquid when you don't need liquidity, and (b) just when you need liquidity most, it tends not to be there."

—HOWARD MARKS

As companies and investors painfully discovered in 2008, liquidity can be most elusive when you need it most. Going forward, for both structural and operational reasons, there is every reason to believe that liquidity will become quite patchy when markets next hit a major air pocket or when the consensus market paradigm shifts suddenly. Yet liquidity tends to be underappreciated by financial investors—both in an absolute sense and relative to corporations that even today tend to carry quite a bit of cash on their balance sheets.

There are two major reasons why financial investors have tended to place so little value on liquidity, thereby underappreciating the considerable optionality that comes with it. First, they have been repeatedly conditioned to believe that central banks will step in to normalize markets—and do so at virtually the first signs of real stress. Second, liquidity is "negative carry" in the sense that it usually involves some give-up of income (and possibly capital appreciation) potential relative to how else the money could be deployed—for example, earning nothing on cash while you could invest in a high-yield bond with a yield of 4–5 percent, but subject to a whole host of risk factors.

As valid as these arguments are, they should not be used to obfuscate structural realities on the ground. Moreover, the longer central banks remain the "only game in town," dedicated to repressing market volatility and artificially boosting asset prices, the greater the subsequent risk to their effectiveness and operational autonomy—and thus also liquidity.

This is not to say that financial investors should rush to liquidate their positions and hold everything in cash. After all, we have argued that the distribution of potential outcomes is bimodal, possessing relatively high probabilities of both good and bad outcomes. What is needed is liquidity positioning attuned to this type of distribution. At the time of the updating of this chapter, this involved the following types of considerations (my apologies if it comes across as too technical for some):

- When positioning in "liquid markets," carefully scale exposures to any specific set of securities that has a repeated history of suddenly losing market liquidity. Examples include (but are certainly not limited to) emerging-market corporates, which are subject to asset-class-specific disruptions and idiosyncratic shocks. Just witness what happened to trading in Russian corporates when the sovereign was hit by the twin shocks of Western sanctions and lower oil prices, or what happened to trading in Brazilian corporates in the context of the Petrobras scandal.
- Trade up in quality, exchanging some of the high-yield exposure for investment grade, as an example, and tilting sovereign exposures in favor of those with sounder creditworthiness.
- Don't concentrate just on the belly of the curve. Instead,

take some of this positioning and barbell it into lower- and higher-risk exposures—namely, accumulating more cash and short-dated high-quality government bonds while investing a smaller part of it in less-trafficked areas that involve new opportunities (including new tech start-ups), directly sourced infrastructure, and the completion of markets in the emerging word.

- When it comes to portfolio positioning in the more highly trodden segments of the markets, recognize that sector- and security-specific portfolio differentiation (or what is known as "alpha" in the marketplace) will likely be a better potential generator of risk-adjusted returns than just market-wide positioning ("beta"); and if you are going to opt for beta anyway, have a look at the work done on getting smarter passive exposures by such thought leaders as Rob Arnott, the CEO of Research Affiliates. Concurrently, investors will need to be more sensitive to specific events, including M&A opportunities and emerging firms using disruptive technologies.

In turn, these considerations speak to four potentially more controversial views.

First, in reallocating beta (asset-class exposures), investors should not rush at these valuations into making large new commitments now to private equity in an attempt to access private markets. This will be the time when smart money in that domain will be looking to monetize existing investment positions with the exception of a few sectors (for example, newer areas of technology) and certain geographical opportunities. Away from these exceptions, end users need to consider waiting for what are likely to be better vintage years.

Second, investors need to enhance their ability to gain exposure to relative as well as absolute positioning. At the time of first writing this chapter (spring 2015), this speaks most importantly to foreign exchange markets, favoring further dollar strength vis-à-vis emerging currencies.[1]

Third, in scaling such relative positioning, investors need to remember that prospective moves in markets implied by the divergence theme would tend to complicate rather than facilitate policy making, and particularly when it comes to sharp currency moves. This is especially true in a world subject to increasingly bimodal distribution of potential outcomes and low availability of broker-dealer liquidity during transitions. It is a world in which the possibility of policy mistakes and market accidents inevitably rises.

Fourth, all this makes the argument for passive versus active investment a lot more nuanced and a lot less extreme. It is not an either/or, which much of the discussion in the financial media would have you believe. Rather, it is about striking the right balance: using smart passive exposures where investor conviction and foundation do not dominate the wisdom of crowds and where broad-based risk exposure is not undermined by construct defects; but, concurrently, being willing to deviate via high-conviction trades, relative positioning, and risk-management-motivated portfolio overlays.

A final point in closing this chapter: The onus on smart communication is central to successfully managing a world in which technological advances engage and empower so many individuals and collectives. At every level—whether of governments, companies, or households—the challenge is to understand the expectations and requirements of a new generation that has leapfrogged previous ones in their online communications, and to engage, empower, and enable them in a productive manner.

Many have understood the need for smarter communication. But their typical response—which tends to focus on establishing a presence on Twitter, LinkedIn, Instagram, and Facebook, among others—has gone only part of the way. Specifically, it has yet to reflect the full appreciation of a generation that expects to be engaged all the time, anywhere, and through multiple channels; a generation that sees communication as a very active two-way interaction, where the right to express themselves and provide feedback is unfettered.

This is a world where, in the vast majority of cases, "earned media" will tend to dominate "paid media" in influencing people and outcomes. It is a world in which failure to engage properly and to help frame the discussions opens up massive opportunities for competitors. The cost is not just in lost business. It also heightens the risk of extremist ideologies manipulating and tipping vulnerable people into awful lives of violence and destruction.

PART VII

BRINGING IT ALL TOGETHER

"It was the absence of doubt—and scientific rigor—that made medicine unscientific and caused it to stagnate for so long."

—PHILIP TETLOCK AND DAN GARDNER

CHAPTER 35

IN SUM

"Success is not final, failure is not fatal: it is the courage to continue that counts."

—WINSTON CHURCHILL

"The ideas of economists and political philosophers, both when they are right and when they are wrong, are more powerful than is commonly understood. Indeed, the world is ruled by little else. Practical men, who believe themselves to be quite exempt from any intellectual influence, are usually the slave of some defunct economist."

—JOHN MAYNARD KEYNES[1]

I magine you are a teacher at the beginning of the academic year and you're told that the average potential of your class this year is somewhat higher than in previous years. You would naturally welcome this as good news. It promises students who are more engaged and more eager to learn. Now you are told that, together with a higher average potential, your new class involves a lot more dispersion. The good students are getting a little better, the challenged students will struggle even more, the middle is less able to anchor the group, and you have a handful of wildcards whose potential disruptive power could be a problem for the whole class. To make things even more interesting, this year's curriculum will be less effective in stimulating your class.

Suddenly you are less confident about the outcome of your academic year, especially since there isn't much you can do about the curriculum. Your hope is that, somehow or other, the good students will help pull up the whole class; your worry is that the year's pace will be determined by the struggling students; and your fear is that the wildcards will continuously disrupt and derail everyone else. Moreover, you are risking a reputation and an operational freedom that took you years to establish, and which you cherish dearly.

This simple characterization speaks to the complexities facing not just central banks in a global economy, but indeed all of us. We are operating in a context of greater differentiation among some key systemically important actors in the national and global economies.

Overall prospects in the advanced world appear to have improved somewhat on the back of economic healing and balance sheet rehabilitation after the shock of the global financial crisis. But the improvements are far from universal, and they are not yet deeply rooted. Quite a few structural impairments remain. Meanwhile, emerging economies have weakened. As such, dispersion is increasing at many levels, accentuating a bifurcation in individual accomplishments and prospects and potentially amplifying inequalities, political instability, the hollowing out of the middle class, and the ability to benefit from exceptionally exciting innovations.

Think of all this as, in effect, constituting a "new new normal" in which the welfare of current and future generations is subject to an increasing barbelling of economic, financial, institutional, political, social, and technological influences.

This is the world that central banks—and all of us—now need to navigate. It is in a meaningful sense the outcome of an unexpectedly long period of time in which they have been the major and, most of the time, the only responsible economic policymakers. It is an outcome that few if any of them imagined when they courageously stepped in to save the global economy in 2008 and subsequently took on greater policy responsibilities.

We all owe a big debt of gratitude to central banks. Acting boldly and innovatively in the midst of a massive financial crisis, they helped the world avert a multi-year depression that would have wreaked havoc on our generation and that of our children. In the process, they partly made up for their earlier lapses, including falling asleep at the switch while a growing number of banks, households, and companies piled one irresponsible bundle of risks on top of another.

Central bank activism did not stop with their success in normalizing utterly dysfunctional markets and calming a financial crisis that had brought the global economy to a virtual standstill. Having succeeded, they then found no one to hand off to for the next stage of the economic recovery. As such, they felt that they had no choice but to take on unprecedentedly large responsibilities for the macroeconomy; and they ended up doing so for much longer than they, and most others, anticipated.

This was not a power grab. Nor was it something that central banks were seeking. Instead, with political dysfunction paralyzing other policymakers with better policy tools, central banks felt a moral and ethical obligation to do whatever they could to buy time for the private sector to heal and for the political system to get its act together and assume its economic governance responsibilities.

In this new role, central banks did more than assume a leadership role. They also supplied almost the entire content of the policy response, and did so with inherently partial and blunt measures.

Being the only game in town, central banks found themselves pushed ever deeper in experimental policy terrain, and they have stayed there much longer than anyone anticipated or may have hoped for initially.

Policy making often entails difficult trade-offs. This phase of modern central banking has been no different, though with one major qualification: This time around, central banks have not been able to resort to reliable insights and information from historical precedents, analytical models, or past policy experience. There are none that can guide them properly and inspire well-placed confidence.

On the positive side, the central banks' unconventional measures did manage to buy considerable time and space for others to get their act together. They facilitated major private-sector balance sheet repair, starting with banks and then corporations and households. They contributed to growth, albeit frustratingly tepid and insufficiently inclusive, and, in the case of the United States, to significant job creation.

Like dedicated engineers, central banks constructed the best bridge possible with the limited materials they possessed. But no matter how long a bridge they have built, the right destination was never theirs to deliver on their own.

Yes, private sector rehabilitation contributes to reenergized growth. In fact, it is a necessary condition. But in the wake of too many years of misdirected and incomplete growth strategies—particularly one that placed way too much emphasis on finance and not enough on genuine investment in productive capacity—it is not sufficient. High inclusive growth and lasting financial stability require a more comprehensive policy response that sees other government entities joining central banks in a steadfast and serious effort.

We should not be too harsh on central banks. After all, as much as they would like it to be otherwise, central banks do not have the policy means to boost productivity through infrastructure upgrades, education modernization, labor market reforms, and the like. They have no ability to minimize the antigrowth elements of antiquated fiscal structures littered with distortionary loopholes that favor vested interests and the rich at the expense of society as a whole. And they are quite powerless to eliminate stubborn pockets of excessive debt that crush economic dynamism and discourage the inflows of new investment funds.

As much as they recognize the need for it, central banks cannot revamp incomplete regional and international economic architectures. In the case of the Eurozone, for example, the most they can do is to complete two of the four needed legs of a stable and prosperous Eurozone, and even here they need the cooperation of their political bosses. At the multilateral level, they are continuously frustrated in translating the success of their BIS interactions into the broader global gathering in which ministries of finance have a much bigger say and influence.

So while many in the private sector—first corporations and banks, and then households—have used the time bought by central banks to heal their balance sheets, the larger global economy has yet to regain its proper growth composure. It also faces a possible damaging decline in future potential. Moreover, despite the mounting evidence, too many mindsets have remained closed to the kinds of operational reboots that are called for on the ground.

While, as discussed earlier in this book, there is a bit more that some central banks can do, this pales in significance given the challenges. Central banks—and all of us—need governments to step up to the plate with a comprehensive policy response in the four critical areas elucidated earlier.

But, undermined by political dysfunction, governments across the world have remained insufficiently responsive. They have appeared relieved by an excuse to focus on central bank hyperactivism, as opposed to their own ineffectiveness. While some have progressed partially, too many others are still paralyzed by political gridlock. A breakthrough awaits either an endogenous political catalyst, which could even include an enlightened impact by antiestablishment forces, or an external shock in the form of economic and financial disruption. In the meantime, high unemployment and the lower labor participation levels have strained already stretched social safety nets and fueled an enormous inequality of income, wealth, and opportunities.

At the same time, other risks have also been mounting, risks we must not ignore.

Our major concern should not be about an upcoming bout of alarming inflation fueled by the expansion of central bank balance sheets and enormous liquidity injections. Nor should it be the rather strange notion that central banks will dump their large holdings of purchased securities, disrupting the functioning of markets. They won't.

Instead, our real concern should be about the potential consequences of excessive financial risk taking, resource misallocations, and threats to the sound functioning and stability of markets—and all this in the context of contractionary pressures on potential growth.

Also, after a period of pronounced uniformity, we have now entered an era of greater divergence, and not just in economic performance but also in policy and politics. This more pronounced differentiation could complicate already serious economic, financial, institutional, political, and social challenges; but it can also be the catalyst for unleashing the considerable economic potential and securing genuine financial stability.

Diverging economic developments within systemically important countries induces different policy stances among the most influential central banks (particularly the ECB on one hand and the Fed on the other). Those engaged in an uberstimulus mode will have to do more to have the same impact. Others, on the exit ramp from prolonged reliance on unconventional monetary policy, will work hard to carefully craft this part of an extraordinary multi-year policy journey without having the markets preemptively and prematurely jump terminal values and thus undermine the orderliness of the exit.

This divergence also poses challenges for the international monetary system as a whole. Lacking comprehensive policy responses and proper multilateral coordination, the bulk of the global reconciliation function (that is, resolving the global reconciliation challenge) falls to the exchange rates—and not because they are well positioned to carry it out effectively but because there are so few alternatives. Yet they, too, are stretched. Moreover, history is not particularly reassuring as to what follows large movements among the major currencies. Such moves tend to break things.

It also remains to be seen how economic and policy divergence will interact with the different influences that antiestablishment movements are having on both sides of the Atlantic. Will they combine to facilitate the required policy breakthroughs or, instead, lead to even less coherent policymaking? What is clear from the immediate aftermath of the 2016 U.S. presidential elections is that markets are inclined to opt for the former at evidence of pro-growth policies.

Before the November 8 vote, many observers warned of the potential for a significant financial market selloff were Mr. Trump to pull off a major upset and defeat Secretary Hillary Clinton. In doing so, they were heavily influenced by his anti-trade campaign rhetoric that pointed to the possibility of imposing crushing tariffs on China and Mexico, dismantling NAFTA, and terminating the free-trade arrangement with Korea. The potential risks to growth were seen to be so large as to overwhelm the pro-growth impulses from Mr. Trump's stated intentions to pursue infrastructure spending, tax reform, and deregulation.

Markets did sell off as the early results suggested that Mr. Trump was on his way to securing the White House. But the losses were reversed as he delivered his acceptance speech in New York early on the morning of November 9—reflecting both content and tone.*

The president-elect strongly reiterated his aim to pursue the pro-growth elements of his programs while making no mention of the anti-growth ones. Also, he adopted a conciliatory and inclusive tone, rather than a combative and provocative one. A similar tone was evident in the subsequent remarks about and from leaders of both political parties, including President Barack Obama, Secretary Clinton, Speaker Paul Ryan, and several others (including those who had gone out of their way to criticize the president-elect during the bruising campaign).

Tone and content, combined with the fact that the Republican party now controlled both Congress and the White House, led the market to upwardly revise their expectations for growth and inflation. U.S. stocks surged, with the major indices setting new record highs while bond yields and the dollar rose on the expectation that this new environment would also encourage the Federal Reserve to hike interest rates. In combination, all this opened up the possibility of a gradual policy rebalancing that, among other things, would reduce the over-reliance on the Federal Reserve and provide it with an opportunity to slowly normalize monetary policy.

As of this book update, it remains to be seen whether comforting policy announcements will be followed by proper design and sus-

---

* El-Erian, Mohamed A. (2016), "Sustaining the Trump Rally," Project Syndicate, November. https://www.project-syndicate.org/commentary/trump-market-rally-economic-growth-by-mohamed-a—el-erian-2016-11.

tained implementation, and whether central banks will finally get some help, thereby easing the heavy policy burden that they have already carried for too long. But what is undeniable is that investors are eager to internalize and reward movement away from the damaging political gridlock that has led to highly unbalanced policies, produced disappointing growth outcomes, and distorted markets.

Potentially, such reactions can (and should) extend well beyond a notable rally in risk assets. Much more importantly, they have the potential to unleash into productive use the sizable amounts of corporate cash that are either held on balance sheets or used for short-term financial engineering (such as stock buybacks).

Then there are the disruptions from below. Never before have individuals been so empowered to influence their destiny. They expect a lot more from those who serve them, be it in the provision of goods and services, or in governance and corporate responsibility. Meanwhile, those who serve them face actual and potential disruptions by competitors from other worlds who passionately apply their own and different core competencies, and few are good at "self-disrupting."

Such disruptions from below will intensify, given the enormous potential of AI and big data in particular. Indeed, as Andrew McAfee likes to say, we are just entering the second half of a chessboard where the scope for innovation amplifies in an expanding, even exponential, fashion.

The world we live in is being shaken from above, from below, and from the side, simultaneously. Whether you take a top-down view or a bottom-up one, this is an extremely fluid and unusually uncertain world, and it is one that has not been fully captured in market prices, for good reason. And it is one that will increasingly challenge the paradigm of stable growth and repressed financial volatility.

The binding constraint to resolving all this is, fortunately, no longer really about a lack of understanding of what is needed in terms of policy responses at the individual, corporate, national, regional, and global levels. It is all about implementation—politically and personally.

While it took a frustratingly long time to break out of its cyclical mindset, conventional wisdom on both sides of the Atlantic has converged on the importance of also factoring in secular and structural responses. The result is a significant amount of real consensus among economists on the four-legged policy response detailed earlier— invigorating structural reforms, rebalancing aggregate demand, lifting crippling debt overhangs, and modernizing regional and global architectures and policy coordination.

The longer the world waits for such comprehensive responses, the more the ten distinct but reinforcing forces discussed earlier will undermine the stability and sustainability path we're on, one that cannot go on for much longer. We are rapidly nearing an inflection point where central banks will find their policy approach increasingly and consequentially ineffective. As financial volatility increases and as growth becomes less stable, a limit will be reached: It will no longer be possible to artificially repress financial risk while also decoupling it from the anchor provided by fundamentals. At some point, and I believe that point is approaching fast, things will tip, one way or the other.

Yet—and this is *very important*—the next phase need not entail heightened economic, financial, geopolitical, institutional, political, and social malaise. Nothing is inevitable here. It is our choices— profoundly consequential choices—that matter. And politics will play a very large and deterministic role.

Naturally, a lot of the current commentary on this potential "boom and doom" junction tends to focus on the horrid outcome, not just economically and financially, but also institutionally, politically, and socially. Granted, it's a scary world—one in which inadequate growth and the return of financial instability could result in lost generations, worsening inequality, spreading poverty, and political extremism. Yet it would be wrong to ignore the second road, whose current probability is similar to the first one. The T junction I've described throughout this book is real.

Powered by an economic liftoff as politicians are finally tipped into pursuing their policy-making responsibilities (the "Sputnik moment"), and amid stronger multilateral policy coordination, this second road out of the T junction leads to unambiguously better outcomes. The improved enabling environment allows for the productive engagement of lots of sidelined cash. With remarkable innovations accelerating and amplifying the beneficial effects—to quote McAfee at the March 2015 conference on the Future of Work, hosted in London by WorldPost, "we haven't seen anything yet . . . [as these are] the best economic developments in human history"—the emergence of high inclusive growth would be underpinned by genuine financial stability, including the ability to grow out of excessive indebtedness.

As hard as we try, it is challenging to predict precisely either when we will get to the neck of the T, or which road we'll take. But, at the same time, this is a reminder that there is nothing preordained about the future. The current situation is less about destiny and more about alternatives that we collectively end up deciding on, either knowingly or unknowingly. As such, a key question is how well we are likely to do when taken out of our comfort zone—after all, as I stressed at that same London conference, throughout history this has constituted an important test for the well-being of societies—and what we can do now to enhance our probability of success.

A tempting approach is to wait for others to make things better for us. Exploiting the bridges that central banks have built for them at great expense and empowered by the political system, governments can and should do a lot to improve the probability distribution of future outcomes, both on their own, through better multilateral cooperation, and via public-private partnerships. And all of us can play an advocacy role.

But this is not just about governments getting their act together. We as individuals can and should take action and not just wait for governments to do so; we can start by recognizing what lies ahead, why it's there, and what to do about it. Thus the emphasis in this book on responses to bimodal distributions that lack the reassuring attributes of normal bell curves.

Remember, most of us are conditioned to deal with expectations about future events that are governed by well-behaved normal distributions encompassing a dominant probability of a certain outcome (that is, a bell curve). Exchange this for a bimodal distribution and our reaction functions risk becoming a lot less effective, threatening outright paralysis or (also suboptimal) active inertia.

Recognizing and understanding this basic point is the first step in better navigating what lies ahead. It is a necessary condition, but it is not sufficient. It needs to be supplemented by appropriate tools, revamped structures, updated processes, open mindsets, and behavior modifications.

As detailed in this book, entities that succeed in the years ahead will be those that possess considerable cognitive diversity, come to terms with their blind spots, and work hard to overcome both overt and hidden biases. They will be smart users of scenario analyses. They will actively pursue external inputs, not necessarily for validating their priors but to enrich their process of further deliberation. They will evolve structures to help with some of the heavy lifting. They will communicate frequently, interactively, and intelligently. And they will internalize at multiple individual levels the microforces that have the potential to drive segment-wide transformations.

These entities will evolve their core competencies and draw from external knowledge. They will be much closer to their clients' rapidly changing preferences and modes of interaction—thereby converting historical "wholesale" orientations to more retail ones. They will better use the internal data they generate as well as outside insights to experiment, consolidate, and respond. They will secure their growing treasure of enabling data. They will selectively self-disrupt.

In simpler terms, these are the entities that succeed in building a remarkable mix of optionality, resilience, and agility, especially as the world gets closer to the neck of the T junction:

- Optionality that helps us deal better with the greater unusual uncertainty;

262   THE ONLY GAME IN TOWN

- Resilience that puts us in a better stead to manage higher and different risks; and
- Agility that enhances responsiveness, including when it comes to exploiting the upside of volatility.

The three together remind us of Churchill's statement: "Success is not final, failure is not fatal: it is the courage to continue that counts." And so let us finish with an example that was brought to my attention a few years ago by Don Sull.

Suitably for a discussion that concludes a book written by a sports fan (though not of this particular sport), the example doesn't come from the corporate or government world, and it doesn't involve business, economics, finance, or policy. Instead, it comes from the world of heavyweight boxing.

In October 1974 in Kinshasa, Zaire (now the Democratic Republic of the Congo), the "Rumble in the Jungle" featured a powerful undefeated world champion (George Foreman) taking on a much older boxer who was well past his prime (Muhammad Ali). The experts were unanimous: Foreman would win easily. After all, he had repeatedly demonstrated overwhelming force, knocking out most of his opponents. Meanwhile, the aging Ali could no longer "float like a butterfly," let alone "sting like a bee."

The major question before the bout was not about who would win. Expert opinion was unanimously favoring Foreman in what was expected to be one of the most lopsided heavyweight championship fights in history.

The uncertainty was elsewhere. It involved varying predictions on the seriousness of the injuries that Ali would incur in his devastating loss—all the way from serious to life threatening.

Ali knocked out Foreman in the eighth round. Game over. It was one of the greatest sporting upsets of all time. And it prompted research interest.

It turns out that Ali's camp understood that they were facing a bimodal distribution, albeit quite an unbalanced one. Either Ali would incur significant injuries (the more probable left mode) or he would come up with essentially a miracle (the much less likely right mode). But it would not be business as usual, and the fight certainly wasn't one where Ali could endure a full fifteen rounds and hope to edge ahead on points.

Ali's trainers recognized that they would have to work differently—and be smartly adaptable—if they were to stand any chance of balancing out even a little the probabilities of the two modes. They needed to find a way to reduce the probability of the bad outcome and increase the probability of the good one. In the process, they had to take Ali out of his long-established fighting style. They needed to consider alternative approaches.

All this led the Ali camp to fundamentally alter his training program with the aim of increasing resilience and agility—and thus provide for a lot more optionality.

Greater resilience would keep Ali in the fight despite the punishment he was likely to receive. Agility would open up the possibility of Ali pouncing on an opening should Foreman's attention wane or his stamina falter. To increase their chances of success, they also thought hard about how to use structure and design modifications to help with some of the heavy lifting.

Recognizing the different distribution of expected outcome, Ali's training program was fundamentally recast. He spent a lot more time standing still in the practice ring and absorbing a tremendous amount of punches and pain—day after day.

But the changes did not stop there. At the start of the fight on that October day, Ali did what until then was deemed unthinkable as a positive strategy.

Instead of going to the middle of the ring and maneuvering there, Ali leaned back against the ropes. He just stayed there, putting his hands and arms up to protect as much of himself as he could.

Initially surprised, most of those watching the fight judged what seemed to be Ali's strategy to be a huge mistake. After all, Ali was a sitting duck, especially in the face of such a powerful opponent. They were wrong. Rather, it was a risky move aimed at using the ropes to help dissipate the force of the blows Ali was receiving from Foreman—a tactic subsequently dubbed the rope-a-dope.

Norman Mailer, the American writer and sometime boxer, described the strategy as follows: "Standing on one's feet, it is painful to absorb a heavy body punch even when blocked with one's arm. The torso, the legs and the spine take the shock. Leaning on the ropes, however, Ali can pass it along; the rope will receive the strain."[2] And it did, giving Ali optionality that would not have been otherwise available to him.

For seven long rounds, Ali absorbed a tremendous amount of punishment from a powerful Foreman intent on knocking him out. But Foreman was getting tired. In the eighth round, Ali saw an opening and, displaying enormous agility, jumped on it and knocked Foreman out.

This story speaks to more than simply recognizing a bimodal distribution, responding accordingly, and, in the process, overcoming narrow mindsets, outmoded framing, and blind spots. It is also about actively working to alter the distribution of the two modes in favor of the better one. It also points to the importance of using structure, incorporating new insights, and altering game plans that worked well in the past but need revamping in the face of an unusually uncertain outcome. And it highlights the close interconnections of optionality, resilience, and agility.

These insights translate to the challenges facing individuals, households, companies, governments, and the multilateral system today.

The time has come for politicians to recognize that policy making can no longer rely on central banks to do the heavy policy lifting. A more comprehensive policy approach is urgently needed and is available. By mastering the political will and leadership required to implement it, political leaders can enable governments to unleash the considerable productive powers of the underemployed and unemployed, idle cash on companies' balance sheets, alienated youths, better global policy coordination, and significant innovations whose beneficial impact is on the verge of going macro. The time has also come for companies and households to do more to gain greater control of their destiny under either road out of the T junction.

Central banks have a huge stake in all this. Having been forced into being the only game in town, they now find that their destiny is no longer entirely or even mostly theirs to control. The legacy of their exceptional period of hyper policy experimentation is now in the hands of governments and their political bosses.

Should the political system finally step up to its economic governance responsibilities, central banks' risky policy bet will have paid off. Their boldness, wisdom, and judgment will be celebrated. And their political autonomy and operational flexibility will be protected.

But if the political system stumbles, central banks will be the worse for it. Rather than being viewed as a critical part of the solution, they will be seen as having contributed to problems that will haunt both current and future generations. Ultimately, the global economy will lose the effectiveness of some of its most critical players.

Seldom has the global economy been engaged on such a path to a T junction; hardly ever have the alternatives been so stark; rarely have the stakes been so high.

Where we actually end up is still a function of choice rather than destiny. Much will of course depend on the willingness and ability of governments to join central banks in more responsible policy making—at the national, regional, and multilateral levels. But this doesn't mean that the rest of us should be passive observers. There is a lot that we can and should do to help improve the prospects for good outcomes, in the process also increasing our ability to better navigate bad outcomes should the world come out of the T on the wrong road. We need to spend a lot more time replenishing our reservoirs of agility, optionality, and resilience, and we need to do so in an open-minded manner, including by acting on the real possibility that some of what has served us well in the past will not be as effective in the future.

ACKNOWLEDGMENTS

This book is the result of several years of reading, observing, thinking, and, most important, discussing. It would not have been written without the amazing support that I have received from family, friends, colleagues, and acquaintances; without the wonderful opportunities I have had to interact with policymakers, thought leaders, and astute observers of the global economy, markets, modern central banking, and behavioral science; without the extremely stimulating environments afforded to me by my professional activities; and without the inspiration, support, and companionship of some truly special people.

By asking me how I would summarize in one sentence some of the most important economic issues facing us in the next few years, Rich Miller first put the idea of this book in my head. It was October 2012 and, along with his Bloomberg News colleague Simon Kennedy, we had met for lunch in the context of the IMF/World Bank Annual Meetings. Walking out of this stimulating get-together, Rich started me on a thought journey that led to what you read in this book. And it is just one of the examples of how Rich and Simon have educated and stimulated me over the years with their insightful comments and columns.

My agent, Andrew Wylie, provided amazing motivation, inspiration, and advice. Will Murphy at Random House was key in guiding me through the production stages of the book and improving its quality. Jiachen Fu and Irene Hill were also instrumental in the production stages and elsewhere, providing tremendous and exceptional help. I owe a lot to all four for their incredible support and encouragement.

Many of the ideas in the book were first pursued in higher-frequency columns that I have written, particularly for *Bloomberg View*, the *Financial Times*, Project Syndicate, *Fortune*, *Business Insider*, *Foreign Policy*, *The Atlantic*, and *The Huffington Post*. They matured through discussions with friends, work colleagues, and other professional acquaintances; and they benefited from the questioning of participants at various seminars, conferences, and panels.

In publishing my regular columns, I have been both privileged and delighted to work and interact with amazing colleagues at some of the very best media platforms. They include Jennifer Ablan, Chris Adams, Becky Anderson, Lionel Barber, Mark Barton, Max Berley, Richard Blackden, Mike Bloomberg, Michelle Caruso-Cabrera, Anna Dedhar, Jonathan Ferro, Jim Greiff, Andrew Hill, Arianna Huffington, Tom Keene, Joe Kernen, Betty Liu, Michael MacKenzie, Ken Murphy, Tim O'Brien, Richard Quest, Becky Quick, Vonnie Quinn, Carl Quintanilla, Sam Ro, Kate Roberts, Alec Russell, Rick Santelli, Andy Serwer, David Shipley, Pauline Skypala, Andrew Ross Sorkin, Alex Steel, Fred Studemann, Scott Wapner, David West, and Mark Whitehouse.

I am extremely grateful for the support and friendship of colleagues at Allianz and PIMCO. They have been a great source of intellectual stimulation and companionship. I could not have written this book without them. Special thanks to Mike Amey, Oliver Baete, Francesc

Balcells, Andrew Balls, Philippe Bodereau, Andy Bosomworth, Petra Brandes, Libby Cantrill, Suhail Dada, Chris Dialynas, Michael Diekmann, Jiachen Fu, Emilio Galli-Zugaro, Bill Gross, Michael Gomez, Irene Hill, Dan Ivascyn, John Maney, Paul McCulley, Sarah Middleton, Thomas Naumann, Lorenzo Pagani, Helmet Perlet, Sara Piccolo, Jay Ralph, Sabia Schwarzer, Marc Seidner, Scott Simon, and Josh Thimons.

Over the years, I have been influenced and enlightened by the thinking, statements, and interactions with individuals whom I regard among the giants of modern central banking, including Ben Bernanke, Mark Carney, Stanley Fischer, Arminio Fraga, Alan Greenspan, Andy Haldane, Mervyn King, Christian Noyer, Raghu Rajan, Jean Claude Trichet, Paul Volcker, and Janet Yellen. Their insights complemented those from other policymakers such as Olivier Blanchard, Josh Bolten, and Christine Lagarde.

Among those who have also influenced my thinking over the years, special thanks to Jared Cohen, Andy Cosh, Mark Dow, Lord Eatwell, Ian Goldin, Krishna Guha, Jon Hilsenrath, Nick Knight, Gayle Lemmon, James Manyika, Jessica Mathews, Colin Powell, Scott Saunders, Eric Schmidt, Ajit Singh, Mike Spence, Anne-Marie Slaughter, Don Sull, Martin Wolf, and colleagues at the BIS.

Finally, a very special word of thanks and deep appreciation to my family and close friends.

I started writing this book in December 2014, during and ahead of years of significant transitions for me. In navigating all the challenges that inevitably accompany change, a small set of incredible people provided me with enormous support and encouragement. I could not have advanced on this book without the steadfast friendship and wise counsel of Caroline Atkinson, Francesc Balcells, Andrew Balls, Laurye Blackford, Shermeen and Suhail Dada, Chris and Sheri Dialynas, Michael and Whitney Gomez, Allison and Nick Knight, Anna and Sandro Leipold, Sindo Oliveros and Titina de Montagut, Dryden and Laila Pence, Scott and Suzanne Saunders, Shakour Shaalan, Mike Spence, and Edi and Josh Thimons. The parents and kids of the Laguna Playhouse Youth Theater, and Donna Inglima, its inspirational leader, also deserve a special mention, as do Anna and Georgia Stylianides, who brought wonderful things into our lives.

Throughout the writing of this book, my mother, my sister, and her family provided me with an amazing mix of support, encouragement, and occasional teasing. They found time for me also during important transitions in their lives. And I still benefit today from the amazing educational opportunities that my late father afforded us, along with his incredible love, guidance, and care. He may have passed more than three decades ago, yet his beneficial influence and inspiration are as strong today as they were during his exceptional life.

Our wonderful dog, Bosa, lay next to me for hours as I typed away on a laptop on the kitchen counter. Whenever she sensed my periodic writer's freeze, she would get up and place her head on my lap, both seeking a quick pat and providing me with that needed refresh and reboot.

Then there is my incredible daughter. Her wisdom, insights, and talents go well beyond her age. Her amazing love and constant encouragement have sustained me, as have her enjoyable companionship, engaging wit, and timely reminders about the book's deadlines (yes, I missed the first one). I am the luckiest dad in the world, with the most amazing daughter in the world. And I will never be able to thank her enough for providing me in mid-2013 with a much-needed wake-up call as to the extent to which my work-life balance had gotten out of whack. The reset she prompted is a source of many great things, and this book would not have been written without it.

In closing this acknowledgment, I have the uneasy feeling that this is far from a complete list of people who were instrumental in enabling me, one way or the other, to write this book. I apologize to all those whom I have inadvertently failed to mention. And none of those whom I have mentioned should be held responsible for any errors that this book may contain.

NOTES

CHAPTER 2: THE ONLY GAME IN TOWN

1. Christian Noyer, "Central Banking: The Way Forward?," opening speech to the International Symposium of the Banque de France, November 7, 2014, https://www.banque-france.fr/uploads/tx_bdfgrandesdates/Allocution-ouverture-Noyer-Symposium-7112014-EN.pdf.
2. Richard Milne, "Denmark Highlights Naked Truth About Negative Lending," *Financial Times*, April 8, 2015, http://www.ft.com/intl/cms/s/0/7f4e2f4c-dde3-11e4-9d29-00144feab7de.html.
3. Ben S. Bernanke, "The Economic Outlook and Monetary Policy," speech to the Federal Reserve Bank of Kansas City Symposium in Jackson Hole, Wyoming, Board of Governors of the Federal Reserve Bank, August 27, 2010, http://www.federalreserve.gov/newsevents/speech/bernanke20100827a.htm.
4. I first came across this term, attributed to a "senior Citigroup executive," in Landon Thomas, Jr., and Neil Gough, "Swiss Move Prompts Fears of Sustained Market Tumult," *New York Times*, January 16, 2015, http://dealbook.nytimes.com/2015/01/16/currency-traders-rattled-in-wake-of-swiss-central-bank-move.

CHAPTER 3: CENTRAL BANKS' COMMUNICATION CHALLENGE

1. "Quarterly Review," media briefing by Claudio Bario, head of the Monetary and Economic Department, and Hyun Shin, economic adviser and head of research, Bank for International Settlements, December 5, 2014, http://www.bis.org/publ/qtrpdf/r_qt1412_ontherecord.htm.

2. "Central Banks Lift the Veil on More of Their Secrets," *Financial Times,* December 14, 2014, http://www.ft.com/intl/cms/s/0/64d1c072-8206-11e4-a9bb-00144feabdc0.html.

3. Alan Greenspan interview with Maria Bartiromo, CNBC, September 17, 2007.

4. Joseph M. Bessette and John J. Pitney, Jr., *American Government and Politics: Deliberation, Democracy, and Citizenship* (Andover, MA: Cengage Learning, 2011).

5. "Central Banks Lift the Veil on More of Their Secrets." *Financial Times,* December 14, 2014, http://www.ft.com/intl/cms/s/0/64d1c072-8206-11e4-a9bb-00144feabdc0.html.

6. Neil Irwin, "The Goal of 2% Inflation, Rethought," *New York Times,* December 21, 2014, http://www.nytimes.com/2014/12/21/upshot/of-kiwis-and-currencies-how-a-2-inflation-target-became-global-economic-gospel.html.

7. "Central Banks Lift the Veil on More of Their Secrets," *Financial Times,* December 14, 2014, http://www.ft.com/intl/cms/s/0/64d1c072-8206-11e4-a9bb-00144feabdc0.html.

8. Nicholas Lemann, "The Hand on the Lever," *New Yorker,* July 2014.

9. Binyamin Appelbaum, "Q. and A. With Charles Plosser of the Fed: Raise Rates Sooner Rather Than Later," *New York Times,* January 30, 2015, http://www.nytimes.com/2015/01/30/upshot/q-and-a-with-charles-plosser-of-the-fed-raise-rates-sooner-rather-than-later.html.

10. Mohamed A. El-Erian, "Why This Market Rally Is So Unloved," *Bloomberg View,* September 2, 2014, http://www.bloombergview.com/articles/2014-09-02/why-this-market-rally-is-so-unloved.

11. Jack Ewing and Binyamin Appelbaum, "A Stress Test for Mario Draghi and the European Central Bank," *New York Times,* January 3, 2015, http://www.nytimes.com/2015/01/04/business/stress-test-for-mario-draghi.html.

12. Janet Yellen, "Monetary Policy and Financial Stability," speech at the 2014 Michel Camdessus Central Banking Lecture at the International Monetary Fund in Washington, D.C., Board of Governors of the Federal Reserve System, July 2, 2014, http://www.federalreserve.gov/newsevents/speech/yellen20140702a.htm.

CHAPTER 4: HOW AND WHY THIS BOOK IS ORGANIZED

1. Andrew G. Haldane, "Growing, Fast and Slow," speech at the University of East Anglia, Norwich, England, February 17, 2015, http://www.bis.org/review/r150219b.pdf.

2. Mohamed A. El-Erian, *When Markets Collide: Investment Strategies for the Age of Global Economic Change* (New York: McGraw-Hill, 2008).

PART II: CONTEXT: THE RISE, COLLAPSE, AND RESURRECTION OF CENTRAL BANKING

1. Martin Wolf, "We Are Trapped in a Cycle of Credit Booms," *Financial Times,* October 8, 2014, http://www.ft.com/intl/cms/s/0/1a9f058e-4d43-11e4 -bf60-00144feab7de.html#axzz3Lfv9pY4D. For a detailed analysis, see Martin Wolf, *The Shifts and the Shocks: What We Have Learned—and Have Still to Learn—from the Financial Crisis* (New York: Penguin Press, 2014).

CHAPTER 5: THE GOLDEN AGE OF CENTRAL BANKS AND "BUBBLISH FINANCE"

1. Joan Robinson, "The Economics of Hyperinflation," *Economic Journal* 48 (September 1938).
2. Mohamed A. El-Erian, *When Markets Collide: Investment Strategies for the Age of Global Economic Change* (New York: McGraw-Hill, 2008).
3. For an insightful discussion of this and more, please see Raghuram G. Rajan, *Fault Lines: How Hidden Fractures Still Threaten the World Economy* (Princeton, NJ: Princeton University Press, 2010).
4. "Paul Krugman: Here Are 5 Big Things Paul Krugman Says He Got Wrong Over the Years," *Business Insider,* November 2014, http://www.business insider.com/big-things-paul-krugman-got-wrong-economy-2014-11.
5. William C. Dudley, "Economics at the Federal Reserve," remarks at the American Economic Association 2014 Annual Meeting, Philadelphia, http://www.newyorkfed.org/newsevents/speeches/2014/dud140104.html.
6. Atef Mian and Amir Sufi, *House of Debt: How They (and You) Caused the Great Recession, and How We Can Prevent It from Happening Again* (Chicago: University of Chicago Press, 2014).
7. Mark Carney, "Inclusive Capitalism: Creating a Sense of the New Systemic," speech at the Conference on Inclusive Capitalism, London, May 27, 2014, http://www.bankofengland.co.uk/publications/Documents/speeches/2014/ speech731.pdf.

CHAPTER 6: CASCADING FAILURES

1. Michiyo Nakamoto and David Wighton, "Bullish Citigroup Is 'Still Dancing' to the Beat of the Buyout Boom," *Financial Times,* July 10, 2007, http:// www.ft.com/intl/cms/s/0/5cefc794-2e7d-11dc-821c-0000779fd2ac.html.
2. As late as September 2014, the popular media was still on this point. As an example, the money section of the September 18 edition of *USA Today* included the headline "Fed Sings Wall Street's Tune." And the drivers of the accusation, both real and perceived, went well beyond what former Treasury secretary Geithner noted in his memoir, *Stress Test,* that "the optics of the institution's governance are awful. The Fed has always been vulnerable to perceptions of capture by the big banks."
3. Robin Harding, "Transcripts Reveal Drama and Fear as Fed Confronted Lehman's Implosion," *Financial Times,* February 21, 2014, http://www.ft .com/intl/cms/s/0/ec1c3a5a-9b0f-11e3-946b-00144feab7de.html.

4. Sam Fleming and Shawn Donnan, "Fed Feared Japan-Scale Crisis in 2009," *Financial Times*, March 5, 2015, http://www.ft.com/intl/cms/s/0/d77aff2c -c28d-11e4-ad89-00144feab7de.html.

5. Jeremie Cohen-Setton, "The 2008 FOMC Transcripts: Did the Committee Obsess over the Wrong Crisis and the Performance of Key Personalities," Bruegel Blog Review, March 3, 2014, http://www.bruegel.org/nc/blog/ detail/article/1258-blogs-review-the-2008-fomc-transcripts/.

6. "A Desperate Plea—Then the Race for a Deal Before 'Sucker Goes Down,'" *Guardian*, September 26, 2008, http://www.theguardian.com/business/ 2008/sep/27/wallstreet.useconomy1.

7. Neal Collins, "Archaic BoE Was Ill-Equipped to Prevent Financial Crisis," *Financial Times*, January 9, 2015, http://www.ft.com/intl/cms/s/0/d3db1f52 -9752-11e4-845a-00144feabdc0.html.

8. Joshua Zumbrun and Alaa Shahine, "Retired Bernanke Harbors Regret on Main Street's View of Bailout," Bloomberg News, March 4, 2014, http:// www.bloomberg.com/news/2014-03-04/bernanke-says-u-s-economy -seeing-progress.html.

9. Timothy F. Geithner, *Stress Test: Reflections on Financial Crises* (New York: Crown, 2014).

CHAPTER 7: CENTRAL BANK RESURRECTION

1. Mario Draghi, speech to the Global Investment Council, European Central Bank, July 26, 2012, http://www.ecb.europa.eu/press/key/date/2012/html/ sp120726.en.html.

2. Jack Ewing and Binyamin Appelbaum, "A Stress Test for Mario Draghi and the European Central Bank," *New York Times*, January 3, 2015, http://www .nytimes.com/2015/01/04/business/stress-test-for-mario-draghi.html.

3. Philip Turner, "The Exit from Non-Conventional Monetary Policy: What Challenges?," BIS Working Paper 448, 2014, May, http://www.bis.org/publ/ work448.pdf.

4. "Monetary Policy Struggles to Normalize," BIS Annual Report, June 29, 2014, Bank for International Settlements, http://www.bis.org/publ/arpdf/ ar2014e5.htm.

5. Mohamed A. El-Erian, "Parsing Draghi's QE Gambit," *Bloomberg View*, January 23, 2015, http://www.bloombergview.com/articles/2015-01-23/parsing -draghi-s-qe-gambit. See also Mohamed A. El-Erian, "The ECB Can Only Buy Time for Europe's Politicians," *Financial Times*, January 22, 2015, http:// www.ft.com/intl/cms/s/0/957b9ddc-a241-11e4-bbb8-00144feab7de.html.

6. Tracy Alloway, "Markets' Misplaced Faith in Central Banks," *Financial Times*, January 23, 2015, http://www.ft.com/intl/cms/s/0/2ad516fa-a2d4 -11e4-ac1c-00144feab7de.html.

7. Hyman Minsky, "The Financial Instability Hypothesis," Working Paper No. 74, Levy Economics Institute of Bard College, 1992.

8. Mohamed A. El-Erian, "Beware of Calls for QE4," *Financial Times*, October 17, 2014, http://blogs.ft.com/the-a-list/2014/10/17/beware-of-calls-for-qe4/.

9. Chris Giles, "Carney Warns on Low Interest Rates," *Financial Times*, January 24, 2015, http://www.ft.com/intl/cms/s/0/c20266fe-a3fb-11e4-b90d-00144feab7de.html.

10. Timothy F. Geithner, *Stress Test: Reflections on Financial Crises* (New York: Crown, 2014).

CHAPTER 8: SETTING THE STAGE

1. Jim Grant, "Monetary Policy Is a Virus That Infects Politics," *Financial Times*, January 5, 2015, http://www.ft.com/intl/cms/s/0/14078740-9277-11e4-a1fd-00144feabdc0.html.

2. "The World Economy: In Need of New Oomph," *Economist*, May 24, 2014, http://www.economist.com/news/leaders/21602698-how-make-rich-worlds-recovery-stronger-and-safer-need-new-oomph.

3. "In Search of a New Compass," Bank for International Settlements, June 29, 2014, http://www.bis.org/publ/arpdf/ar2014e1.htm.

4. E. S. Browning, "The 'Investor's Dilemma': Everything Is Expensive," *Wall Street Journal*, August 24, 2014, http://blogs.wsj.com/moneybeat/2014/08/24/the-investors-dilemma-everything-is-expensive/.

5. Lawrence H. Summers, "Reflection on the 'New Secular Stagnation Hypotheses,'" in Coen Tuelings and Richard Baldwin, eds., *Secular Stagnation: Facts, Causes, and Cures* (London: CEPR Press, 2014), http://www.voxeu.org/sites/default/files/Vox_secular_stagnation.pdf.

CHAPTER 9: THE QUEST OF A GENERATION

1. Mohamed A. El-Erian, "The Global Growth Quest," Project Syndicate, April 9, 2013, http://www.project-syndicate.org/commentary/the-worldwide-search-for-new-growth-models-by-mohamed-a--el-erian.

2. Matt O'Brien, "Greece's Poor Are Back to Where They Were in 1980," *Washington Post*, April 10, 2015, http://www.washingtonpost.com/blogs/wonkblog/wp/2015/04/10/greeces-poor-are-back-to-where-they-were-in-1980/.

3. "Mohamed A. El-Erian Discusses PIMCO's Secular Outlook and Investment Implications," Economic Outlook, PIMCO, May 2009, http://europe.pimco.com/EN/Insights/Pages/Secular%20Outlook%20Q%20and%20A%20May%202009%20El-Erian.aspx. Also, Mohamed A. El-Erian, "Navigating the New Normal in Industrial Countries," Per Jacobsson Lecture, IMF, October 10, 2010.

4. Jim Pearce, "The New Normal—Six Years Later," *Investing Daily*, January 30, 2015, http://www.investingdaily.com/22053/the-new-normal-six-years-later-2/.

5. Mohamed A. El-Erian, "The 'New Normal' and Its Consequential Morphing," *Journal of Indexes*, November 22, 2013, http://europe.etf.com/europe/publications/journal-of-indexes/articles/9398-the-new-normal-and-its-consequential-morphing.html?start=6&Itemid=200.

6. Mohamed A. El-Erian, "'The New Normal' Has Been Devastating for America," *Business Insider*, March 22, 2014, http://www.businessinsider.com/el-erian-state-of-the-new-normal-2014-3.

7. Mohamed A. El-Erian, "Europe Must Pay Heed to Japan's New Slide," *Bloomberg View*, November 18, 2014, http://www.bloombergview.com/articles/2014-11-18/europe-must-pay-heed-to-japans-new-slide.

8. Mohamed A. El-Erian, "Could America Turn Out Worse than Japan?," Reuters, October 31, 2011, http://blogs.reuters.com/mohamed-el-erian/2011/10/31/could-america-turn-out-worse-than-japan-2/.

9. Lawrence H. Summers, "U.S. Economic Prospects: Secular Stagnation, Hysteresis, and the Zero Lower Bound," *Business Economics* 49, no. 2 (2014), http://larrysummers.com/wp-content/uploads/2014/06/NABE-speech -Lawrence-H.-Summers1.pdf.

10. Christine Lagarde, "The Challenge Facing the Global Economy: New Momentum to Overcome a New Mediocre," speech to Georgetown University School of Foreign Service, October 2, 2014, http://www.imf.org/external/np/speeches/2014/100214.htm.

11. Gauti Eggertsson and Neil Mehrota, "A Model of Secular Stagnation," NBER Working Paper No. 20574, National Bureau of Economic Research, April 2014, http://www.nber.org/papers/w20574.pdf.

12. Mohamed A. El-Erian, "Confronting Persistent U.S. Economic Slump," *Bloomberg View*, April 21, 2014, http://www.bloombergview.com/articles/2014-04-21/confronting-the-u-s-economic-slump.

13. Martin Wolf, "Why America Is Going to Win the Global Currency Battle," *Financial Times*, October 12, 2010, http://www.ft.com/intl/cms/s/0/fe45eeb2-d644-11df-81f0-00144feabdc0.html.

14. Janet Yellen, "Monetary Policy and the Economic Recovery," speech to the Economic Club of New York, Board of Governors of the Federal Reserve System, April 16, 2014, http://www.federalreserve.gov/newsevents/speech/yellen20140416a.htm.

15. Mohamed A. El-Erian, "Trial by Fire: What Crises Lie in Wait for Janet Yellen," *Foreign Policy*, January 7, 2014, http://foreignpolicy.com/2014/01/07/trial-by-fire/.

16. Raghuram Rajan, "Global Policy: A View from Emerging Markets," Brookings Institution, video, April 10, 2014, http://www.brookings.edu/events/2014/04/10-global-monetary-policy-view-from-emerging-markets.

17. See, for example, "The BIS Quarterly Review for December 2014: Buoyant Yet Fragile?," December 7, 2014, Bank for International Settlements, http://www.bis.org/publ/qtrpdf/r_qt1412.htm.

18. Michael Chui, Ingo Fender, and Vladyslav Sushko, "Risks Related to EME Corporate Balance Sheets: The Role of Leverage and Currency Mismatch," Bank for International Settlements, 2014, http://www.bis.org/publ/qtrpdf/r_qt1409f.pdf.

CHAPTER 10: REDUCING THE RISK
OF THE UNEMPLOY*ED* BECOMING UNEMPLOY*ABLE*

1. Stanley Fischer, "The Great Recession: Moving Ahead," speech to conference sponsored by the Swedish Ministry of Finance, Board of Governors of

the Federal Reserve, August 11, 2014, http://www.federalreserve.gov/news
events/speech/fischer20140811a.htm.

CHAPTER 11: THE INEQUALITY TRIFECTA

1. "Focus on Inequality and Income," Organisation for Economic Co-operation and Development, Directorate for Employment, Labor and Social Affairs, December 2014, http://www.oecd.org/social/Focus-Inequality-and-Growth-2014.pdf.
2. Emmanuel Saez and Gabriel Zucman, "Wealth Inequality in the US Since 1913," NBER Working Paper No. 20615, October 2014.
3. Estelle Sommiller and Mark Price, "The Increasingly Unequal Income States of America," Economic Policy Institute, January 26, 2015, http://www.epi.org/publication/income-inequality-by-state-1917-to-2012/.
4. "17 Things We Learned About Income Inequality in 2014," *Atlantic*, December 23, 2014, http://www.theatlantic.com/business/archive/2014/12/17-things-we-learned-about-income-inequality-in-2014/383917/.
5. Federal Reserve Board of Governors, "Changes in US Family Finances from 2010 to 2013: Evidence from the Survey of Consumer Finances," *Federal Reserve Bulletin* 100, no. 4 (September 2014), http://www.federalreserve.gov/pubs/bulletin/2014/pdf/scf14.pdf.
6. Rakesh Kochhar and Richard Fry, "Wealth Inequality Has Widened Along Racial, Ethnic Lines Since the End of the Great Recession," Pew Research Center, December 12, 2014, http://www.pewresearch.org/fact-tank/2014/12/12/racial-wealth-gaps-great-recession/.
7. Thomas Piketty, *Capital in the Twenty-First Century* (Cambridge, MA: Belknap Press of Harvard University Press, 2014).
8. Mohamed A. El-Erian, "The Inequality Trifecta," Project Syndicate, October 17, 2014, http://www.project-syndicate.org/commentary/imf-world-bank-annual-meetings-and-inequality-by-mohamed-a--el-erian-2014-10.
9. Madeline Ostrander, "What Poverty Does to the Young Brain," *New Yorker*, June 4, 2015, http://www.newyorker.com/tech/elements/what-poverty-does-to-the-young-brain.
10. Frank Bruni, "Class, Cost and College," *New York Times*, May 17, 2014, http://www.nytimes.com/2014/05/18/opinion/sunday/bruni-class-cost-and-college.html.
11. McKinsey Global Institute, "QE and Ultra-Low Rates," 2013.

CHAPTER 12: THE PERSISTENT TRUST DEFICIT

1. Ian Fraser, *Shredded: Inside RBS, the Bank That Broke Britain* (Edinburgh: Birlinn, 2014).
2. Joshua Zumbrun and Alaa Shahine, "Retired Bernanke Harbors Regret on Main Street's View of Bailout," Bloomberg News, March 4, 2014, http://www.bloomberg.com/news/2014-03-04/bernanke-says-u-s-economy-seeing-progress.html.

3. Timothy F. Geithner, *Stress Test: Reflections on Financial Crises* (New York: Crown, 2014).

4. Binyamin Appelbaum, "Yellen Says Restraining the Fed's Oversight Would Be a 'Grave Mistake,'" *New York Times,* July 16, 2014, http://www.nytimes .com/2014/07/17/business/yellen-says-constraining-fed-would-be-a-grave -mistake.html.

5. Panel discussion remarks quoted in Jeff Kearns, "Fed's $4 Trillion Assets Draw Lawmaker Ire Amid Bubble Concerns," Bloomberg News, December 17, 2013, http://www.bloomberg.com/news/2013-12-17/fed-s-4-trillion-assets -draw-lawmaker-ire-amid-bubble-concern.html.

6. Ibid.

7. Peter Eavis, "New York Fed Is Criticized on Oversight," November 21, 2014, http://dealbook.nytimes.com/2014/11/21/new-york-fed-chief-faces -withering-criticism-at-senate-hearing.

8. Liz Alderman, "Netherlands Asks Bankers to Swear to God," *New York Times,* December 12, 2014, http://dealbook.nytimes.com/2014/12/12/ netherlands-asks-bankers-to-swear-to-god.

9. Mohamed A. El-Erian, "The Threat to the Central Bank Brand," Project Syndicate, June 4, 2013, http://www.project-syndicate.org/commentary/ the-growing-risk-to-central-bankers--credibility-by-mohamed-a--el-erian.

10. Guy Kawasaki, *Enchantment: The Art of Changing Hearts, Minds, and Actions* (New York: Penguin Books, 2012).

CHAPTER 13: NATIONAL POLITICAL DYSFUNCTION

1. "The Great Fracturing," *Economist,* February 21, 2015, http://www.econo mist.com/news/leaders/21644147-britains-slide-six-party-politics-presages -instability-and-crisis-legitimacy-great.

2. Mohamed A. El-Erian, "I Don't Know What Will Happen If We Default, and I Don't Want to Find Out," *Atlantic,* October 10, 2013, http://www.theatlantic .com/business/archive/2013/10/i-dont-know-what-will-happen-if-we -default-and-i-dont-want-to-find-out/280467/.

3. For an insightful discussion of the various components of this balancing act, see Eric Schmidt and Jared Cohen, *The New Digital Age: Reshaping the Future of People, Nations and Business* (London: John Murray, 2014).

4. Mohamed A. El-Erian, "The Very Messy Politics of Economic Divergence," Project Syndicate, March 2015, http://www.project-syndicate.org/com mentary/economic-divergence-global-politics-by-mohamed-a--el-erian -2015-03.

CHAPTER 14: THE "G-0" SLIDE INTO
THE "INTERNATIONAL ECONOMIC NON-SYSTEM"

1. The term was coined more than ten years ago by Jim O'Neil, Goldman Sachs's chief economist at that time. It now refers to the grouping of countries consisting of Brazil, Russia, India, China, and South Africa.

2. Mohamed A. El-Erian, "The Real Message of the BRICS Summit," *Bloom-*

berg View, July 17, 2014, http://www.bloombergview.com/articles/2014
-07-17/the-real-message-of-the-brics-summit.

3. Mohamed A. El-Erian, "U.S. Opposition to Asian Bank Is Self-Destructive,"
Bloomberg View, March 31, 2015, http://www.bloombergview.com/articles/
2015-03-31/el-erian-u-s-opposition-to-asia-bank-is-self-destructive.

4. Richard Dobbs, James Manyika, and Jonathan Woetzel, *No Ordinary Disruption: The Four Global Forces Breaking All the Trends* (New York: Public-
Affairs, 2015).

5. Mohamed A. El-Erian, "Is the World Bank Losing Asia?," *Bloomberg View,*
July 10, 2014, http://www.bloombergview.com/articles/2014-07-10/is-the
-world-bank-losing-asia.

CHAPTER 15: THE MIGRATION
AND MORPHING OF FINANCIAL RISKS

1. See, for example, the December 9 press release by the Board of Governors
of the Federal Reserve System, http://www.federalreserve.gov/newsevents/
press/bcreg/20141209a.htm.

2. Greg Ip, "Post-Crisis Risk Casts a Darkening Shadow," *Wall Street Journal,*
April 8, 2015, http://www.wsj.com/articles/post-crisis-risk-casts-a-darkening
-shadow-1428499827.

3. Brad Jones, "Asset Bubbles: Rethinking Policy for the Age of Asset Management," IMF Working Paper, February 2015, http://www.imf.org/external/
pubs/ft/wp/2015/wp1527.pdf.

4. Jaime Caruana, "Macro-Prudential Policies: Opportunities and Challenges,"
speech to the Tenth High-Level Meeting for the Middle East and North
Africa, Bank for International Settlements, December 9, 2014, http://www
.bis.org/speeches/sp141219.pdf.

5. Banque de France, "Macroprudential Policies: Implementation and Interactions," *Financial Stability Review,* April 2014.

6. Mohamed A. El-Erian, "3 Steps to Remove Financial System Risk," Harvard
Business School, August 15, 2007, http://hbswk.hbs.edu/item/5745.html.

7. Mohamed A. El-Erian, "Creative Self-Disruption," Project Syndicate,
April 7, 2015, https://www.project-syndicate.org/commentary/consumer
-sharing-economy-adaptation-by-mohamed-a--el-erian-2015-04.

8. Steve Lohr, "Banking Start-ups Adopt New Tools for Lending," *New York
Times,* January 19, 2015, http://www.nytimes.com/2015/01/19/technology/
banking-start-ups-adopt-new-tools-for-lending.html.

9. For full disclosure, I have been recently involved in one of these efforts—
"Payoff"—as an investor and board member of a start-up seeking to improve the financial services offered to households and small businesses.

CHAPTER 16: THE LIQUIDITY DELUSION

1. Tracy Alloway and Michael MacKenzie, "Anatomy of a Market Meltdown,"
Financial Times, November 18, 2014, http://www.ft.com/cms/s/0/cac64efe
-6b34-11e4-ae52-00144feabdc0.html.

2. Jamie Dimon, "Annual Letter to Shareholders," JPMorgan Chase, April 2015, http://files.shareholder.com/downloads/ONE/15660259x0x820077/8af78e45-1d81-4363-931c-439d04312ebc/JPMC-AR2014-LetterToShareholders.pdf.

3. William Finkbarr Flynn and Takako Taniguchi, "Prudential Chief Echoes Dimon Saying Liquidity Is Top Worry," Bloomberg News, April 13, 2015, http://www.bloomberg.com/news/articles/2015-04-14/prudential-chief-says-biggest-worry-is-liquidity-echoing-dimon.

4. Mohamed A. El-Erian, "The Market 'Sucking Sounds' Are Getting Louder as Four Forces Come Together," Business Insider, June 11, 2013, http://www.businessinsider.com/el-erian-on-the-liquidity-gap-2013-6.

5. Mohamed A. El-Erian, "Is the Market Confident or Too Complacent?," Bloomberg View, June 9, 2014, http://www.bloombergview.com/articles/2014-06-09/is-the-market-confident-or-too-complacent.

CHAPTER 17: BRIDGING THE GAP
BETWEEN MARKETS AND FUNDAMENTALS

1. Jim Puzzanghera, "Yellen Upbeat About Growth in the Coming Quarter," Los Angeles Times, May 7, 2014, http://www.latimes.com/business/la-fi-yellen-economy-20140508-story.html.

2. Binyamin Appelbaum, "Q. and A. With Charles Plosser of the Fed: Raise Rates Sooner Rather Than Later," New York Times, January 30, 2015, http://www.nytimes.com/2015/01/30/upshot/q-and-a-with-charles-plosser-of-the-fed-raise-rates-sooner-rather-than-later.html.

3. Claire Jones, Robin Wigglesworth, and James Politi, "Fed Fights Back Against 'Feral Hogs,'" Financial Times, June 24, 2013, http://www.ft.com/intl/cms/s/0/9d8fa63e-dce6-11e2-b52b-00144feab7de.html.

4. Mohamed A. El-Erian, "Big Money vs Bernanke: Who's Right About the Economy," Atlantic, July 3, 2013, http://www.theatlantic.com/business/archive/2013/07/big-money-vs-bernanke-whos-right-about-the-economy/277548/.

5. Joshua Zumbrun, "Fed Hears Warning That Tightening Policy May Spark Market Tumult," Bloomberg News, February 28, 2014, http://www.bloomberg.com/news/2014-02-28/fed-hears-warning-that-tightening-policy-may-spark-market-tumult.html.

6. Andrew Filardo and Boris Hofmann, "Forward Guidance at the Zero Lower Bound," BIS Quarterly Review, March 2014, Bank for International Settlements, http://www.bis.org/publ/qtrpdf/r_qt1403f.htm.

7. Robin Harding, "Federal Reserve Dissenter Kocherlakota Attacks New Guidance," Financial Times, March 21, 2014, http://www.ft.com/intl/cms/s/0/1607d9b8-b105-11e3-bbd4-00144feab7de.html.

8. Mohamed A. El-Erian, "Here's Why Jeremy Stein's Departure from the Federal Reserve Matters," Business Insider, April 5, 2014, http://www.businessinsider.com/why-jeremy-steins-departure-is-important-2014-4.

9. Jeremy C. Stein, "Challenges to Monetary Policy Communication," speech to the Money Marketeers of New York University, Board of Governors of the Federal Reserve System, May 6, 2014, http://www.federalreserve.gov/newsevents/speech/stein20140506a.htm. A similar point was made by Hyun Song Shin, "Commentary on Robert E. Hall, 'The Routes into and out of the Zero Lower Bound,'" speech delivered at conference on Global Dimensions of Unconventional Monetary Policy, Federal Reserve Bank of Kansas City, Jackson Hole, Wyoming, August 22–24, 2013.

10. Janet Yellen, "Monetary Policy and Financial Stability," speech at the 2014 Michel Camdessus Central Banking Lecture, International Monetary Fund, Washington, D.C., July 2, 2014, Board of Governors of the Federal Reserve System, http://www.federalreserve.gov/newsevents/speech/yellen20140702a.htm.

11. Mohamed A. El-Erian, "Yellen Lays Out Her Policy Blueprint," *Bloomberg View,* July 7, 2014, http://www.bloombergview.com/articles/2014-07-07/yellen-lays-out-her-policy-blueprint.

12. Stanley Fischer, "Financial Sector Reform: How Far Are We?," Martin Feldstein Lecture at the National Bureau of Economic Research, July 10, 2014, Board of Governors of the Federal Reserve System, http://www.federalreserve.gov/newsevents/speech/fischer20140710a.htm.

13. Jeremy C. Stein, "Overheating in Credit Markets: Origins, Measurement, and Policy Responses," Board of Governors of the Federal Reserve System, February 7, 2013, http://www.federalreserve.gov/newsevents/speech/stein20130207a.htm.

14. Jaime Caruana, "Macro-Prudential Policies: Opportunities and Challenges," speech to the Tenth High-Level Meeting for the Middle East and North Africa, Bank for International Settlements, December 9, 2014, http://www.bis.org/speeches/sp141219.pdf.

15. "Staff Guidance Note on Macro-Prudential Policies," International Monetary Fund, December 2014, http://www.imf.org/external/np/pp/eng/2014/110614.pdf.

CHAPTER 18: IT IS HARD TO BE A
GOOD HOUSE IN A CHALLENGED NEIGHBORHOOD

1. Martin Wolf, "A Rebuff of China's Asian Infrastructure Investment Bank Is Folly," *Financial Times,* March 24, 2015, http://www.ft.com/intl/cms/s/0/0dff595e-d16a-11e4-86c8-00144feab7de.html.

2. Mohamed A. El-Erian, "M&A Boom Must Evolve to Create Growth," *Financial Times,* August 20, 2014, http://www.ft.com/intl/cms/s/0/d3b11b24-26c5-11e4-8df5-00144feabdc0.html.

3. Michael MacKenzie and Eric Platt, "US Companies on Course to Return $1 Trillion to Shareholders in 2015," *Financial Times,* April 12, 2015, http://www.ft.com/intl/cms/s/0/2c1a34d8-dfa5-11e4-a06a-00144feab7de.html.

CHAPTER 19: ADDRESSING THE TEN BIG CHALLENGES

1. "Q and A with Charles Plosser, President of the Fed: Raise Interest Rates Sooner Rather than Later," *New York Times,* January 30, 2015, http://www.nytimes.com/2015/01/30/upshot/q-and-a-with-charles-plosser-of-the-fed-raise-rates-sooner-rather-than-later.html.

2. Chris Giles and Ferdinando Giugliano, "Raise Rates or Face 'Devastating Bubbles,' Says Fed Official," *Financial Times,* March 23, 2015, http://www.ft.com/intl/cms/s/0/62c65f4c-d15f-11e4-86c8-00144feab7de.html.

3. Stanley Fischer, "Monetary Policy and the Way Ahead," speech to the Economic Club of New York, March 23, 2015, http://www.federalreserve.gov/newsevents/speech/fischer20150323a.htm.

CHAPTER 20: THE REDUCED-FORM
APPROACH TO A GRAND POLICY DESIGN

1. Special thanks to Professor Michael Spence, who has been instrumental in helping me think through these issues.

2. The 2015 Economic Report of the President, White House Council of Economic Advisers, February 19, 2015, http://www.whitehouse.gov/sites/default/files/docs/cea_2015_erp.pdf.

3. Michael Spence, "Five Reasons for Slow Growth," Project Syndicate, September 29, 2014, http://www.project-syndicate.org/commentary/slow-economic-growth-reasons-by-michael-spence-2014-12.

4. "The Fund's Lending Framework and Sovereign Debt," International Monetary Fund, Washington, D.C., June 2014, http://www.imf.org/external/np/pp/eng/2014/052214a.pdf.

5. See, for example, "Debt Relief Under the Heavily Indebted Poor Countries (HIPC) Initiative," IMF Factsheet, Washington, D.C., September 2014, https://www.imf.org/external/np/exr/facts/hipc.htm.

6. Carmen M. Reinhart and Kenneth S. Rogoff, "Financial and Sovereign Debt Crises: Some Lessons Learned and Those Forgotten," IMF Working Paper, WP/13/266, December 2013, https://www.imf.org/external/pubs/ft/wp/2013/wp13266.pdf.

7. "Bleak Words and Difficult Homework from the IMF," *Financial Times,* October 5, 2014, http://www.ft.com/intl/cms/s/0/53516aec-4af6-11e4-b1be-00144feab7de.html.

8. Mohamed A. El-Erian, "The New Isolationism: Why the World's Richest Countries Can't Work Together," *Atlantic,* September 3, 2013, http://www.theatlantic.com/business/archive/2013/09/the-new-isolationism-why-the-worlds-richest-countries-cant-work-together/279282/.

CHAPTER 21: WHEN DESIRABLE AND FEASIBLE DIFFER

1. Mohamed A. El-Erian, "Obama Sets Terms of 2016 Debate," *Bloomberg View,* January 21, 2015, http://www.bloombergview.com/articles/2015-01-21/obama-sets-terms-of-2016-debate.

2. Amartya K. Sen, "Rational Fools: A Critique of the Behavioral Foundations of Economic Theory," *Philosophy and Public Affairs* 6, no. 4 (Summer 1977), http://www.jstor.org/discover/10.2307/2264946?sid=21105866957553&uid =3739256&uid=4&uid=2&uid=3739560.

3. Mohamed A. El-Erian, "The 1 Equation Investors Need to Know to Understand the World Today," *Atlantic,* May 22, 2013, http://www.theatlantic .com/business/archive/2013/05/the-1-equation-investors-need-to-know-to -understand-the-world-today/276124/.

CHAPTER 22: TURNING PARALYZING
COMPLEXITY INTO ACTIONABLE SIMPLICITY

1. Mohamed A. El-Erian, "What We Need from the IMF/World Bank Meetings," *Financial Times,* October 6, 2013, http://blogs.ft.com/the-a-list/2013/ 10/06/what-we-need-from-the-imfworld-bank-meetings/.

CHAPTER 23: THE BELLY OF THE
DISTRIBUTION OF POTENTIAL OUTCOMES

1. "The World in 2015," *Economist,* December 2014.

2. Michael J. Casey, "Flattening Yield Curve Latest Complication for Fed," *Wall Street Journal,* April 12, 2015, http://blogs.wsj.com/moneybeat/2015/ 04/12/flattening-yield-curve-latest-complication-for-fed/?mod=WSJ_hps _MIDDLE_Video_Third.

3. Mohamed A. El-Erian, "The Instability in Central Bank Divergence," *Financial Times,* February 26, 2014, http://blogs.ft.com/the-a-list/2014/02/26/ the-instability-in-central-bank-divergence/.

CHAPTER 24: A WORLD OF GREATER
DIVERGENCE (I): MULTI-SPEED GROWTH

1. Mohamed A. El-Erian, "A Year of Divergence," Project Syndicate, December 8, 2014, http://www.project-syndicate.org/commentary/economic -monetary-policy-divergence-2015-by-mohamed-a--el-erian-2014-12.

2. Mohamed A. El-Erian, "Missteps and Miscalculations That Could Cost Greece the Euro," *Financial Times,* March 25, 2015, http://www.ft.com/intl/ cms/s/0/a28549d6-d303-11e4-a792-00144feab7de.html.

CHAPTER 25: A WORLD OF GREATER
DIVERGENCE (II): MULTI-TRACK CENTRAL BANKS

1. Mohamed A. El-Erian, "An Accidental Currency War," Project Syndicate, February 10, 2015, http://www.project-syndicate.org/commentary/monetary -policy-central-bank-activism-by-mohamed-a--el-erian-2015-02; and Mohamed A. El-Erian, "Rising Risk of Currency Market Instability," *Financial Times,* August 26, 2014, http://www.ft.com/intl/cms/s/0/a82d9c14-2ce4 -11e4-911b-00144feabdc0.html.

2. Ben S. Bernanke, "The Logic of Monetary Policy," remarks by Governor Ben S. Bernanke before the National Economists Club, Washington, D.C., De-

cember 2, 2004, http://www.federalreserve.gov/Boarddocs/speeches/2004/
20041202/default.htm.

CHAPTER 26: A WORLD OF GREATER
DIVERGENCE (III): NON-ECONOMIC, NON-POLICY HEADWINDS

1. Mohamed A. El-Erian, "Greece Can Learn from Brazil and Argentina,"
   Bloomberg View, January 13, 2015, http://www.bloombergview.com/
   articles/2015-01-13/greece-can-learn-from-brazil-and-argentina.

CHAPTER 27: A WORLD OF GREATER
DIVERGENCE (IV): DISRUPTIVE INNOVATION GOES MACRO

1. Daniel Yergin, "Who Will Rule the Oil Market?," *New York Times,* January 23, 2015, http://www.nytimes.com/2015/01/25/opinion/sunday/what
   -happened-to-the-price-of-oil.html.
2. Mohamed A. El-Erian, "Good, Bad and Ugly of Lower Oil Prices," *Bloomberg View,* December 1, 2014, http://www.bloombergview.com/articles/
   2014-12-01/good-bad-and-ugly-of-lower-oil-prices.
3. Erik Brynjolfsson and Andrew McAfee, *The Second Machine Age: Work,
   Progress, and Prosperity in a Time of Brilliant Technologies* (New York: Nor-
   ton, 2014).
4. See, for example, Erik Brynjolfsson and Andrew McAfee, *Race Against the
   Machine: How the Digital Revolution Is Accelerating Innovation, Driving Productivity, and Irreversibly Transforming Employment and the Economy* (Lex-
   ington, MA: Digital Frontier Press, 2011).

CHAPTER 28: PUTTING IT ALL TOGETHER

1. Richard Dobbs, James Manyika, and Jonathan Woetzel, *No Ordinary Disruption: The Four Global Forces Breaking All the Trends* (New York: Public-
   Affairs, 2015).
2. Mohamed A. El-Erian, "Creative Self-Disruption," Project Syndicate, April
   7, 2015, http://www.project-syndicate.org/commentary/consumer-sharing
   -economy-adaptation-by-mohamed-a--el-erian-2015-04.

CHAPTER 29: WHAT HISTORY TELLS US

1. Richard Dobbs, James Manyika, and Jonathan Woetzel, *No Ordinary Disruption: The Four Global Forces Breaking All the Trends* (New York: Public-
   Affairs, 2015).
2. Daniel Kahneman, *Thinking, Fast and Slow* (New York: Farrar, Straus & Gi-
   roux, 2011).
3. Lea Wineman, "A Machine for Jumping to Conclusions," *Monitor on Psychology* 43, no. 2 (February 2012).
4. Daniel Kahneman, *Thinking, Fast and Slow* (New York: Farrar, Straus & Gi-
   roux, 2011).

CHAPTER 30: RECOGNIZING
BLIND SPOTS AND OVERCOMING BIASES

1. Mohamed A. El-Erian, "Remarks at the Launch of USAID's Policy on Gender Equality and Women Empowerment," PIMCO Viewpoint, March 2012.
2. Mahzarin Banaji and Anthony Greenwald, *Blindspot: Hidden Biases of Good People* (New York: Random House, 2013).
3. Don Lovallo and Olivier Sabony, "The Case for Behavioral Strategy," *McKinsey Quarterly*, March 2010.
4. Sheryl Sandberg and Adam Grant, "Speaking While Female," *New York Times*, January 12, 2015, http://www.nytimes.com/2015/01/11/opinion/sunday/speaking-while-female.html.
5. Patricia Sellers, "El-Erian: A Gender Bias Lesson from My Daughter," *Fortune*, August 8, 2013, http://fortune.com/2013/08/08/el-erian-a-lesson-on-gender-bias-from-my-daughter/.

CHAPTER 31: ADVANCING AND ENHANCING COGNITIVE DIVERSITY

1. Scott Page, *The Difference: How the Power of Diversity Creates Better Groups, Firms, Schools, and Societies* (Princeton, NJ: Princeton University Press, 2007).
2. Scott Page, "Making the Difference: Applying a Logic of Diversity," *Academy of Management Perspectives*, November 2007.
3. Scott Page, *The Difference: How the Power of Diversity Creates Better Groups, Firms, Schools and Societies* (Princeton, NJ: Princeton University Press, 2007).
4. Scott Page, "Making the Difference: Applying a Logic of Diversity," *Academy of Management Perspectives*, November 2007.
5. Mohamed El-Erian, "Why CEOs Should Read Sheryl Sandberg's Book," *Fortune*, March 11, 2013, http://fortune.com/2013/03/11/why-ceos-should-read-sheryl-sandbergs-lean-in/.
6. Sheryl Sandberg, *Lean In: Women, Work, and the Will to Lead* (New York: Knopf, 2013).

CHAPTER 32: TRANSLATING AWARENESS
INTO OPTIONALITY, RESILIENCE, AND AGILITY

1. Eric Schmidt and Jonathan Rosenberg, *How Google Works* (New York: Grand Central, 2014).
2. Ibid.
3. Sheryl Sandberg, *Lean In: Women, Work, and the Will to Lead* (New York: Knopf, 2013).
4. Mohamed A. El-Erian, "Getting Real About Diversity," *American Banker*, September 18, 2013, http://www.americanbanker.com/magazine/123_10/pimcos-mohamed-el-erian-on-getting-real-about-diversity-1062068-1.html.

CHAPTER 33: THE POWER OF SCENARIO ANALYSES

1. Further information and demonstration tests may be found on the website of Project Implicit, https://implicit.harvard.edu/implicit/demo/.
2. Gary Klein, "Performing a Project Premortem," *Harvard Business Review,* September 2007, https://hbr.org/2007/09/performing-a-project-premortem.
3. Gary Klein, *The Power of Intuition: How to Use Your Gut Feelings to Make Better Decisions at Work* (New York: Crown Business, 2004).

CHAPTER 34: VALUING LIQUIDITY AND OPTIONALITY

1. Mohamed A. El-Erian, "Global Tug of War Is Focus for Investors," *Financial Times,* February 9, 2015, http://www.ft.com/intl/cms/s/0/1e0e8662-ac80 -11e4-9d32-00144feab7de.html.

CHAPTER 35: IN SUM

1. John Maynard Keynes, *The General Theory of Employment, Interest, and Money* (N.p.: CreateSpace Independent Publishing Platform, 2014).
2. Norman Mailer, *The Fight* (New York: Vintage International, 1975).

INDEX

Page numbers in *italics* refer to figures.

Author of the *New York Times* and *Wall Street Journal* best-seller *When Markets Collide* and winner of the *Financial Times*/Goldman Sachs Business Book of the Year, Mohamed A. El-Erian was named to *Foreign Policy*'s list of "Top 100 Global Thinkers" four years in a row. He chairs President Obama's Global Development Council and is a columnist for *Bloomberg View,* a contributing editor at the *Financial Times,* and chief economic adviser of Allianz, the corporate parent of PIMCO, where he served as CEO and co-CIO (2007–2014). He has also been deputy director of the International Monetary Fund, CEO of the Harvard University endowment, managing director at Salomon Smith Barney, and chair of Microsoft's Investment Advisory Board. An honorary fellow of Queens' College (Cambridge University), he was awarded a master's degree and a doctorate at Oxford University after completing his undergraduate degree at Cambridge University.

@elerianm

ABOUT THE TYPE

This book was set in Minion, a 1990 Adobe Originals typeface by Robert Slimbach (b. 1956). Minion is inspired by classical, old-style typefaces of the late Renaissance, a period of elegant, beautiful, and highly readable type designs. Created primarily for text setting, Minion combines the aesthetic and functional qualities that make text type highly readable with the versatility of digital technology.